BORROWED LAND, STOLEN LABOR,
and the HOLY SPIRIT

BORROWED LAND, STOLEN LABOR, *and the* HOLY SPIRIT

The Struggle for Power and Equality in Holmes County, Mississippi

Diane T. Feldman

University Press of Mississippi / Jackson

The University Press of Mississippi is the scholarly publishing agency of
the Mississippi Institutions of Higher Learning: Alcorn State University,
Delta State University, Jackson State University, Mississippi State University,
Mississippi University for Women, Mississippi Valley State University,
University of Mississippi, and University of Southern Mississippi.

www.upress.state.ms.us

The University Press of Mississippi is a member
of the Association of University Presses.

Publisher: University Press of Mississippi, Jackson, USA
Authorised GPSR Safety Representative: Easy Access System Europe
Mustamäe tee 50, 10621 Tallinn, Estonia, gpsr.requests@easproject.com

Library of Congress Cataloging-in-Publication Data

Names: Feldman, Diane T. author
Title: Borrowed land, stolen labor, and the Holy Spirit : the struggle for
power and equality in Holmes County, Mississippi / Diane T. Feldman.
Other titles: Struggle for power and equality in Holmes County, Mississippi
Description: Jackson : University Press of Mississippi, [2025] |
Includes bibliographical references and index.
Identifiers: LCCN 2025007319 (print) | LCCN 2025007320 (ebook) |
ISBN 9781496857477 hardback | ISBN 9781496857460 trade paperback |
ISBN 9781496857491 epub | ISBN 9781496857507 epub |
ISBN 9781496857484 pdf | ISBN 9781496857514 pdf
Subjects: LCSH: African Americans—Civil rights—Mississippi—
Holmes County—History | African Americans—Civil rights—Religious aspects |
African Americans—Mississippi—Holmes County—Social conditions |
Civil rights movements—Mississippi—Holmes County—History |
Holmes County (Miss.)—Race relations—History | Holmes County (Miss.)—History |
Holmes County (Miss.)—Religious life and customs
Classification: LCC F347.H6 F45 2025 (print) | LCC F347.H6 (ebook) |
DDC 323.1196/0730762625—dc23/eng/20250424
LC record available at https://lccn.loc.gov/2025007319
LC ebook record available at https://lccn.loc.gov/2025007320

British Library Cataloging-in-Publication Data available

CONTENTS

PREFACE

At the end of 2018, I closed the research company in Washington, DC, that I had run for thirty years and retired to Jackson, Mississippi. There were multiple reasons for the move, but among them was the opportunity to nurture my long-standing admiration for the Mississippi civil rights movement.

As a child in New York City in 1964, I was captivated by the events of Freedom Summer. The violence shocked me. It was nearly unimaginable to me that people would be subjected to violence for trying to vote, which I thought was simply responsible adult behavior. I was also inspired as I saw young people, not all that much older in my view than my eleven years, helping set the stage for change. As an adult in the 1980s and 1990s, I read volumes about that summer and the efforts leading up to it. Many veterans of the Student Nonviolent Coordinating Committee settled in Washington, DC, and I came to know and work with several of them, deepening my respect and appreciation for what they had done. They, in turn, celebrated the local people who had been on the front lines of the Mississippi civil rights movement. They always told me the civil rights movement was both local and continuous. I nodded as if I understood, but I didn't really know what they meant. I knew I had more to learn and to understand.

So, after I finished arranging the furniture in my new home, I decided to dig deeply into the history of one county to learn more from a local perspective. I did not know initially that it would be a book. It began as a learning project. I chose Holmes County because it played a storied role in the civil rights movement. Part of Holmes County is in the Mississippi Delta, and the county provided an early outpost of Delta organizing. It was home to the Mileston Co-op, a Black-owned cooperative farm enterprise founded during the Roosevelt administration. The farmers of Mileston, with more economic independence than those who did not own their land, were leaders in the local civil rights movement. I was curious how Mileston came to be and about the history of activism among African American farmers. The Holmes County border is also about forty-five minutes from Jackson, so I didn't have to go very far to get there.

My first drive through Holmes County taught me that you can go a very long way in forty-five minutes. Holmes County—like much of the Delta—does not look like a place where segregation has been vanquished. It is one of the lowest-income counties in Mississippi. It has areas of beauty and charm but also downtown strips and old railroad stations that are boarded up and deserted. Few people are on the streets of any town. Front porches are collapsing, and businesses have been abandoned. The visible poverty is set against a backdrop of still-rich land—flat expanses with seemingly unending rows of cotton, soybeans, and corn; cattle grazing on green fields in front of deeply forested hills. Still, the poverty is profound. I felt as if I had traveled farther in some ways from my Jackson neighborhood to Holmes County than from DC to Jackson.

Over the next few years, however, I found that Holmes County had a great deal to teach me. It taught me how deep history can be in a place that looks, at first glance, like flyover—or drive-through—country. Its civil rights movement did not spring up in the early 1960s like rain lilies after a storm. The civil rights leaders in Holmes County were heirs to a century-long progression by Black people there to gain land and self-sufficiency. The success of those efforts has receded in part, but that is not the first time that has happened either.

As I began to understand how little I knew, I searched more broadly, taking less for granted. Of course, COVID hit, and for a time Holmes County people and sources—and some archival sources—were unavailable to me. But I had already spent time in Holmes County and with land records there. Local newspapers from earlier times are online, and I began to absorb all I could from secondary sources, which were more available during the pandemic. Much of that time I focused on learning about the Native heritage of Holmes County, about the land itself, and about the history of enslaved people in Mississippi.

The land, I discovered, is like an independent character in the Holmes County story. The land itself changes through time in relationship to those who occupy it. A geologist advised me that "geology is destiny." In the case of Holmes County, geology explains why the earliest Native Americans made it their home and why it was developed earlier than most of the Mississippi Delta—first by Europeans and later by Americans. Geology also explains why, thousands of years after it was initially settled, land speculators made such a frenzied grab for this land, expelling the Native population and bringing in enslaved African Americans to plant and harvest it. The richness of its land also partially explains why large, often corporate, farm operations took it back from smaller farmers in the twentieth century, contributing to the current poverty in Holmes County and altering the land once again.

The land has always been the county's wealth. The question of who owns and occupies the land has been a center of struggle from its beginning—and still is today. Native Americans chided early European settlers, telling them they had merely "borrowed" the land. Yet Europeans—and, later, Americans—believed they had dominion over property, a concept that was foreign to Native peoples. The story of how the land "was took," as a formerly enslaved person once described it, begins with European settlers and continues with the US government—all three branches—and land speculators who either planted it or sold it for cotton, the early nineteenth century's most profitable crop.

African American land ownership began immediately after the Civil War as individuals who managed to get a little cash during enslavement put it into land. They bought land—platted and sold in the European and American manner—but not merely as a commodity. They knew the biblical story of the promised land—of land that belonged to God and was granted to people who abided by His laws. Land ownership had spiritual value. It allowed people to free themselves from the plantation and fulfilled a desire to achieve independence and self-sufficiency.

Over the coming decades, many bought their land, but most literally borrowed it as sharecroppers or tenant farmers. Tenants rent land for a set fee. Sharecroppers live on the plantation and farm a section, keeping a portion of the proceeds after the landowner has deducted his estimate of their expenses. In the 1960s, civil rights leaders would also speak of the Delta as borrowed land. It was a recognition that the land had been taken from Native Americans. It was also an admonishment that previously enslaved people—and their descendants who worked borrowed land—had rights as well.

The ongoing story of African American land ownership makes visible the long-term strength of Black agency in Holmes County. Scholarship on the Jim Crow period usually stresses the violence and victimization of Black people during that time. There is no shortage of violence in the Holmes County story, and no shortage of victimization. But African American agency during the late nineteenth and early twentieth centuries laid foundations that allowed the later civil rights movement to flourish as Black people in Holmes County built their own institutions and formed their own networks of economic support.

The most important institutional development of the Jim Crow period in Holmes County was the birth of the Church of God in Christ, founded in the county seat of Lexington. The denomination is in the Holiness-Pentecostal tradition and combines practices from African religions with a Christian doctrine of sanctification and service to the poor. From its beginning, the COGIC rejected the formalism of other denominations. Anyone could experience the indwelling of the Holy Spirit and commit to a life of sanctification. For many, it brought a strong sense of self and a new feeling of freedom. The denomination now has millions of members across the country and around the world.

My new understanding of Holmes County history gave context to the civil rights movement there. The 1960s was a brief period of dramatic change brought by courageous and clear-thinking people. It is the period I thought I knew about, but I still had much to learn. Local people had begun the effort for voting rights long before Freedom Summer. The Student Nonviolent Coordinating Committee and others offered critical support, but the movement was local. It was part of a continuity of change. Looking at the civil rights movement nationally—or even on a state level—misses the long view. Of course, much of what I learned about Holmes County applies to other places in Mississippi. Much of it is also unique. In either case, I do not believe I would have learned as much about the history of the civil rights movement—or of Mississippi—had I not adopted a local perspective.

As the pandemic receded, archival sources were again available and so, too, were people in Holmes County. I gained deep respect for the community of people I met there. There are leaders in Holmes County whose families have worked on the same issues for generations—sometimes with success and sometimes not—but bravely, selflessly, and continually. They welcomed me. They told me their histories. They were patient in explaining much that I did not know or understand. They encouraged me to dig for the realities behind vaguely recalled remnants from earlier times.

It is now over five years since my first drive to Holmes County. My interest in the civil rights movement has held, but it has matured as I have learned about the extensive root system of that moment. I have learned how closely political rights and economic realities are intertwined, and I have learned much more about the spirit of commitment and community that is integral to creating change. I understand far better both the local and continuous nature of the struggle for equality. I also have a new understanding of how Holmes County—and, indeed, the Mississippi Delta—has been shaped by what people have wanted from its land.

This book shares what I have learned.

INTRODUCING HOLMES COUNTY

For those who are new to it, modern Holmes County is right about in the middle of Mississippi. Interstate 55, the main north-south highway through the state, passes through it. Along I-55, it lies about 150 miles from the Tennessee line to the north and about 160 miles from the Louisiana line to the south.

Just under seventeen thousand people live in Holmes County, according to the 2020 US Census. Eighty-three percent of the population is African American, and 16 percent is white. It is a low-income county: The median household income is just under $25,000 a year, about half the median for the state of Mississippi and just over a third of the median household income of $71,000 in the United States. Thirty-eight percent of the population lives in poverty. Among adults over age twenty-five, 78 percent are high school graduates. Under 13 percent have bachelor's degrees compared to 23 percent of adults in the state.[1]

Holmes County is rural, with a population of about twenty-two people per square mile. Less than half the population live in one of three Holmes County towns—Tchula, Lexington, or Durant. The western third of the county lies in the Mississippi Delta, where the most populous town is Tchula, with just over a thousand people. Mileston is there too, the home of the Mileston Co-op founded by the Farm Security Administration.

East of the bluffs that frame the Delta is Lexington, the county seat, with a population of about 1,600. It has an iconic courthouse square surrounded by early twentieth-century buildings. Heading farther east is Durant, which is the largest town in Holmes County and the only one with a population over 2,000. Durant, and the other towns in the eastern part of Holmes County—West, Goodman, and Pickens—were railroad towns. The Mississippi Central Railroad broke ground in 1853, and the rail line from Tennessee down to Canton, near Jackson, was completed in 1860. Downtown Goodman and Pickens are mostly boarded up now since trains no longer stop there. The trains do not stop in Durant either, but they did until the 1990s.[2]

For a time, Holmes County was a transportation hub. The Mississippi Central ran through it, and freight rail through the Delta. The county is bordered by the Yazoo and Big Black Rivers, which were both navigable in the eighteenth and nineteenth centuries. The rivers brought Europeans and then Americans to Holmes County far earlier than to the northern part of the Delta, which was largely unsettled until after the Civil War.

Holmes became a county in 1833. It is named for David Holmes, the final governor of Mississippi Territory and the first elected governor after Mississippi became a state in 1817. David Holmes had nothing in particular to do with his namesake county—he was born in Pennsylvania and had served as a member of Congress from Virginia before President Thomas Jefferson appointed him the governor of Mississippi Territory. The county is likely named for him because he had died the year before.[3]

That is a foreshortened version of Holmes becoming a county. Its two-hundred-year-old jurisdictional lines are less critical to its history, however, than the shape of the land it occupies. The land was initially shaped by natural forces. The resulting contours help explain why people settled on it. The ways in which different peoples used the land, what they did to it, and what it meant to them have in turn shaped the history of Holmes County—and of Mississippi.

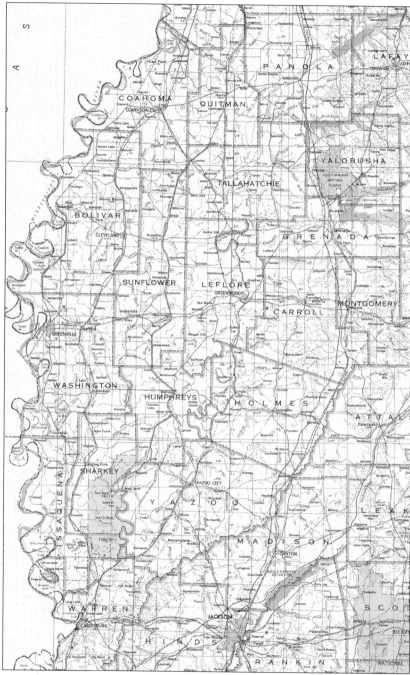

Holmes and nearby counties. Cropped from Geological Survey, US State of Mississippi, base map with highways and contours. Washington: The Survey, 1972. Map. https://www.loc.gov/item/79691506/. Library of Congress, Geography and Map Division.

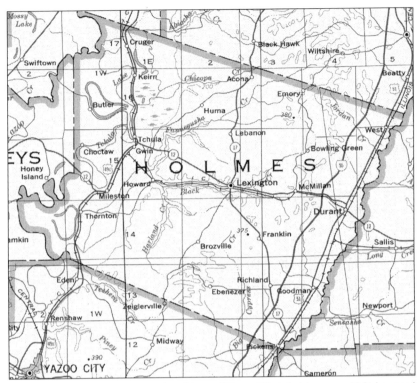

Map of Holmes County. Cropped from Geological Survey, US State of Mississippi, base map with highways and contours. Washington: The Survey, 1972. Map. https://www.loc.gov/item/79691506/. Library of Congress, Geography and Map Division.

BORROWED LAND, STOLEN LABOR, *and the* HOLY SPIRIT

Chapter 1

THE LAND IS MINE—BEFORE 1860

The land shall not be sold in perpetuity, for the land is mine;
for you are strangers and live as foreigners with me.

—LEVITICUS 25:23 (WORLD ENGLISH BIBLE)

I don't want you telling me to go back to Africa, unless you going back where you come from. I got a note one day telling me to go back to Africa and ever since that time—it's been three times a week I say it when I am in a white audience—I say, 'We'll make a deal. After you send all the Koreans back to Korea, the Chinese back to China, the Jewish people back to Jerusalem, and you give the Indians their land back and you get on the Mayflower from which you come'... We all here on borrowed land. We have to figure out how we're going to make things right for all the people of this country.

—CIVIL RIGHTS LEADER FANNIE LOU HAMER

(BROOKS AND HOUCK, *SPEECHES OF FANNIE LOU HAMER*, 126)

NATIVE LAND

The land that would become Holmes County was the home of Native people until about thirty years before the Civil War. Having grown up on land from which Native people had been expelled far earlier, the comparative recentness of Native culture in Mississippi remains striking to me. The Mississippi Band of Choctaw Indians still live in the state. Native history is visible through mounds that remain, projectile points found frequently in fields and streams, and in old names like Tchula, Yazoo, and, for that matter, Mississippi, which means big river in the language of Native people at the river's headwaters. Native people have lived in Holmes County for about ten thousand years, longer than virtually anywhere else in Mississippi, and longer than any other peoples have lived there. Still, for the land's first forty million years, no one resided on it.

3

The land was first shaped when glacial ice across the North American continent melted. The melt became a vast sea stretching from what is now Illinois south to the gulf. Erosion and changes in the Earth's crust created a path to the ocean. Forty-one percent of the continent drained into the new path, which became the Mississippi River, out through the gulf to the open sea. On the way, it sculpted the alluvial plain known as the Yazoo-Mississippi Delta. The Delta has some of the most fertile land in the world, with topsoil that is over one hundred feet deep in some places, including near Tchula in what has become Holmes County.

In prehistoric times, as the glacial water level dropped, the ice-cold waters met with the heat of the new ground, creating powerful winds that blew across the land and receding water. The winds blew silt, sand, gravel, and rocks into loess bluffs that frame the Delta's eastern edge. The sediment formed alluvial fans on the face of the bluffs—concentrations of rock and gravel that became freshwater streams. The bluffs are higher in Holmes County than elsewhere in the Delta because they rest on an ancient rock formation that protects them from erosion. They rise up to two hundred feet in Holmes, laced with fresh-water alluvial streams.[1]

The Mississippi River changed shape as it evolved. Like most rivers, it was initially braided—a network of small channels—and then meandered with deeper, more permanent channels defining the land in between. Remnants of the river's ancestral course are found in long, twisted-shape lakes like Tchula Lake, Horseshoe Lake, and Bee Lake in Holmes County.[2]

For the first thirty-nine million plus years, no human beings lived in the area. Then, around ten thousand years ago, some of the very first people who came to Mississippi settled along the top of the bluffs in Holmes County. Game for food was especially abundant in the wet woodlands of the Delta below while the height of the hills protected the land from floods—and gave relief from the mosquitoes that plagued Mississippi even then. The streams through the bluffs were a source of clean, fresh water. For the first people who came there, the rock and gravel in the streams provided critical lithic material for making tools, unavailable in the silt-filled, rock-free swamp of the Delta alluvial plain.

The first people to settle in what would become Holmes County were hunter-gatherers. They did not have the stationary and often hierarchical societies that relied on agriculture for food. They lived at that time in mobile villages, moving to find fresh game and edible plants. The oldest site in Holmes is a pre-historic quarry found in 2021 that may be ten thousand years old. There Native Americans mined rock for tools. Projectile points from that earliest period of occupation are still found in the woods and fields around Holmes County.[3]

After a millennium or so, villages were occupied for longer and native people grew their own food. There are fourteen archeological sites along the bluffs that show evidence of longer-term occupation through agricultural tools and pottery left behind. Some archeological findings are from what is called the Poverty Point period, named after a similarly early location in Louisiana, about 1100 to 1700 BCE. Others still have particularly rich artifacts from what is called the Marksville period, roughly 100 BCE to 400 CE, again named for a site in Louisiana and known in part for its ceremonial pottery with stylized birds. Still others show evidence of occupation by the Mississippian culture, which lasted from about 800 to 1600 CE, about a thousand years.[4]

"Mississippian" culture was named for the river that defined it. The Mississippians built large mounds along the Mississippi River and its tributaries from Louisiana north to Cahokia, Illinois, which was the largest site with more than one hundred mounds and an estimated population of forty thousand people. Some mounds were ceremonial—the site of temples or other buildings—and others were burial mounds. Differing sites were interconnected as people communicated and traded with each other up and down the river. Archeologists frequently find shells or pottery in one location clearly derived from up- or downriver from where they were dug.[5]

There are hundreds of mound sites in the state of Mississippi. Most mounds are on private land and inaccessible to the public. Many have been plowed under over the years and are no longer archeologically useful or, often, visible. In Holmes County, in addition to the sites along the bluffs, archeologists have described mounds on private property on the western side of Tchula Lake that included artifacts and forty-seven burials. The site, now known as the Frances Lee mound group, is still on private land with restricted access. Providence Mound, on land now owned by the state, dates to around 500 CE and appears to be a largely undisturbed burial mound.[6]

In the Mississippian period, villages grew and agriculture expanded around the mounds. Land just outside the village was farmed communally by the women while men were hunters. The women of the villages grew squash, wild spinach, and other vegetables and, increasingly over time, corn or maize. Corn was developed in Central America, but as seed corn made its way to Mississippi, it became a staple here too.[7]

The Mississippian sites in Holmes County may be related to a large mound site at Lake George in neighboring Yazoo County, fifty miles from Holmes down the Yazoo River. Some speculate that Lake George was home to the chiefdom of Quigualtam, who was a significant figure in chronicles of the first European figure to visit the area. There were thirty mounds at Lake George when it was first excavated in 1908, making it one of the most formidable sites in Mississippi, with remnants of cultures dating back to 1300–1700 BCE. Forty years later, after farming and cattle grazing in the fields, only twenty-five mounds could be identified.[8]

Quigualtam led the effort to chase Spaniard Hernando de Soto out of Mississippi, according to chronicles of his expedition. The de Soto expedition, which arrived in 1542, was the first significant European incursion into Mississippi. The expedition had come up through what is now Florida and Alabama to northern Mississippi. Quigualtam sent a squadron of 1,500 warriors in hundreds of large canoes to observe de Soto crossing the river in northern Mississippi and to warn him to stay out of Quigualtam's turf to the south. If the mound sites in Holmes are satellites of the Lake George site, people who lived in Holmes were likely associated with that effort.

Quigualtam was also responsible for organizing other chiefdoms on both sides of the river to oppose de Soto. After de Soto died from fever on the Arkansas side of the river, Quigualtam's warriors chased the remainder of his expedition downriver to the gulf without the Spanish making landfall anywhere near Lake George.[9]

No known organized group of Europeans came to Mississippi for nearly another 150 years. The British had established colonies as far south as Georgia. The Spanish had claimed Florida and much of the Caribbean and South America. The French had colonized eastern Canada and the Great Lakes region but had not yet traveled south. Then, in 1682, René-Robert Cavelier, Sieur de La Salle, canoed down the Mississippi River from French territory south to the gulf and claimed the lower Mississippi River valley for France. The French had come to stay, founding the first permanent European settlements in Mississippi.[10]

Native cultures in Mississippi had changed in the years between the de Soto expedition and the arrival of the French. Mississippian culture, as de Soto found it, had not survived. Native people were no longer building mounds near the river nor living clustered near them. Instead, they had moved inland and lived in chiefdoms—some smaller and some larger, some part of loose confederacies and some in independent villages. Their heritage was Mississippian, but the culture had changed.

No one knows exactly what happened to the Mississippians, but there are several possible explanations. First, the de Soto expedition, before it was chased downriver by Quigualtam, had a major impact on the preexisting culture. De Soto had burned villages, killed thousands of Native Americans, and enslaved hundreds more. His expedition left behind new diseases from contact with Native people—smallpox, tuberculosis, bubonic plague, influenza, and venereal disease—and trichinosis through the swine he brought whose descendants still roam the woods of the Delta. Still, death and disease from direct contact seems insufficient on its own to obliterate Mississippian culture.

European arrival likely compounded a process of change that had already begun. Mound Builder culture had been in decline when de Soto arrived. The largest Mississippian sites had already lost population as the Mound Builder populations along the river were competing for resources and territory. Contact and conflict with Europeans apparently accelerated a dispersion of the population that was already in progress. Surviving populations moved farther inland from the Mississippi River to settle along its tributaries, where there was more room and more territory. There was also less flooding, and the dispersion may also have been the result of particularly virulent Mississippi River floods.[11]

At the time of French arrival in Mississippi, the Native population was governed by chiefdoms of varying sizes and levels of organization. In some cases, a few family villages were allied but with little authority structure. Some groups, in contrast, had inherited leadership and multilevel hierarchical organization in which lesser leaders paid some form of tribute to recognize the authority of a paramount chief. All these peoples were amalgams of Mississippians and other nearby groups.

The Choctaw Nation was the largest in Mississippi. Choctaw territory included parts of Louisiana and much of Alabama, stretching into northern Florida. The Chickasaw were in northern Mississippi with territory that stretched north through Tennessee and east to the Savannah River. The Choctaw and Chickasaw, in their own histories, have shared origins, and many aspects of their language and culture overlap.[12] In one important origin story, they were descended from two brothers who both emerged from a mound, Nanih Waiya, about eighty miles east of Holmes County.[13] There were also more than a dozen other Native groups with shared heritage present in Mississippi when La Salle arrived.

Far more is known of Choctaw culture than that of their predecessors, the Mississippians. Knowledge of the Mississippians comes exclusively from the interpretation of archeological remnants and from the chronicles of the de Soto expedition. There is more written history of the Choctaw, although early histories were often written from a Eurocentric viewpoint. We know that the Choctaw villages were a loose confederacy in the seventeenth century, not a tight hierarchy, with villages reflecting kinship organization, which was matrilineal, with husbands moving into their wives' families and larger clans.[14]

Choctaw religious and spiritual beliefs were complex. The Choctaw aimed to live within a sacred circle signified in their art by an enclosed cross, illustrating the four directions, inside a circle. The upper world was the realm of Aba, the sun god. The sun itself was a hole in the sky through which their deity watched. The underworld was the home of the moon, water, and disorder. In between was their own world, which required a balance between the other two for fertility and continued life. Choctaw religious laws include multiple taboos. Breaking those taboos would let loose forces of disorder and magic, requiring religious cleansing ceremonies to restore balance. Many themes from

Choctaw religion are seen in Mississippian artifacts, demonstrating continuity with the earlier culture.[15]

The land that was to become Holmes County was in Choctaw territory. It also shows on seventeenth- and early eighteenth-century maps as the "ancient home of the Ibitoupa." The Ibitoupa, which means people of the headwaters, lived along the top of the loess bluffs at that time, moving later to above the Yalobusha River. The Ibitoupa were a branch of the Chakchiuma people, who had larger settlements in nearby Carroll and Grenada Counties, and were, in turn, closely related to the Choctaw.[16]

Unlike the Choctaw, however, the Chakchiuma had a multigenerational reputation for violence dating back to Mississippian times. Their chief, Miko Lusa, which means "Black Chief," was hostile to de Soto, and his expedition recounted their burning the village of a rival group. A seventeenth-century diary by La Salle's deputy speaks of the "Chacoumas" killing a scout. Later, Jean-Baptiste Le Moyne de Bienville, the eventual governor of New France, complained to the Natchez Indians about their refusal to avenge the death of a French missionary family killed by the Chakchiuma. The Chakchiuma were, concluded nineteenth-century historian H. B. Cushman, "a warlike and very overbearing tribe of Indians."[17]

Tales of the Chakchiuma aside, most Native peoples were living quite peaceably together before colonization. In the eighteenth century, Europeans began fostering conflict among Native Americans motivated by their own competing ends. The British allied with the Chickasaw, whose territory, principally north and east of Mississippi, overlapped with British colonies. The British were also looking for labor to work their lands as they were already growing tobacco in Virginia, rice in Carolina, and sugarcane in the West Indies. The British armed the Chickasaw with muskets and paid them handsomely for attacking and delivering other Indians as slaves. The Chickasaw captured approximately five hundred Choctaw during this period, selling them to the British.[18]

Choctaw territory overlapped mostly with French territory in Mississippi and Louisiana. When the French first arrived in Mississippi, they were more interested in trade than in land possession and agriculture. The French would develop tobacco plantations near Natchez, in southwestern Mississippi, and sugarcane plantations in Louisiana. But the earliest French settlers were explorers and "coureurs des bois"—runners of the woods—who harvested fur pelts rather than tobacco. The Choctaw welcomed trading relationships with them. Besides, by the time the French established a permanent settlement on the Mississippi coast in 1699, the Choctaw were seeking protection from the Chickasaw. They allied with the French for protection as well as trade.

The Chakchiuma, for their part, were not large enough to be valuable allies to the Europeans and did, apparently, attack French settlers and disrupt the alliances of larger groups. In 1770, in a rare display of unity between them for the time, the Choctaw and Chickasaw teamed up to eliminate the Chakchiuma.[19] The Chakchiuma's reputed last stand was at Lyon's Bluff, near Starkville, southeast of Holmes County. The site had a horseshoe-shaped enclosure. The Chickasaw took the north and the Choctaw the south until every warrior was killed. Only a couple hundred women and children survived, and they were absorbed into other peoples.[20]

One Chakchiuma woman who survived was named Shumaka, and she, with her children, became absorbed into the Choctaw Nation. Shumaka's children—and especially her grandchildren—will play a significant role in the history of Holmes County—and of Mississippi—as we get to the nineteenth century.[21]

Meanwhile, the need to strengthen alliances with the increasing number of European (and a little later, American) settlers led to reorganizations of Choctaw leadership. Economic interdependence had deepened as the Choctaw began to raise pigs, cattle, and horses to sell to settlers and to trade for manufactured products like guns. The Choctaw had lived in loose confederations of independent villages through the middle of the eighteenth century. In the latter part, they organized themselves into three divisions: The Okla Hannali, or Six Towns people, were in the south. The Okla Tannap were in eastern Mississippi, and the Okla Falaya were in the west. The chiefs of each division played an economic as well as a political role.[22]

Holmes County had few Choctaw settlements by the late 1700s, but those that remained were in the Okla Falaya region. Okla Falaya means the long people, which was not a reference to height but to greater distance or dispersion among settlements.[23]

In the late 1700s, three coureurs des bois arrived in central Mississippi and settled in and around Holmes County. Their names, or the anglicized versions of them, are familiar to Mississippians today. Louis LeFleur, his brother Michael, and Louis Durant arrived together in Mississippi around 1790. They eventually settled in Holmes and neighboring Attala Counties. The City of Durant is named for Louis Durant. There are multiple sites in Mississippi named for members of the LeFleur family, usually with the name in its anglicized form, Leflore. It's worth learning a little about Louis Leflore, who settled in Holmes County as his better-known son, Greenwood Leflore, became a formidable player in Mississippi and Choctaw history.

Louis LeFleur was born Louis Lefleau in 1762 in Mobile, then part of French West Florida. His father, Jean Baptiste Lefleau, came to Mobile with the French army to help colonize the area. He went to work building ships and married his boss's daughter, Marie Jeanne Girard. After his father's death, Louis LeFleur began operating boats along the coast and up the rivers. According to one of his descendants, he specialized in the river route from Pensacola to Natchez. He also explored the Pearl River, which flows through what is now Jackson and also forms part of the border between Louisiana and Mississippi. LeFleur founded a trading post at what became known as LeFleur's Bluff. He later established a trading post along the Natchez Trace, the main route between the Mississippi port town of Natchez and Nashville, at a place that became known as French Camp. He settled, finally, in Holmes County, in a town that has since disappeared, called Rankin, between present-day Lexington and Tchula, where he raised cattle and anglicized his name.[24]

All three coureurs des bois—Louis Leflore, his brother Michael, and their friend Louis Durant—married Choctaw women. As membership in the Choctaw Nation was matrilineal, the children of these unions were Choctaw. Leflore married two sisters of Native heritage, Rebecca and Nancy Cravat, in 1790, and by some reports, a third Native woman, Hoke Hoke, on the Gulf Coast in 1794. Having multiple wives was common among the Choctaw, as was the communal raising of children. The Cravat sisters were daughters of another French trader, Jean Cravat, and his wife, Nahotima. The Cravat sisters were considered Choctaw through Nahotima, and they passed on their ancestry to the children of Louis Leflore.[25]

Nahotima's heritage was Chakchiuma. Her mother was Shumaka, one of the few surviving members of the Chakchiuma people. Shumaka was born in the late 1730s, in the early days of European settlement in Mississippi. She married a European, Roscoe Cole, who had originally been a Chakchiuma captive. Shumaka herself lived until 1838 and died at her home near the town of Chocchuma in what became Grenada County.[26] The town of Chocchuma will also appear in the nineteenth-century part of this story.

As for Louis Durant, LeFleur's fellow traveler, he built a home on bluffs overlooking the Big Black River across from the town later named for him. He married a Choctaw woman, Sheniya Hanak. His three sons and two daughters became part of the Hanak Iksa clan, into which Louis Durant was also adopted. His son, Pierre, married a Choctaw woman, further cementing Durant family relationships in the iksa and solidifying that family's Choctaw identity.[27] The Leflores and Durants arrived together, but their family histories will diverge dramatically a little later.

But first, both the Leflores and the Durants were active members of the alliance between the French and the Choctaw. Both families, after all, had heritage from both parties to that alliance. The Choctaw-French alliance lent tacit support to the United States during the Revolutionary War, while the Chickasaw generally supported the British.

After the American Revolution, the Choctaw transferred their allegiance to the new Americans. The French presence in Mississippi had dwindled, but the Choctaw-French alliance fought for the United States during the War of 1812, while the Chickasaw continued to side with the British. During the War of 1812, both the Leflores and Durants joined General Andrew Jackson at the Battle of New Orleans. Louis Leflore even named his youngest son, born in 1815, Andrew Jackson Leflore, after the general under whom the Choctaw fought. It would not, in the end, do the Choctaw much good to have allied with the Americans, although the Leflores would prosper nonetheless.[28]

THE LAND OF COTTON

The first inhabitants of Holmes County—Native Americans—came for the fresh water and lithic material. Later, de Soto came looking for gold. Later still, Choctaw women farmed the land to grow food, and the French coureurs des bois arrived for the fur trade. By the end of the eighteenth century, the Americans who traveled south wanted the land in Mississippi because they had discovered its potential to grow another commodity: cotton.

In 1800, cotton was the raw material of the world's largest and most important industry. There was no auto industry and almost no oil industry. There were obviously no computers or microchips. People wore skins and leathers, linen, silk, wool, or cotton. There were no synthetic fibers for clothing, boat sails, blankets, or upholstery.

Cotton was not new. People had grown cotton for thousands of years as it had been cultivated, spun, and woven in East Africa for millennia. The Mayan people of Central America wore clothing from their own native cotton. And in 1800, India was the world's largest producer of cotton.[29]

The demand for cotton kept growing. Cotton production had started as a small-scale, household-based enterprise. But as it became more profitable, and as the places where it was produced were colonized by Europeans, production expanded. By the eighteenth century, French and British colonies in the Caribbean produced a significant share of cotton. Cotton plants love the heat and growing cotton was labor intensive. Cotton producers learned the value of enslaved labor in growing the plants to scale. Producers could demand that a captive labor force put in the long, hot days required for volume cultivation. The transatlantic slave trade, which had begun during the sixteenth century, accelerated to grow cotton and sugar in the Caribbean and South America and tobacco and indigo in the Upper South. Still, as late as 1780—around the time the Leflores and Durants came to Holmes County—no cotton arrived in Europe from North America. People grew cotton as far north as Virginia for domestic use, but it was not yet a large-scale or export crop in the Western Hemisphere outside the Caribbean.[30]

All that changed very rapidly. In 1793, Eli Whitney invented the cotton gin, making large-scale separation of cotton from its seeds more efficient. In 1798, Mississippi Territory became an uncontested part of the United States. Haiti's very violent revolution expelled its French colonizers in 1803, and that revolution and other political unrest in the Caribbean brought with it higher cotton prices. The potential that a large swath of land might become available in a climate warm enough to grow cotton brought a rush of interest in its purchase.[31]

The process of claiming the land for cotton began on the eve of the nineteenth century. It began with a scandal featuring a colonial charter, corrupt state legislators, the US Supreme Court, and the US Congress. The tale may seem, at first, to have little to do with Holmes County. Its outcome, however, is that when the land eventually went up for sale, speculators could purchase land in Holmes County for almost no money down because they had purchased Mississippi "stock" years earlier. They could purchase land elsewhere in the Delta with that stock too, but Holmes and its immediate neighbors, bordered by the Yazoo and Big Black Rivers, were more accessible.

Mississippi stock undergirded the purchase of land in large tracts, not small homesteads, and these large tracts became the vast cotton plantations of the Mississippi Delta. Questionable alliances between land speculators and politicians recur at other moments in Holmes County history. So, it's a complicated story, and not much discussed these days, but it is pivotal in how cotton became king in the Mississippi Delta—and how enslaved people in Holmes County would become its subjects.

Before Mississippi became an official US territory, part of its land arguably belonged to the State of Georgia. The original colonial charter of the State of Georgia extended west to the Mississippi River and granted dominion over what were known as the Yazoo lands. The Yazoo lands extended across thirty-four million acres—fifty-four thousand square miles—including much of central Mississippi and the Delta and all of what would become Holmes County.[32]

An initial, if futile, effort to purchase Yazoo lands began in 1789 with a group of Virginians who wanted to expand plantation lands free from the strictures of the then brand-new federal government. They offered Georgia $200,000 for options on fifteen million acres of Yazoo lands. Georgia was amenable, but since Spain still claimed part of the land, the first effort came to naught. Then, six years later, Spain relinquished its claim to Mississippi in the Treaty of San Lorenzo. Another politically well-connected group of speculators moved in to purchase the Yazoo lands. This group bought the lands on a fee simple basis—not options—from the State of Georgia for a sum of $500,000. Even in those days that was nothing short of a steal.

Georgia sold the land because it needed cash to pay its militia, and selling Yazoo lands was a quick way to obtain cash. Plus, the speculators who bought the land had freely bribed most members of the Georgia legislature. In doing so, however, they aroused the ire of both Georgia voters and President George Washington. Washington asserted that neither speculators nor the State of Georgia were empowered to negotiate with Indian nations and thus were out of bounds in selling what was still Indian land. The result was a US Senate request for President Washington to negotiate a treaty and extinguish Native titles to the land so speculators could take possession of it. Washington resisted. Meanwhile, Georgia voters rejected the Yazoo land deal and the bribery and corruption that were part of it. They elected a new legislature in 1796, which repealed the deal.

The repeal barely paused the effort. Speculators had already bought and, in some cases, already resold Yazoo land before the new legislature voted for repeal. Indeed, on the very same day the legislature repealed the deal, speculators who had bought Yazoo lands resold to a new group of investors, mostly from New England, and dubbed the New England Mississippi Land Company (NEMLC). The NEMLC paid over a million dollars—a hefty profit already from the original purchase price of half a million. The land that would become Holmes County was included in the sale to the NEMLC.

The Supreme Court of the United States entered the fray in 1810 in the case of *Fletcher v. Peck*. Fletcher had bought Yazoo land from Peck before Georgia repealed the law authorizing the sale. The two litigants were colluding to clarify title, and, in the process, they aimed to undercut Native claims to the land. The court upheld the legitimacy of their contract. The ruling declared the Georgia legislature's repeal of the Yazoo land sale unconstitutional because the US Constitution prohibited states from repudiating private contracts. The court also hinted at the illegitimacy of Native claims to the land, an issue to which they would return in a later case.

The Supreme Court ruling meant those who bought Yazoo land were entitled to compensation even though Georgia had sold land that, in fact, belonged to the federal government. Congress was drawn into the matter to determine a means of compensating the buyers. The NEMLC led a substantial congressional lobbying effort. They were a politically connected bunch—the chair of one key congressional committee had been an NEMLC agent—and key members of both the Georgia delegation and delegations from the New England states supported compensation for buyers of Yazoo land.

In 1814, Congress determined that compensation would be in the form of "Mississippi stock," which could be redeemed for land when federal land offices opened in Mississippi Territory. The stock could be exchanged for cash after land was sold or could be presented for a 95 percent discount on purchases at federal land sales in Mississippi.

The NEMLC sold its stock as shares on the securities market. Those who owned shares were entitled to the 95 percent discount. The sales drove up the price of Mississippi stock, bringing a profit to the NEMLC. The stock remained a good deal for land, however. While purchases of federal land generally required 25 percent down, the discount for stockholders meant that they could purchase land in Mississippi (and Alabama) for 1.25 percent down, applying their 95 percent discount once land was put up for sale.

The Yazoo land sale—which was complex and took a generation to resolve—receives little attention now, but it was high profile at the time. "There was not a child of 10 years old in the country who would not have heard of this business" of the Yazoo land sale, declared Maryland congressman Roger Nelson in 1808.[33] His declaration was certainly an exaggeration, but there seems little doubt that the Native American leadership knew their land was up for grabs. The process undoubtedly encouraged Native American leaders to sign treaties, aware that the combined forces of land speculators, plantation owners, Congress, and the Supreme Court were to rampage their heritage.

As the legal processes were underway for taking Choctaw lands to grow cotton, the stage was also being set for the importation and regulation of the enslaved people who would provide plantation labor. In 1820, there were already over thirty-two thousand enslaved Black people in Mississippi—over a third of the population—mostly in the southern half of the state. Natchez had developed early and had a thriving slave market by the end of the eighteenth century. Firms like Franklin, Armfield, and Ballard grew enormously wealthy bringing slaves from the Upper South to Mississippi, for sale in Natchez and other slave markets. Enslaved people were transported by overland coffle, which means people were shackled together and walked more than a thousand miles. A young, enslaved person in the Upper South faced a roughly one in three chance of being taken in the slave trade and brought to the Deep South.[34]

In theory, the African slave trade to the United States ended in 1808. In reality, illegal slave trading continued until the Civil War: The arrival of the *Clotilda*, a slave ship from Benin that docked in Mobile Bay in 1860, is well documented.[35] Slave ships also came to New York illegally, and slave trading in Cuba continued, with some slaves arriving in New Orleans from there. As late as 1920, there were still a handful of elderly African Americans in Mississippi who had been born in Africa and brought to Mississippi as slaves.[36]

As the importation of enslaved people grew, their numbers made white settlers nervous. In 1812, David Holmes, as territorial governor, complained, "Scarcely a day passes without my receiving some information relative to the designs of those people to insurrect . . . certain facts and expressions of their views have justly excited considerable alarm amongst the citizens."[37]

Mississippi had especially harsh slave codes in the territorial period. In 1807, it passed a law that if a slave ran away, the fugitive would be burned in the hand by the sheriff in open court. False testimony against another slave yielded an ear nailed to a pillory while standing there for one hour, and then the ear was cut off. As territorial governor, Holmes instituted slave patrols under supervision of the local militia. Any slave found off the slaveholder's property without a pass was subject to up to twenty lashes. Thirty-nine lashes were the punishment for attending a literacy class. Slave offenses were adjudicated by a special three-person panel, not in a regular court system, and slaves had no representation in front of the panel except in capital cases, which had an appeals procedure.[38]

Enslaved people were not allowed to congregate, particularly for religious worship, since in the minds of plantation holders that, too, risked organized insurrection. An 1822 law required that two whites be present in a supervisory capacity at religious meetings of enslaved people, which could not be held on Sunday. Later revisions of the law allowed slaveholders who so desired to provide religious instruction to slaves but banned slaves from preaching at religious services.[39]

Holmes County was not a center of action at that time. In 1820, Holmes County was still Choctaw land, with some Native villages, and scattered farms and settlements, very little cotton, and only a few enslaved people. The next fifteen years would bring major change. By 1836, the land would have become Holmes County and sold to new owners who had bought it for cotton production. First, the Native Americans would have to go.

EXPULSION

The Choctaw lost about a third of their land and more than half of what would be Holmes County in signing the Treaty of Doak's Stand in 1820. The rest was ceded in 1830 through the Treaty of Dancing Rabbit Creek.

The Treaty of Doak's Stand was controversial and flawed from the start. In exchange for their land in Mississippi, the Choctaw were to receive land in Arkansas. After the treaty was ratified, the federal government swapped the land it had promised, which had already been settled by whites, for less fertile land in Oklahoma. The treaty was also to provide land in Mississippi to any Choctaw who wanted to stay and farm, and to support Choctaw schools both in Mississippi and in the new territory. Neither of those promises were fulfilled.

The three chiefs in the early nineteenth century were Apuckshunnubbee in the Okla Falaya region in the north, Mushulatubbee in the central region and Pushmataha to the south. They were the second and third generations who had traded with Europeans and then with the Americans. They had adapted to the market economy. A century earlier the Choctaw had traded deerskins for muskets; by the 1820s, they owned taverns that sheltered travelers along the Natchez Trace and livestock that they sold to newly arrived settlers.[40]

Pushmataha, who was reputedly related to Nahotima and therefore to the Leflores, had led the alliance between the Americans and the Choctaw during the War of 1812. The Shawnee chief Tecumseh had worked to unite all the Native American nations to side with the British, who had promised them land and sovereignty. Tecumseh came to persuade the Choctaw to ally with other nations, but Pushmataha rejected Tecumseh's arguments and declared that any Choctaw who followed Tecumseh would not be welcome back. Pushmataha joined with the Leflores and Durants in fighting alongside Andrew Jackson to defeat the British at the Battle of New Orleans in 1815.[41]

Just five years later, in 1820, Andrew Jackson and Thomas Hinds met with the three chiefs to negotiate the Treaty of Doak's Stand. Pushmataha and Mushulatubbee signed the treaty with reservations. Apuckshunnubbee of the Okla Falaya reportedly never signed. As the United States swapped out the originally promised land in Arkansas, the three chiefs traveled to Washington to negotiate a revised treaty. Apuckshunnubbee said before leaving that he would not sign a treaty that gave away one foot more of Choctaw land. He never made it to Washington. He fell—or some speculate, was pushed—from a cliff in Maysville, Kentucky, and was buried there.

Pushmataha became ill in Washington and died there. Pushmataha asked that "the big guns be fired over him." He was buried with full military honors and a twenty-one-gun salute in the Congressional Cemetery about a mile from the US Capitol. On his deathbed, Pushmataha spoke in Choctaw. Recalled and translated by those there at the time, he argued for prudence, saying the Choctaw people are "warm in battle but cool in the hours of debate." He added that the Choctaw had held Americans' hands for so long that "like the claws of an eagle they will not let them go." He observed that neither his nation nor any of his ancestors had fought against the United States, and that the Choctaw have "given of our country until it has become very small."[42]

The Treaty of Doak's Stand remained in place without amendment. But in 1823, three years later, the United States Supreme Court ruled in *Johnson v. M'Intosh* that the Indians did not own their land after all, a decree that reinforced federal dominion over Indian lands.[43] The court held that Indians had no right to sell their land because they never owned it in fee simple terms in the first place. Rather, Indians had rights of occupancy but could not transfer those rights to others. The only impediment to the sale of remaining Native lands in Mississippi was the natives' continued presence on them.

The final expulsion of virtually all Choctaw from Holmes County—and the rest of Mississippi—followed the signing of the Treaty of Dancing Rabbit Creek in 1830. The head of the Choctaw at that time was Greenwood Leflore. He was the son of Louis Leflore and great-grandson of Shumaka. He was both reviled and admired and was certainly a tangle of contradictions. He did very well for himself, and for some of his kin. He was no hero to his people, although by some accounts he tried to protect them. By all accounts he was wily and sophisticated. He most certainly knew of the Yazoo land sales and related Supreme Court decisions and recognized the inevitability of Choctaw land loss.

Greenwood Leflore was born on June 3, 1800, in the camp that became known as LeFleur's Bluff, now in the City of Jackson. He was named Greenwood for one of his father's shipping colleagues. He was raised in French Camp along the Natchez Trace. He spoke Choctaw as his first language as a child. The family later settled in Holmes County. A few historians name Greenwood as Nancy Cravat Leflore's child, but family genealogies list him as Rebecca's son. In either case he would have been raised by both women in the Choctaw tradition.[44]

From ages twelve to seventeen, Greenwood Leflore lived in Nashville with the Donly family. Major John Donly had the contract to carry mail from Nashville to Natchez, and he stopped along the way at French Camp, where he became friendly with the Leflore family. He was apparently impressed with young Greenwood and invited him to live with his family in Nashville and obtain an English-language education there. Greenwood was fully bilingual by adulthood.

When he was seventeen, Greenwood left Nashville. He eloped with Donly's older daughter Rosanah, called Rosa. The couple had one son, John Donly Leflore, in 1824 and two daughters, Elizabeth and Jane. After Rosanah died in childbirth in 1829, Leflore married Elizabeth Cody, a relative of Cherokee chief John Ross. When she died a year later, he wed his first wife's younger sister Priscilla Donly in 1834, thereby continuing the family—and Choctaw—tradition of marrying sisters. They had a daughter, Rebecca.

Back in Mississippi after Rosa's death, Greenwood converted to the Methodist Church. He used to translate services at the church in Ebenezer in Holmes County and opposed the continued practice of Choctaw religion. He advocated for education including Christian religious instruction for Native children and written laws modeled after European laws. He was virulently opposed to the sale of alcohol, believing it harmed his people and disrupted their culture. He helped prosecute his own brother-in-law for violations of liquor laws.[45]

In 1824, Greenwood succeeded his uncle, Robert Cole, as Okla Falaya chief. Cole had served only two years following the death of Apuckshunnubbee. Cole resigned to allow Greenwood to succeed him because others felt a bilingual chief could best lead negotiations on the Treaty of Dancing Rabbit Creek, which the Choctaw leadership anticipated. Andrew Jackson, under whom the Choctaw had fought during the War of 1812, became president in 1829 and immediately called for Indian removal.

The Treaty of Dancing Rabbit Creek was signed by the Choctaw chiefs on September 27, 1830. It was the final and most important agreement leading to the removal of most members of the Choctaw Nation from lands they and their ancestors had occupied since at least 7000 BCE. The treaty pledged perpetual peace and friendship between the United States and the Choctaw, and the United States promised a tract of land in Oklahoma in return for the Choctaw ceding "the entire country they own and possess, east of the Mississippi River" and agreeing to move "as early as practicable." They were promised, but most never received, annuities from the US government.[46]

There are indications that Leflore worked to get a better deal for the Choctaw Nation than they received in the end. He reached out to Cherokee chief John Ross, to whom he was related through his second wife. Eyewitness accounts of treaty negotiations also report that the chiefs argued to keep their traditional lands. They were told that if they did not sign, the US Army would come to forcibly remove or exterminate them. Leflore had already acknowledged to the federal agent for Mississippi the power of greater numbers on the president's side.[47]

Negotiations with the full group of chiefs were paused after the acrimony, in favor of a smaller group meeting. A supplement was then added to the treaty granting Mississippi land to specific Choctaw leaders and family members who did not wish to be removed. The list includes widows and orphans of recent chiefs, family members of chiefs, Louis Durant, and other prominent members of the Choctaw Nation. The allocations by one count included forty sections of land (a section is a square mile) in Mushulatubbee's district, thirty-three and a half in Leflore's district, and twenty-two sections in Nitakechi's district.

An entire article in the treaty supplement is devoted to grants to non-Indians. It begins by granting a full section of land to Greenwood's father-in-law, John Donly, noting he has Choctaw grandchildren and carried the mail through the Choctaw Nation. It also grants the proceeds of the sale of land to creditors of Indian leaders and a half section "at the earnest and particular request of the Chief Greenwood Leflore" to David Haley, who had apparently served as a courier on a trip to Washington on Leflore's behalf.[48]

In many cases, the Choctaw named in the treaty supplement never received the land. The federal agent assigned to the Choctaw, William Ward, was reputedly corrupt and had been the subject of complaints for twenty years. He simply refused to enroll Choctaw claimants.[49] The Durants, for example, were never compensated for the land granted them in the treaty.[50]

But the treaty did well by the Leflore family. Holmes County land records alone show Greenwood reserved a full section under the treaty, as well as plots or sections for Louis Leflore, Greenwood's brother-in-law Samuel Long, members of the Brashear family who were also in-laws, and to David Haley, some of which is patented to Greenwood Leflore. Land owned by Samuel Long later became the site of the city of Lexington. Felicity Leflore Long, Samuel Long's wife and Greenwood's sister, is buried there.

Other land in Holmes County was allocated to the widows and orphans of Pushmataha, and to Chiefs Nitakechi and Mushulatubbee. Other plots are listed as "selected for Choctaw orphans." A few of those to whom land was allocated in Holmes took possession. The Mushulatubbee family occupied their land in Holmes and changed their name to King. Others exchanged the land allocated in Holmes for land elsewhere.[51] Much of Choctaw and Chickasaw land had not yet been platted and therefore was not sold or allocated until 1833 or later. Reserving land in Holmes (and likely other counties as well) allowed for a later swap when more land went up for sale.

After the Treaty of Dancing Rabbit Creek, the Choctaw stripped Greenwood Leflore of his role as chief and replaced him with George Washington Harkins, who was the son of Greenwood's older sister Louisa and John Harkins, a European descendant who had come to Mississippi from North Carolina. The federal government, however, seemed not to recognize Harkins. President Jackson had named John Eaton as lead negotiator with the nations, and Eaton and Leflore continued to correspond about the circumstances and processes of removal.[52]

George Harkins wrote a letter "to the American People," widely published in newspapers at the time, which closed with the following: "We go forth sorrowful, knowing that wrong has been done. Will you extend to us your sympathizing regards until all traces of disagreeable oppositions are obliterated, and we again shall have confidence in the professions of our white brethren? Here is the land of our progenitors, and here are their bones; they left them as a sacred deposit, and we have been compelled to venerate its trust; it is dear to us, yet we cannot stay, my people are dear to me, with them I must go."[53]

Greenwood Leflore remained in Mississippi and prospered, as did most of his sisters. His brother Forbis Leflore had been raised in the Harkins household and evidently had greater allegiance to George Harkins than to Greenwood. Greenwood's brother Basil Leflore also removed and briefly served as governor of the Choctaw Nation. In the end, only about 4,000 out of 25,000 Choctaw remained in Mississippi. They formed the Mississippi Band of Choctaw Indians. Today, the band has 11,000 members and owns just shy of 34,000 acres of land.[54] The Choctaw Nation of Oklahoma, headquartered in Durant, Oklahoma, has 225,000 members.[55]

The Durant family tried to remain in Mississippi, but after a decade of harassment and the death of Louis Durant they left for Oklahoma. On December 30, 1844, Louis Durant's son Pierre led eight wagons of Durants with a total of 550 Choctaw west along the Trail of Tears. They traveled over land, by steamship, and again over land in midwinter. Seven group members died of exposure and pneumonia along the way. They arrived in Fort Coffee, Oklahoma, in early February of 1845, where they were paid a stipend of ten dollars each. They were never paid for their land, nor did they receive the equipment or annuities promised.

The Durants settled in Oklahoma just north of an area called Pigeon Roost in late March. Pierre's son Fisher settled about twenty-five miles away and founded a station stop there instead of farming. It was called Carriage Point and later named Fisher's Station. Fisher's son, Dixon Durant, erected the first permanent structure there. Durant, Oklahoma, where the Choctaw Nation is headquartered today, is named for him. William A. Durant, a direct descendant of Pierre's son Sylvester, served as principal chief of the Choctaw Nation from 1937 to 1948. Few if any members of the Durant family remained in Mississippi.[56]

THE NEW OWNERS

By the end of the 1830s, virtually all the land in Mississippi that had been Native American land had been sold to new owners. Many were speculators who held the land for a short time and then sold it at a profit, including members of the NEMLC who had obtained Mississippi stock through the Yazoo land deal. Others held on to their land and profited from growing cotton on it. Those who held on to large tracts of land became Holmes County's new elite and were responsible for populating the county with enslaved people brought from elsewhere. Most of this book is about those enslaved people, who replaced the Choctaw as the county's new majority in the 1830s, and their descendants. First, let us take a closer look at who came to own the land in the 1830s and the process by which they purchased it.

The new owners were white and generally recent arrivals from the Carolinas, Virginia, or even farther north. They most often purchased land from new federal land offices, or from those who purchased land from the land office to sell at a quick profit in a second wave of land speculation. Native Americans who wanted to stay technically had preemptive rights—as did other squatters on the land—but the land purchase process did not respect those rights. Companies of wealthy purchasers and speculators took over, rolling those who were already on the land, particularly in the Delta portion of the county where the land was best for growing cotton.

Native Americans who wanted to stay had been required to register with federal agent William Ward. Ward, however, failed to properly register or retain records of Choctaw who wished to remain in Mississippi. Land companies also regularly forced out those with preemptive rights—often by force—so the companies could buy land in large parcels and keep it at a bargain price or resell it at a profit.[57]

In Holmes County, Robert Cole, who gave up the Okla Falaya chiefdom to his nephew Greenwood Leflore, finally agreed to sell the twelve hundred acres granted him in the Treaty of Dancing Rabbit Creek, although the sale noted the name of a settler already on the land who should also have had preemptive rights. Similarly, Isaac Impson, an Englishman who had married into the Choctaw Nation and settled in Holmes, appointed an attorney to receive compensation for his quarter section of land, but when that effort failed, he removed to Oklahoma instead.[58]

Greenwood Leflore, not surprisingly, had better luck than other Native Americans. He swapped the land reserved for him in Holmes County (and presumably elsewhere) for acreage in Carroll County, once it was platted. The land he chose had been Chakchiuma land. He ended up with 15,000 acres in Carroll County, the equivalent of twenty-three sections of land. As one descendant lists, "15,000 acres of land, 400 slaves, sawmills, brickyards, steamboats, warehouses, and other enterprises."[59] Leflore's descendants recount that when he was accused of accepting a bribe to sign the treaty, he responded, "Which is worse, for a great government to offer a bribe or a poor Indian to take one?"[60] Greenwood Leflore certainly did not live his life as a poor Indian.

Land purchasers who were neither Native nor squatters—the settlers and speculators from the Upper South or the North—bought Native land through the federal government, allowing Mississippi stock from the Yazoo land sales to be used for purchase. Congress had set the minimum price for land at $1.25 an acre. It had also banned the use of credit for purchasing federal land, which encouraged wealthy speculators and those who owned Mississippi stock. A federal land sales office opened in Mt. Salus in 1822 to sell land ceded by the Treaty of Doak's Stand. Two offices opened in 1833 to sell the land ceded by the Treaty at Dancing Rabbit Creek. The sale of land east of the Pearl River was through the federal land office in Columbus. Federal land in the state's western half was through the federal land office in Chocchuma, a town on historic Chakchiuma land in what was then Carroll County. Federal government sales of Mississippi land climbed from 236,894 acres in 1832 to more than a million acres in 1833. Sales peaked at 3,267,299 acres in 1836.[61]

The Chocchuma Land Company was organized shortly before the land sales at Chocchuma by major land speculators and buyers. Its constitution provided that each individual joining would put up $1,000 for land purchases and that profits from resale of land would be shared equally. By pooling resources, the company could purchase large tracts. The company reputedly allowed squatters on the land to purchase at resale for the minimum federal government price of $1.25 an acre—provided they did not bid on the land at auction and limited the quantity of their purchase. In at least one instance, the Chocchuma Land Company bought an 840-acre parcel for $800 and sold it within a day for more than $8,000.[62]

The company membership was mostly secret and details are scarce, but the company had sufficient capital to purchase approximately 376 square miles of land, including at least tens of thousands of acres in Holmes County.[63] With a secret membership, and all the buying and selling of Mississippi stock, we do not know whether the same people were involved with both the Chocchuma Land Company and the purchase of Mississippi stock from the New England Mississippi Land Company. There was likely overlap, however, as both groups were mostly speculators who were new to Mississippi, if, indeed, they ever lived in the state.

One leader of the Chocchuma Land Company, who did most of the bidding for land, was Robert J. Walker, soon to become a United States senator from Mississippi. Walker was born in Pennsylvania in 1801 and graduated from the University of Pennsylvania, married a great-granddaughter of Benjamin Franklin, and threw himself wholeheartedly into the Democratic Party and support for Andrew Jackson. He arrived in Mississippi in the 1820s, with the purpose of gaining wealth through land speculation.[64]

President Jackson appointed Samuel Gwin as the federal land agent for Mississippi despite the Senate's refusal to confirm him. Samuel Gwin's brother, William McKendree Gwin, had been Jackson's personal secretary for a time, prior to his appointment as federal marshal for Mississippi. William Gwin became a Mississippi congressman, then headed out west, where he became a US senator from California. In the latter role, William Gwin is perhaps best known for his efforts to establish a Confederate colony in Mexico. A branch of the Gwin family would continue to play a prominent role in Holmes County history through the twentieth century.[65]

The anticompetitive nature of the Chocchuma Land Company drew contemporaneous criticism. George Poindexter, one of Mississippi's two US senators, was a member of the Whig Party and a long-standing critic of President Andrew Jackson, a Democrat. Poindexter accused Samuel Gwin of collusion with Walker and the Chocchuma Land Company. According to Poindexter, Gwin was marking as already sold parcels of land that Walker and the Chocchuma Land Company wanted to buy, making that land unavailable to other bids and giving the Chocchuma Land Company a virtual monopoly on the choicest land. Poindexter authored a report to the US Senate, entitled *Fraud in Land Sales*, that described "companies of speculators . . . united for the purpose of monopolizing all the good lands then offered at a public sale, of overawing bidders, and driving all competition out of the market." Those companies then "established an office in the vicinity of the register's office, at which they opened, on each day, a regular sale of the lands purchased by them at public sale, and, at this company sale . . . the company claimed and actually enforced a complete monopoly."[66]

Poindexter's objections were not an effort to protect the Choctaw. He opposed Walker's politics and objected to the competitive advantages of the Chocchuma Land Company.[67] Poindexter himself bought and sold land in Holmes County in the 1830s. He sold to William Ferriday "land reserved for Cullishuba as an Indian reservation and the same tract conveyed to him by Aaron W. Davis." There were twenty-eight enslaved people on the land, mostly children, and the sale lists their names and ages together with all "horses, stock, cattle farming utensils," and the unharvested corn crop.[68]

Walker ultimately won the fight with Poindexter. Walker called on counties to pass a series of resolutions in support of his role in the process. One resolution "adopted by very large meetings in Holmes and Yalobusha Counties" said in part, "We entertain the most exalted respect for the abilities, political principles, and estimable moral qualities of our fellow citizen, R. J. Walker, Esq. and feel the warmest gratitude for his generous and manly protection of the interests of the settlers at the Chocchuma land sales."[69] In 1835, the state legislature replaced Poindexter with Walker as US senator. Samuel Gwin was a casualty of the fracas, however. He died in 1838, some say of a lung disease, although most reports say George Poindexter's law partner, Judge Isaac Caldwell, and Gwin shot each other in a duel.[70] Gwin progeny, however, would remain in Holmes County.

The Chocchuma Land Company, together with the Yazoo land deal, helped make Holmes County a place of large, wealthy plantations—among the most affluent in the state. Nearly two-thirds—63 percent—of Holmes County farms had more than one hundred acres of improved land and ten had more than one thousand acres. In comparison, just over a third—37 percent—of farms in Mississippi were larger than one hundred acres—and only 26 percent of the farms in the United States. The average net worth of Holmes County farmers was more than a half a million in today's dollars.[71]

Several of the largest landowners—and soon, largest slave holders—in Holmes County with ties to Walker had lasting impacts on Holmes County. Walker sold land to Wiley and Aaron Davis, and to Garrett Keirn, endorsed by Richard T. Archer.[72] The Davises were major investors in the Tchula area when they bought large parcels in the 1830s. The Archer family owned 245 slaves over two properties in Tchula and Eulogy.[73]

The Keirn family held 211 slaves at their properties north of Tchula. Garrett Keirn had come south from Maryland. He bought land in Holmes County from Robert J. Walker in 1835 and added to his holdings in the 1840s.[74] Garrett

Keirn married Lucy Leake, whose father at the time of their 1823 wedding was Governor Walter Leake. Their son, Walter Leake Keirn, was born in Holmes County in 1830. He would become one of the wealthiest men in Mississippi and play a significant role in the county's future, adding over time to the property he inherited from his father.

In one instance, Walter Leake Keirn bought a large plantation from the Pinchback family. The Pinchback family had come from Georgia, where William Pinchback had freed a mixed-race woman, Eliza Stewart, and married her. Their second son, Pinckney Benton Stewart (P. B. S.) Pinchback, was to become, briefly, governor of Louisiana and a US senator from that state (although he was never sworn in). Under Georgia law, the Pinchback children born there were also free. The family moved to Holmes County around 1837 when Pinckney was an infant. After William Pinchback died in 1848, Eliza Stewart Pinchback moved the family to Cincinnati as she feared they would be enslaved if they remained in Holmes County.[75]

Another prominent Mississippian, William Raphael Miles, held 174 slaves near Tchula. Miles, a native of Kentucky and an attorney, had homes in Yazoo City and New Orleans as well as his Holmes County property. He served in the Mississippi State Legislature from 1844 to 1848. He represented New Orleans at the Louisiana Secession Convention and then raised and largely financed the Confederacy's Thirty-Second Louisiana, known as Miles' Legion. His land became the town of Mileston, where the African American co-op is located today.

Not all the new landowners in Holmes County held large plantations. Smaller farms were concentrated in the eastern part of Holmes, in the area near Durant and West, where the land was more hilly and less fertile. There, farmers held fewer enslaved people and often farmed their own land. Farmers from the Durant area would take the lead during a brief period of small farmer rebellion and populism in Holmes County in the 1880s.

Holmes County also had a small Jewish community. The county's first Jewish resident was a former peddler named Jacob Sontheimer, who in the early 1840s cared for a customer, Henry Johnson, on a plantation near what is now Ebenezer. At the time, the town was known as Bucksnort Landing with a tavern known for heavy drinking, gambling, and carousing, located next door to a Methodist church where Greenwood Leflore translated sermons for Choctaw tribal congregants. Sontheimer and Johnson helped the Methodists clean up Bucksnort Landing and its name was changed to Ebenezer. Members of the Sontheimer family fought for the Confederacy with Nathan Bedford Forrest, who became the first grand wizard of the Ku Klux Klan.[76]

Between 1820 and 1860, the population of the state of Mississippi grew from 75,000 to 791,000 people, a majority of whom were enslaved Black people. In

Holmes County, in the same period, the population grew from a few hundred to over 16,000. Nearly two-thirds were enslaved Black people.

The land itself had been transformed from forest to fields. In 1839, Holmes County had produced just over six thousand bales of cotton. Twenty years later it produced nearly forty-two thousand bales of cotton. Nearly half of that cotton was produced in the Delta portion of Holmes, which produced over eighteen thousand bales in 1860.[77]

ENSLAVED PEOPLE IN HOLMES

The profitability of the land purchased by these new owners relied on enslaved labor. The new owners brought nearly ten thousand enslaved people into Holmes County to clear and then work the land. The people brought to Holmes County as slaves carried their own cultures and values that would forever change the nature of the place they were brought to farm. They all had African origins—and some Native American as well—but they had origins in different parts of Africa, encompassing multiple languages and belief systems. The diverse origins of enslaved people in Holmes County and, indeed, throughout Mississippi, is important to the development of music, religion, and a culture that became a syncretic mix of the beliefs and traditions people came with while assimilating to conditions in Mississippi.

Most enslaved people in Holmes County had origins in British West Africa, although more than a few were from the French colonies of the Senegambia, and most—but by no means all—were brought to Holmes County after a generation or more of slavery in the Upper South.

Enslaved people in the Upper South—Virginia, Maryland, and North Carolina—had been brought there as part of the British slave trade. The British brought slaves from their colonies—present-day Cameroon through Ghana—although African slave traders took people to British-held West Africa from a wider area. The French were more likely to enslave people from the Senegambia, as present-day Senegal was a French colony.

African people from British West Africa and the Senegambia had different musical and religious traditions. The melding of those was important in the practice of religion and in the development of music in Mississippi. People in British West Africa practiced Yoruba religion. Yoruba traditions have parallels to Christianity and became especially important in developing religious practices.[78] "At some points, the parallels are amazing, as with the omnipotence, justice, omniscience, and providence of God. . . . None of these attributes of God had to be learned first in slavery."[79] People from the Senegambia traded with the Arab world. Some were Muslim, as most of Senegal is now, and others practiced a combination of Muslim and Yoruba religion.

West Africa had a deep tradition of drum music. The djembe drum is found throughout West Africa in what were both British and French colonies. The music of the Senegambia embeds Arab influence as well, in its greater reliance on stringed instruments and vocal song.[80] The iconic blues music of the Delta is an amalgam of the music of the Bambara people from Mali, West African drum rhythms, and sounds all its own.[81]

As slaves were brought to Mississippi, they were separated from their families, which also happened once they arrived. One estate sale ad from 1839 reads in part: "I will sell for ready money at the court house door in the town of Lexington, in the county of Holmes, and State of Mississippi, on Monday the thirteenth of May next, the following descried Negro Slaves, the property of said John White, viz: one Negro man named Daniel, about twenty three years old, one Negro woman named Jane, about twenty years old, one Negro girl named Mary, about four years old, and one Negro child named Isaac, aged ten months."[82] This was self-evidently a family but each enslaved person was advertised for sale individually.

The diversity of enslaved people in Holmes and separation from family had a formidable impact on the development of its culture. Whether brought from the Upper South or New Orleans, and whether sold or resold individually, Black people in Holmes County—and throughout Mississippi—needed to form new families, new communities, and new traditions there. They clearly did so, despite both the requirements of extremely hard labor and ongoing efforts to repress their religion and culture.

The process of clearing the land was accomplished in Holmes by enslaved labor in the 1830s and early 1840s. Before it was cleared, the Delta looked more like the Amazon rain forest than it did the setting of row-crop agriculture it is today. Once the land was cleared, enslaved people were generally required to work from dawn until dusk six days a week with Saturday off. The season began when women and children beat down the old plants and burned the stalks in late winter or early spring. Men then plowed the furrows using a sequence of horse- or mule-drawn ploughs and hand hoes. Women spread the seeds from a collection held in their aprons followed by a light harrowing to cover the seeds. Gangs of slaves then "scraped," or chopped, the cotton fields in spring and early summer, thinning the plants, reducing weeds, and "moulding" the plants to further reduce weeds. Repeated scraping passes helped reduce weeds and chop out weaker plants. They then turned to other crops, usually corn, until the bolls opened on the cotton plants.

During cotton picking, work began two hours before sunrise and did not finish until full darkness—fourteen or fifteen hours a day. Each boll was picked by hand, separating the cotton fibers from the sharp edges of the boll. At the height of the season, each person picked more than one hundred pounds of cotton a day. An overseer weighed each basket of cotton and punished people if the quantity of cotton was inadequate or if it contained leaves or dirt.[83]

Enslaved people were pushed to work fast. Planters measured productivity by "bales per acre per hand," a measure that contributed to exhausting the labor and depleting the land. The size of the crop per slave—a measure of productivity—was four times greater in the 1850s than in the 1820s. That may have been partly due to the development of a more productive cotton strain but also to more aggressive efforts in pushing enslaved labor.[84]

The mass insurrections white people had long feared did not happen in Holmes County, but enslaved people rebelled in other ways against the strictures placed on them. They continued their own religious practices despite a ban on them. They held religious meetings at night in the woods in "brush arbors" with services that incorporated traditional African practices as well as Christian ones.

Early post–Civil War African American churches grew from these brush arbor meetings. As one former slave described, "Us Niggers didn' have no secret meetin's. All us had was church meetin's in arbors out in de woods. De preachers 'ud exhort us dat us was de chillun o' Israel in de wilderness an' de Lawd done sent us to take dis lan' o' milk an' honey. But how us gwine a-take lan' what's already been took?"[85] Asia Missionary Baptist Church in Lexington, founded in 1871, has roots in a brush arbor meeting called Mount Pleasant. Other early African American churches likely did as well, given the timing of their founding. The United Methodist Church was founded near Pickens in 1865 and the Colored Methodist Church of Durant in 1865. A landowner donated property for the Mount Valley Baptist Church near Cruger in 1866.[86]

Interviews conducted in the 1930s tell of an incident that may have reflected Yoruba religious beliefs. Mrs. Sue Hallie Brennan of Franklin, clearly frightened by the incident, told of "Uncle Roberson, a negro slave owned by Edmund Noel and whose wife cooked for the Noel family, organized a form of religion that came very near destroying the entire community. He was called the Shepherd and he had disciples on each of the adjoining plantations. Whenever new members joined, they were given a new name, some of them were Sarah Hope Zion Leader, Laura Prince Bells of Badja, etc. He prophesied that three men would be killed within three days and that he would be one of them and sure enough they were all three killed the same day."[87] One explanation of the "success" of the prophecy may be that it was a suicide pact. Suicide among slaves, particularly those who came from Africa, was not uncommon, as some believed they would return to Africa upon their death.[88]

Continuing banned religious activity was one way that slaves showed resistance. Another was to run away. The slaveholder would send a posse after them and sometimes they were caught and jailed by the sheriff in another county. The sheriff would try to locate the slaveholder, sometimes using newspaper advertisements, and the slaveholder would pay a fine and any associated costs. If the slaveholder did not recover the escapee, they were sold at auction.

One example of such an advertisement for a Holmes County runaway reads:

> Committed, to the jail of Warren County, State of Mississippi, by S. L. George, an acting Justice of the Peace, in and for said county, of the 4th day of March, 1861, a negro man runaway slave, who says his name is MOSES, and that he belongs to Robt. Guinn [Robert Gwin], of Holmes County, State of Mississippi. The said boy is 40 to 45 years of age, five feet nine inches high, weighs 175 pounds, has a high forehead and a scar on the right side of the forehead, caused from the fall of a fence rail when small. Had on when committed white Linsey pants, white Linsey sack coat, russets and a black soft hat. The owner of said negro is requested to come forward, prove property, pay charges, and take him away, or he will be dealt with as the law directs. WM McRae, Sheriff.[89]

Another ad finds George, from South Carolina, in the Holmes County jail. The ad says that he "reads and writes very well, and appears to be about 20 years old," apparently running away to Mississippi looking for family. Holmes County also held Creesey, who said she belonged to William Barrow of Carroll County, and the ad noted, "She has a band of iron on each ankle, and a trace chain around her neck, fastened with a common pad lock."[90]

An early study of slavery in Mississippi concludes that "the chief difference between a slave and a free agricultural laborer lay outside the realm of food, clothing, shelter and work; his food and clothing were allowanced; his movements were restricted; his every act was watched; he was sometimes punished, and he might be sold. How distasteful life was under these conditions depended on two variable factors: the character of the masters and the desire for freedom in the hearts of the slaves."[91]

That 1933 study missed the reality that enslaved people from different parts of Africa and America banded together to continue their own religious practices, to develop their own artistry and music, to teach each other skills and trades, and to protect each other. They acted in accordance with their own worldviews and so bypassed many of the strictures placed on them. Slaves did not launch the insurrection plantation owners feared, which would surely have ended badly for them; neither did they all absorb whites' presumption of superiority over them. They were guided by their own values, grounded in their own Christianity that celebrated an exodus from slavery that they believed was sure to come. Spiritual songs of the period tell of the Lord telling Moses to "let my people go," and call on people "to weep no more," with the reminder that "Pharaoh's army got drown-ded" in the end.[92] The enslaved people of Holmes County were already fighting back in their own way before the war began. Soon, hundreds would join the Union army.

Chapter 2

CIVIL WAR TO JIM CROW—1861 TO 1890

Our position is thoroughly identified with the institution of slavery—the greatest material interest of the world. Its labor supplies the product which constitutes by far the largest and most important portions of commerce of the earth. These products are peculiar to the climate verging on the tropical regions, and by an imperious law of nature, none but the black race can bear exposure to the tropical sun. These products have become necessities of the world, and a blow at slavery is a blow at commerce and civilization.

—FROM MISSISSIPPI DECLARATION OF SECESSION

Mr. Lincoln, don't you think you oght to stop this thing and make them do the same by the colored men they [whites] have lived in idleness all their lives on stolen labor and made savages of the colored people, but they now are so furious because they are proving themselves to be men, such as have come away and got some edication.

—HANNAH JOHNSON, MOTHER OF A FEDERAL SOLDIER, TO PRESIDENT ABRAHAM LINCOLN
(QUOTED IN GIENAPP, *CIVIL WAR AND RECONSTRUCTION*, 222)

HOLMES COUNTY GOES TO WAR

Holmes County's first twenty-eight years—from its founding in 1833 to the beginning of the Civil War in 1861—were certainly eventful. Its Native population, descendants of people who had been there ten thousand years—were expelled; its land was sold, and the new population of owners brought in thousands of enslaved people of diverse origins to work it. Its next thirty years were similarly dramatic: The Civil War was fought, enslaved people were legally emancipated, and in a brief period of Reconstruction, African American men took positions of political leadership. Then, in 1890, roughly thirty years after the war began, white conservative Democrats who had returned to power wrote Mississippi's Jim Crow Constitution. That constitution, a much-amended version of which remains the state constitution today, took back many of the rights African Americans had gained through emancipation and Reconstruction.

The war is the headliner of those thirty years. Its impact on the nation then and now is incalculable—especially in the South. It was brutal, bloody, and deadly. It changed everything—for a time, at least. As part of the story of civil rights and land in Holmes County, the years after the war—the Reconstruction period—were a critical new beginning. It didn't last long. But Black people bought land and founded schools and churches. In so doing, they began processes that would sustain them into the future. First, however, Holmes County people had to survive the war.

The history of the Civil War has been the subject of over eighty thousand books, and Mississippi figures in virtually all of them. This chapter will focus on the war in Holmes—some of the players and a story of the skirmish that was fought there. It tells a little of the African American troops who fought with federal troops. African Americans were not passive observers in the fight, although many details of those from Holmes who fought for the Union are lost in history. There were likely hundreds of African Americans from Holmes County who fought with federal troops, even as many more hundreds, virtually all white, fought for the Confederacy.

The war effectively began in Mississippi on January 9, 1861, when the state seceded from the United States. Before Abraham Lincoln won the presidency in the 1860 election, Holmes County had been divided on secession, as shown by their votes in the 1860 election, but support for the Confederacy largely consolidated after Lincoln won. Doubts would return during the war, however, as individuals sought substitutes—paying someone to fight in their stead—and others came home early to protect their plantations and families.

In 1860, only white men could vote for president. Even that subset of the population was less than unanimous in its support for the most pro-secession of the presidential candidates. The candidates for president in 1860 were John C. Breckinridge, the choice of southern Democrats who had walked out of their party's convention when it nominated Stephen Douglas from Illinois; Douglas himself; and Constitutional Union Party candidate John Bell, who opposed secession from the United States while supporting slavery. Republican Abraham Lincoln was not on the ballot in Mississippi. He was a threat to slavery, although his actual position fell short of what it would become, and far short of how it is often perceived historically. Breckinridge was described as the secession candidate, although that, too, exaggerated his actual position.

Breckinridge won the state with 59 percent of the vote, losing only sparsely populated Delta counties to Bell. His majority was narrower in Holmes—just under 55 percent—with over 46 percent for Bell and less than 1 percent for Douglas (who received only 9 votes out of 1,416 cast). The *Lexington Advertiser* referred to Breckinridge as the secession candidate and endorsed Bell, who won over 40 percent of the vote in Lexington. Bell also won majorities in the western part of the county, which had smaller farms and fewer slaves, with a majority in Durant and the nearby precinct of "Lockharts." Notably, Absalom Madden West, whose family had helped settle that part of the county, was a former Whig and strongly for Bell.[1] The Lockhart family were in the same political orbit as Absalom West. Both would help make Durant politically distinctive a little later in its history as well.

Lincoln's victory, and his opposition to slavery, changed the calculus on secession. Less than a month after Lincoln won, Mississippi governor John J. Pettus sent a message to the legislature saying, "The existence or the abolition of African slavery in the Southern states is now up for final settlement." He asked for a convention to determine secession and to decide how Mississippi would arm itself. The legislature acted quickly, with delegates elected on December 20 and the secession convention called to order on January 7, 1861.[2]

Holmes County chose two delegates, both of whom supported secession, although one was willing to entertain delay. The two delegates were Walter Leake Keirn, son of early settler Garrett Keirn, and Lexington attorney James Monroe Dyer. Like these two, most of the one hundred convention delegates were lawyers or planters—and some were both. Almost all owned slaves, although most white Mississippians did not. Only twenty-one delegates had a net worth of less than $10,000, comparable to about $350,000 in today's dollars. Fourteen delegates had a six-figure net worth—what would be millions now—including Walter Leake Keirn.[3]

Dyer, like Keirn, was a multigeneration slave owner. In addition to being a practicing attorney, Dyer owned land and twenty-one slaves. Dyer had come to Holmes County from Tennessee, where his father, Joel Henry Dyer, born in Virginia, had been an army major during the Revolutionary War, and received a land grant in Tennessee in partial compensation.

At the convention, Dyer and Keirn voted similarly. Keirn supported immediate secession and was on the pro-secession side of every vote. Dyer voted for an amendment that would have delayed secession but otherwise voted with the secessionists. Dyer was an especially active delegate. He spoke out for funding the war with bonds rather than taxation, for protection for the river, and against the need for commercial banks in Mississippi's agricultural economy. As a member of the Citizenship Committee, Dyer advocated allowing people to return to Mississippi from the North, an issue for Andrew Jackson's nephew, Earl Van Dorn, who had been born in Mississippi but was then serving in the US Army.[4]

At the end of the convention, a committee of delegates was charged with producing a document outlining the reasons for secession. The Declaration of Causes states, "Our position is thoroughly identified with the institution of slavery—the greatest material interest of the world. Its labor supplies the product which constitutes by far the largest and most important portions of the commerce of the earth. These products are peculiar to the climate verging on the tropical regions, and by an imperious law of nature, none but the black race can bear exposure to the tropical sun . . . a blow at slavery is a blow at commerce and civilization."[5]

Even before conscription, white men in Holmes County began volunteering in locally formed companies. Most volunteers did not own slaves. Whether they were motivated by sectionalism, white supremacy, or fealty to local leadership, many volunteered early and enthusiastically. Four years later, at the end of the war, whether killed or wounded in battle, felled by disease, or deserting in fear or frustration, only a fraction remained with their units.

The Holmes Volunteers, under Keirn's leadership, recruited 113 men and became part of the Thirty-Eighth Infantry Regiment. The Thirty-Eighth would suffer very heavy losses. More than 1 in 10 members were casualties of the Battle of Corinth in the fall of 1862. Keirn was wounded at Corinth and returned to Holmes for the duration of the war. By the time of the siege of Vicksburg in 1864, only a third of the Thirty-Eighth Infantry remained. The Durant Rifles, with 129 men from Holmes, folded into the Twelfth Mississippi Regiment and fought in Virginia and at Gettysburg. At the end of the war, less than a third of them remained as well.[6]

The Black Hawk Rifles, Company G of the Twenty-Second Mississippi Infantry, had a similar survival rate but an especially noteworthy return. They were recruited by Captain—later Colonel—H. J. Reid and came principally from Carroll and Holmes Counties. Company G of the Black Hawk Rifles began with 64 members in April of 1861. They trained on their own for six months, growing to 78 volunteers, before being mustered into the Confederate army. Approximately 20 were killed in action or died of disease when spinal meningitis swept through the unit.[7] Another 24 were wounded or taken prisoner, and 14 had deserted or were absent without leave. At the end of the war, 27 men remained. The surviving members were to form a vigilante group called Heggie's Scouts that folded into the early Ku Klux Klan—more on them and their activities in the next section.

Most Holmes County white leaders served in the war along with most white men in the county. James Monroe Dyer, who had been a convention delegate, was an exception, although his son Joel Henry Dyer served in the Eighteenth Mississippi Regiment with Burt's Rifles. The elder Dyer held a seat in the state legislature during the war, which could have exempted him, although his son's unit was founded by Oktibbeha County legislator Erasmus Burt, who was killed in the war. The elder Dyer may have avoided conscription under the twenty-slave rule, which exempted those who owned more than twenty slaves from conscription.

The twenty-slave rule meant wealthy plantation owners did not have to fight. It also served to calm the fears of the women they had left behind. A group of women from five families in Holmes County petitioned Governor Pettus in February of 1863 to release one of their men so that he might supervise their slaves:

> The undersigned Citizens of the county of Holmes State of Mississippi, being willing and active supporters in our struggle for Independence and as such still willing to give not only fortune, but life if necessary in the consummation of said object: hence, we desire to do that which will best promote our efforts; knowing too, the fearful consequences attending neglect of Agriculture, we therefore respectfully beg leave to call your attention to the following facts; viz; That the following Farms, Messrs. Godfrey's Hamilton, Mrs. King, Weems, Mrs., Boyett & Mrs. Lockhart, lying contiguous & containing respectively, 31, 21, 16, 33, 17 & 12 negroes, are left without any male adult or suitable person for the governing of said negroes; we therefore respectfully ask and do pray that, for the above consideration, you release Sam W. Weems of Capt. R. L. Adam's "Guerilla" Company. Your Petitioners know Mr. Weems to be both efficient and faithful in regarding our interest and feel assured that the community will receive a benefit correlative to that of the Confederate Government; hence we petition his release and as duty bound will ever pray.[8]

As the war—and conscription—continued, there are signs that the burst of enthusiasm for it following Lincoln's election waned. Some soldiers sought a substitute for their service. One of those who sought a substitute was Jeremiah Gage, born in Holmes County in 1837. Jeremiah Gage's letter to his mother as he lay dying is an icon of Confederate heroism. On July 3, 1863, at Gettysburg, Jere Gage, as he was called, suffered a mortal stomach wound. The surgeon acknowledged to him that he would not make it. The young man, just nineteen, wrote, on a letter spattered with his own blood:

> My dear mother, this is the last time you may ever hear from me. I have time to tell you that I died like a man. Bear my loss as best you can. Remember that I am true to my country and my greatest regret at dying is that she is not free and that you and my sisters are robbed of my worth, whatever that may be. I hope this will reach you and you must not regret that my body cannot be obtained. It is a mere matter of form anyhow. This is for my sisters too as I cannot write more.[9]

Jere Gage's correspondence is part of the Gage Family Collection at the University of Mississippi, which he attended before joining the University Grays. Gage retained optimism about the Confederacy winning the war, but he was ready to come home. He wrote repeatedly of looking for a substitute— someone who for a thousand dollars would fight in his place.[10] His fiancée and his mother disapproved, so he delayed.

But then a few months later, Jere wrote to his sister Mary,

> I am right glad to hear that Jerrie [his brother-in-law] is about to succeed in getting me a substitute. I should be rejoiced to receive a telegram from him this morning stating that the boy is on the way. He will find me at Fredericksburg now instead of Ivor Station. If, up to the time you get this, he has not forwarded me one tell Jerrie that it would be well enough to send the written consent of the boy's father for him to go as a substitute, and that he (Jerrie) might state that the boy is a good honest kind of a boy and well calculated to make a good soldier. I have consulted the Colonel on the subject and he says he will take him for me.

Jeremiah Gage died twenty-three days later.

Black men from Holmes County also fought in the war as federal troops. Following the Emancipation Proclamation, which took effect in January of 1863, the Union army began to actively recruit African Americans. The United States Colored Troops (USCT) became 10 percent of federal troops toward the end of the war. Lincoln himself acknowledged that USCT were critical to victory, both because of their bravery in battle and because as locals they knew the terrain and the opposition. People who were still enslaved helped Union troops as well by reporting what they saw and heard of Confederate activity, and many African Americans who were not in USCT regiments traveled with the Union army in civilian roles.[11]

African Americans' willingness to fight and their effectiveness in the war came as a shock to many in the Confederacy. After a generation of fearing a slave insurrection that did not come, some had convinced themselves enslaved people were satisfied with their lot. They were surprised at the willingness to take up arms and treated the USCT with deep hostility on those occasions when their members were captured. One of the worst incidents involved Company F of the Fifth Mississippi Cavalry. That company, with members from Holmes and Carroll Counties, was recruited by James Z. George from Carroll County.[12] George would play a prominent role in white supremacist politics over the next forty years.[13]

The Fifth Mississippi Cavalry joined with General Nathan Bedford Forrest's brigade for a time and fought with them in Tennessee. Company F was with Forrest's brigade at the Fort Pillow Massacre in which troops under Forrest's command killed or mortally wounded 350 African American Union soldiers after they had surrendered. They took white Union troops prisoner and slaughtered the Black Union troops. The Fort Pillow massacre is excoriated as one of the most brutal events of a very brutal war.[14]

Several regiments of USCT were recruited primarily from Mississippi. It is difficult to identify individual members of the USCT from Holmes County. There were over seventeen thousand USCT from Mississippi paid as soldiers— and many more as civilian personnel. The records are not, however, sorted by county of residence at the time the war broke out. Many African Americans who joined federal troops went to Vicksburg to sign up and did not return to their home counties. A handful from Holmes County can be identified in various records. Interpolating from statewide numbers, there were likely hundreds from Holmes County who joined the USCT. The few names I could confirm are listed in the appendix.[15]

One notable regiment, recruited largely from Mississippi, and including members from Holmes County, was the Third Cavalry, African Descent, originally formed near Vicksburg and led by Embury Osband of Illinois. The history of the Third Colored Cavalry is especially well documented as one of the regiment's officers, Major Edwin Main, wrote a memoir detailing their activities. Main's book tells of an encounter with Greenwood Leflore and travels through the area of Holmes County. It includes a lengthy description of the battle at Franklin Church in Holmes County in which the Third Colored Cavalry, with members from Holmes County, defeated the Thirty-Eighth Infantry, which included the remainder of Keirn's Holmes County volunteers.[16]

First, we re-meet Greenwood Leflore. Leflore had opposed secession and supported the Union during the Civil War. His support for the Union was counter to the perspective of the Choctaw leadership who had removed to Oklahoma and fought for the Confederacy. Many of the Choctaw were slave owners who brought enslaved people with them when they removed. They also believed that because the United States had failed to live up to the terms of the Treaty of Dancing Rabbit Creek, they might be better served under state sovereignty.[17] Greenwood Leflore instead believed that his signing of the Treaty of Dancing Rabbit Creek was tantamount to pledging support for the United States.[18]

Main recounts how Greenwood Leflore welcomed the regimental officers— all white—of the Third Colored Cavalry to Carroll County in February of 1864.[19] Main introduced Leflore by explaining,

He had fought with General Jackson, "Old Hickory," in the Florida war and had imbibed a great love for the Union and the flag. He had preserved a small American flag, keeping it concealed in his house, and when the troops landed, he met them, waving the flag, and raising his hands exclaimed, "Thank God I have lived to see the old flag again carried by United States soldiers. Take of my supplies what you will. I give freely. My negroes too, shall fight for the Union." And so they did. After that, the Third US Colored Cavalry had many men on its rolls who bore the old Chief's name.[20]

In December of 1864, the Third Colored Cavalry joined other troops as part of General Benjamin Henry Grierson's second raid on Mississippi. The skirmish at Franklin Church in Holmes County was part of that raid. The Grierson command had destroyed railroads and Confederate property through northern Mississippi.[21] The raiders then headed west, demolishing railroads and factories and, in one instance, slaughtering pigs meant to feed the Confederate army.

On January 1, 1865, the command separated into detachments. The Fourth Illinois Cavalry headed out to destroy the rail line from Winona to Vaiden, and the Third Colored Cavalry headed out to destroy the rail line from Vaiden, in Carroll County, to West, in Holmes County. After destroying the railroad as planned, the two detachments met up on the Franklin turnpike heading toward Benton, in Yazoo County, where they were to rejoin the rest of the brigade. The Third Colored Cavalry was at the head of the column, led by Company G.

Then at Franklin Church, the Third Colored Cavalry encountered the Thirty-Eighth Infantry—including the remaining members of Keirn's Holmes Volunteers. The Thirty-Eighth Infantry swept down at the crossroads near the church. Company G of the Third Colored Cavalry responded with a volley that killed the commanding officer of the Confederate company. Main writes that "a hasty survey" found a larger force in position at the church behind the woods. So, eight companies of the Third Colored Cavalry dismounted and went through the woods to outflank the Confederates while four companies mounted and moved down the road toward the church. The forces met in a series of charges. The Fourth Illinois arrived during the battle. The battle was intense, and the fighting lasted several hours. The Union lost one commissioned officer and five other men while seventy-five Confederate soldiers were killed. The dead were buried near Franklin, and the brigade proceeded to Benton and then on to Vicksburg.

Main notes that "the numerous examples of personal bravery displayed by officers and men—Union and Confederate—entitles the fight at Franklin to rank with the most spirited Cavalry fights of the war." The skirmish was not important militarily—Grierson, who was not present, gives it less than a paragraph in his own memoirs. The behavior of the brigade did, however, draw contemporaneous praise beyond Main. Levi Naron, who was Grierson's scout on both his raids through Mississippi, was known as Chickasaw as he had lived in Chickasaw County, Mississippi, before the war. Naron wrote, "Too much praise cannot be awarded the whole brigade for their conduct in this fight, and particularly that of the Third US Colored Cavalry, commanded by Major Mann [sic]. They alone repulsed several desperate charges, having their adjutant killed and several wounded."[22]

Franklin Church still stands. The building itself has been renovated, although a few scars remain. The churchyard has a cemetery where several early settlers are buried, and some who lost their lives in the fighting are buried in the woods around the church. The dirt road leading to the church has a historical marker that references the encounter. It was not officially a battle but a mere skirmish, although it caused Wirt Adams to abandon his pursuit of Grierson. It is also the place in Holmes County where African American federal troops met Confederate troops in combat on shared home ground during the last six months of the war.

CHAOS AND VIOLENCE

The war ended in Mississippi on May 22, 1865, when Mississippi governor Charles Clark was escorted from his office by federal troops. The troops were under the command of Embury Osband, who had been promoted to brigadier general after commanding the Third Colored Cavalry. What immediately followed was not peace, but chaos. There was not enough food to eat. Federal troops had taken what there was to support their own men and burned much of the rest to pressure Confederate surrender. Crops failed throughout the state, as there were few people available to plant or tend them in the spring of 1865. White landowners returned from war and often found their plantations in ruins. Buildings had been burned down and the land was overgrown. Few of their previously enslaved people were still on the land.

There was massive displacement of people as soldiers slowly returned home and tens of thousands of refugees—Black and white—were uncertain where they would find a home. At least a third of Black people in the state had traveled behind Union lines to join the army, to seek employment, or simply to experience freedom. Refugee freedmen had gone to towns like Vicksburg, behind Union lines, or to refugee camps where they often lived in dire poverty. There were epidemics of disease—cholera, yellow fever.[23]

Interviews in the 1930s with older Holmes County residents recount the time: "Transportation in the county was slow and difficult. The dirt roads were rough and narrow. . . . The Mississippi Central which ran through Holmes County was a wreck from Canton [Mississippi] to Jackson, Tennessee."[24] Information was scarce as only one daily newspaper in Mississippi had continued to publish through the war and there were no newspapers in Holmes County at the time of surrender.

The historiography of the Reconstruction period that followed has changed radically over time. After the war, southern historians wrote of the Lost Cause, recasting the war to be less about slavery than about southern honor, and asserting—in self-evident error—that enslaved people had not sought freedom. The southern perspective folded into what is known as the "Dunning School," named for the professor at New York's Columbia University who led it. Dunning's sympathies were with the southern conservative Democrats who were to take back power a decade later. He argued that Reconstruction had been flawed and corrupt. The Dunning school did not believe in Black people's ability to govern and portrayed African American leaders as controlled by corrupt northern whites.[25]

In the last fifty years, historians have instead praised those who brought reform and who supported African American suffrage, placing blame for failures on those who fought against change. Historians are increasingly recognizing African Americans' efforts to win their own freedom and their effective governance after the war. I was taught the Dunning school perspective in high school. I had read much since then endorsing the efforts of reformers who came south to help during the Reconstruction. I had anticipated that I would share the later perspective in examining Holmes County. I found, however, that Reconstruction in Holmes County does not quite fit the broader narratives. Holmes County, like much of Mississippi, received an influx of outsiders, both Black and white, during the 1860s. In the Dunning school, they were excoriated as "carpetbaggers." In more recent work, they are credited as reformers.[26]

Those who came to Holmes County were, in fact, a collection of individuals who arrived with varied motivations. Some evinced a genuine desire to help. Others seemed there for political or economic opportunity. They were neither uniformly corrupt, as the Dunning school would portray them, nor uniformly beneficent. As a smaller rural county, Holmes did not perhaps attract the best of them, although there were individuals among them who made important positive contributions.

The uneven skills and commitment of the outsiders meant federal policies were also not always carried out as distant policymakers intended. In Holmes County the Black community was mostly on its own as Reconstruction evolved from early violence and chaos through self-government to the redemption of power by conservative white Democrats. Holmes County had some outstanding African American leaders, some who had been free before the war and came to help, and others who had acquired both education and leadership skills while enslaved in Holmes County. There was a semblance of a coalition with the white outsiders, although it fell apart, with much of the blame falling on the white outsiders, who then left abruptly when conservative Democrats took back state government. In contrast, African American newcomers stayed and became part of the Holmes County community.

The first step toward Reconstruction was the federal government specifying the circumstances under which states would be readmitted to the Union. In June of 1865, the month after Osband had escorted Governor Clark out of his office, President Andrew Johnson appointed William Sharkey as provisional governor. Sharkey had been a Whig congressman and a judge. He not only opposed secession but retained Union allegiance during the war while preserving cordial working relationships—and sympathies—with his fellow landowners. As provisional governor, he was charged with calling for a Reconstruction convention and a new constitution that would allow Mississippi to again become a state. As counties elected delegates to that convention, Sharkey effectively granted landowners a blanket pardon so they could reclaim their plantation lands.[27]

The delegates elected to that first constitutional convention were white and mostly former Whigs or Constitutional Union Party advocates who supported slavery but had opposed secession. Secessionists boycotted the convention rather than participate, and Black people would not be allowed to vote for nearly three more years. Holmes County elected R. H. Montgomery and T. F. Sessions. Montgomery was a real estate broker and collections attorney from Durant who apparently looked to profit from land sales. Sessions is something of an enigma as his public record appears to begin and end with the 1865 convention.[28]

The convention took ten days of heated debate to resolve that slavery was abolished in Mississippi. The debate was on how to talk about ending slavery and whether to include in the constitution that the state did so only under duress. The convention allowed Black people, now referred to as freedmen, some legal and property rights. Freedmen were not granted any voting rights even though President Johnson had recommended granting suffrage to Black men who owned property and could interpret the constitution. Under the presumption that its new constitution would allow Mississippi to reenter the Union—a presumption that turned out to be false—the convention called for an election for governor, state representatives, and members of Congress to be held in October of 1865.[29]

Despite his recommendation for limited Black suffrage, President Johnson generally sympathized with southern plantation owners—a sympathy that

Congress did not share. Congress refused Mississippi readmission to the Union, finding the mere acknowledgement that slavery had ended insufficient. A poorly administered 1865 election took place anyway. It elected former Confederate general and Democrat Benjamin G. Humphreys as governor over the old-line Whig who had been the unofficial choice of the convention and a third candidate, a Democrat who had opposed secession.

The election was so poorly administered that some counties failed to include all candidates on their ballots.[30] Holmes County voters supported Democrat Humphreys, and, for Congress, former Whig and now Democrat Absolom Madden West.[31] But Congress refused to seat West and the rest of the delegation because Mississippi had not been readmitted to the Union.

The 1865 election did, however, seat a new Mississippi state legislature. The 1865 legislature wrote Mississippi's infamous "Black Codes" that governed formerly enslaved people separately from whites and effectively forced them to live on plantations and to work for plantation owners. Under the Codes, Black people were not allowed to assemble, preach without a license, carry a weapon, or make comments or gestures that white people found insulting. Freedmen could not own or lease rural land and were required to carry written proof of residence and have contractual employment. Without a written employment contract, formerly enslaved people could be arrested as vagrants. Those working on plantations would forfeit all wages if they moved off the plantation before the end of the contractual term.

Under the Codes, any white person could confront a Black person suspected of violation of the vagrancy law and win a cash reward for arresting the vagrant. Once vagrants were arrested, sheriffs had the right to lease out their labor without pay. Black children whose parents were deemed to lack the means to support them were also apprenticed in exchange for food, clothing, and shelter until age twenty-one for boys and age eighteen for girls.[32]

The Black Codes also effectively ratified an extant epidemic of violence against newly freed Black people by vigilante groups. In 1865, Heggie's Scouts, made up of surviving members of the Black Hawk Rifles, were active in Holmes, Carroll, and Montgomery Counties. The leader was Ramsey Heggie, an original member of the Twenty-Second Infantry, Company G—the Black Hawk Rifles. He and his younger brother, Aurelius Heggie, joined the Black Hawk Rifles early, before the unit was mustered into the Confederate army.[33]

The story of Heggie's Scouts comes from an article by Fred Witty, which served as his graduating thesis from the University of Mississippi in 1907. Witty was from Winona, in what became Montgomery County, about twenty miles north of the Holmes County line. Witty writes of Heggie's Scouts killing hundreds of Black people in Holmes County. Witty's own sympathies are with the conservative Democrats and perpetrators of violence as he recounts proudly that the area of Holmes, Montgomery, and Carroll Counties is "perhaps unexcelled by any in the State for genuine bravery and love of white supremacy."[34]

According to Witty, the Scouts were organized into companies of six to eight men, commanded by captains. "These men did not disguise themselves, operated in open daylight, and their object was to make the negroes humble by visiting terrible punishment upon them. Carpetbaggers and scalawags were also proscribed."[35]

Witty recounts multiple incidents of violence against freedmen. The Scouts "often whipped negroes who refused to work." In one particularly horrendous incident the Scouts came upon a large group of freedmen in a field and Heggie ordered a charge. When the men ran, the Scouts opened fire and 116 Black men were killed and their bodies dumped in the Tallahatchie River. Witty reports some of the freedmen were armed but does not report that any white men were injured.

Federal authorities reportedly arrested forty-eight of the Scouts and sent them to trial in Oxford, where James Z. George and Edward Walthall defended them free of charge in front of federal judge Robert Andrews Hill. Hill had been nominated by President Andrew Johnson in March of 1866 and was confirmed by the Senate in May. He was a Whig who had opposed secession. Like many former Whigs, however, his opposition to secession did not signal support for the rights of freedmen. Indeed, Hill was known for lenient sentencing, often a twenty-five-dollar fine for those who had terrorized Black people, arguing that "the certainty of punishment was more important than its severity."[36] In the case of Heggie's Scouts, Witty reports, they were fined one dollar each.

The story is egregious—both the horror of the Scouts shooting over a hundred Black men and the leniency of the sentences received. If the details are true, the violence of the Scouts warrants more attention. However, I was unable to find any primary source verification of the shooting or the trial. The federal court records at the National Archives begin in 1867, after the incident Witty cites.[37] I did find other primary source references to accusations of violence by members of the Heggie family. Ramsey Heggie was accused of killing a Black man but produced an alibi and was freed. Ramsey and Aurelius's father, James L. Heggie, was tried for murdering a former Union officer in 1865 but was found not guilty by a jury of his white male peers.[38] Given the information I could find, I concluded that some of the details Witty reports may be apocryphal, but the context of the times and other elements of Heggie family history argue that the story has considerable truth to it.

Even during the early and chaotic immediate postwar years, the federal government in Washington provided limited counterbalance. The military were still present—and reputedly arrested Heggie's Scouts. In 1865, Congress had also established the Bureau of Refugees, Freedmen, and Abandoned Lands, known as the Freedmen's Bureau. The bureau was charged with allocating abandoned and confiscated property, supervising labor contracts, and helping to establish schools. It had a broad agenda and a weighty structure and was always underfunded for what it was to accomplish. Particularly in the beginning, it had scant staff and few teeth.[39]

Holmes County did not get its first Freedmen's Bureau agent until 1867 and had three different agents in the three years the bureau operated there. The first Freedmen's Bureau agent in Holmes County was Henry W. Barry, assigned to the office in Goodman from July to September of 1867. Barry seems to fit with the opportunist model of white newcomers. He was born in New York but organized a Kentucky regiment in 1861 and in 1864 became a colonel in a Black artillery regiment. After the war, he established a law practice in Columbus, Mississippi, and rose through the postwar political ranks, eventually becoming a member of Congress from Mississippi. Barry was succeeded as a Freedmen's Bureau agent by Charles A. Shields, who remained with the bureau in Holmes County for only three months.[40] Some bureau correspondence from Holmes County was also signed by D. M. White.

The Freedmen's Bureau agents in Holmes County helped with labor contracts, which were required by the Black Codes, and with contract disputes, but apparently little else. Some of the contracts written before Freedmen's Bureau oversight were patently unfair. One example from Holmes County is a handwritten contract from the Stainback plantation. Stainback received half the cotton at no expense to himself, and the thirteen freedmen on his property had to pay all expenses from their half. They could grow only cotton but no other crops, which made them dependent on Stainback for food, and they were required to perform any work he requested. The handwritten Stainback contract, not designed for clarity and presented to freedmen who likely could not read, said:

> Articles of agreement made and entered into the 4th day of January 1866 between E. B. Stainback and Peter Stainback, Amanda his wife, Sandy Phillips, Milly his wife, George Suber, Kate his wife, Jimmie, Mary, Fanny, Liz, Sally, Betsy and Lina, freedmen of the second part. Witnesseth that the said party of the first part agrees to and with the said parties of the second part to furnish them with land of sent team to work the same and provision from each and to give them one half of the cotton crop that may be grown. And the said parties of the second part agrees to work with and for the said party of the first part during the [illegible] and to be at all times governed by the party of the first part to do any and all kinds of work that he may require. And it is further agreed between the parties that the said parties of the second part are to

pay the said party of the first part for all provisions that he may furnish them out of their part of the crop.[41]

Walter Leake Keirn also signed an early contract with the formerly enslaved people he employed. It was preprinted and presumably standard. That contract also said freedmen would need to perform all work required by Keirn but placed limitations on the number of hours they would work and allowed them to plant a patch of food crops. All produce of their labor belonged to Keirn until all debts were paid.[42] One of Keirn's former slaves later complained that her children were not allowed to leave the property and were required to work without compensation.[43]

Freedmen pushed back against contracts like these and the contract requirement itself. A former slave from Fayette, Mississippi, wrote to the Freedmen's Bureau to ask why he could not rent the land instead of sharecropping, which he believed should be his right. The writer, who apologizes for his spelling, writes, "I thought when a man was once free he was free indeed and was entital to all the laws and rights of a free people."[44]

Among those rights was land ownership. African Americans in Holmes County received little if any help purchasing land but, instead, were encouraged to become sharecroppers, as described in postwar labor contracts. Sharecroppers farmed someone else's land for a share of proceeds after the landowner deducted expenses. Sharecropping—and tenant farming in which land is rented for a set fee—remained the most common form of African American farming in Mississippi past the middle of the twentieth century.

FORTY ACRES AND A MULE

With virtually no help from the federal government, and against the odds created by chaos, violence, and labor contracts, Black farmers began purchasing land in Holmes County during the 1860s. For many formerly enslaved people, land ownership was not only an economic advantage but a spiritual imperative. It was a culmination of the Exodus story. Land provided the promise of autonomy and their own "nation space," as one scholar calls it.[45] For Native peoples, the land had been their heritage and their ancestry. To land speculators it was a commodity. To many formerly enslaved people, land ownership was freedom itself as it carried the promise of self-sufficiency.

Freedmen throughout the South presumed—falsely as it turned out—that they would be granted land after the war. The presumption of land grants derived from a limited effort during the war. In January of 1865, General William T. Sherman had met with African American leaders near his Georgia headquarters in Savannah. Former slave and Baptist minister Garrison Frazier led the group. James D. Lynch, a Methodist minister who became secretary of state in Mississippi, was one of those present at that meeting. After the meeting, Sherman issued a field order allocating forty-acre plots of land along the St. John's River in Georgia to Black families. Sherman was thus responsible for the presumption that Black people would receive forty acres, which evolved into a much-discussed but never fulfilled expectation.[46]

Even Sherman's original promise fell flat. A total of 400,000 acres were set aside at $1.25 an acre. However, the land went to open bidding, and most of it was sold for far more. Only 2,276 acres went to freedmen at the agreed upon price.[47] A year later, after the war ended, the Southern Homestead Act of 1866, in theory, provided preferential access to freedmen in the sale of 46 million acres of land in five southern states, including Mississippi. However, the effort "collapsed from poor preparation, clumsy administration, local opposition, and corruption."[48] Much of the land would, instead, be returned to its original owners, and the Freedmen's Bureau, which was supposed to help, was variously unwilling or unable to do so.

Congress had charged the Freedmen's Bureau with assisting Black families in purchasing land, but, in Mississippi, the state Freedmen's Bureau was unstable with four different assistant commissioners—the lead administrators for the state—over four years. Each seemed to have a reason not to help with land purchase. The first assistant commissioner was Colonel Samuel Thomas, who held the position from June of 1865 to April of 1866, a period during which no Freedmen's Bureau agent was assigned to Holmes County.[49] The Black Codes at the time also prohibited rural land ownership. Thomas was reluctant to assign land to Black people, ostensibly because he could not protect them. Instead, he encouraged share tenancy—sharecropping in which the tenant received rights to the land if wages were not paid as promised—leaving the burden of enforcing the contract and claiming the land on the tenant.[50]

Thomas's successors, Thomas Wood and then Alvan Gillem, promoted straight sharecropping without any opportunity for land purchase. Gillem, who was from Tennessee, had been the military commander during occupation and was known for especially lenient treatment of former Confederate soldiers. His successor, Wood, did not enjoy administrative work and held the position for only eight months. The final assistant commissioner in Mississippi was Adelbert Ames, who served in that capacity for a month before becoming military governor.

In addition to transient leadership, there were issues of the availability of confiscated land. Thomas initially reported that there were 3.5 million acres of available land in Mississippi, although of undetermined quality, confiscated from those who had fought for the Confederacy. Then, President Johnson—and in Mississippi, Governor Sharkey—granted amnesty to most former Confederates, restoring their property rights and adding confusion to what land was available. After amnesty, the federal Treasury Department transferred only fifty-eight Mississippi plantations to the Freedmen's Bureau. Johnson then required a court decree before land could be confiscated and thus available to freedmen. By the end of 1865, the available land had diminished to 43,500 identified acres under bureau control, then to 22,600 in 1866 and to none in 1868.[51]

The third issue hampering land efforts was that the timing of most employment contracts effectively blocked land purchase. The Southern Homestead Act set-aside land for freedmen, but it expired in January of 1867. Most employment contracts began in 1866—again, before there was a Freedmen's Bureau agent in Holmes County—and were to last a year. Thus, most freedmen were still under the requisite contract to their employers at the time the act expired.

The combined result of these issues was that in 1870, only 2,009 rural Black families in the state of Mississippi owned any real estate at all, a ratio of 1 out of 43 families, and there were only 1,600 Black farmers who owned their land.[52] Those who did own land most often simply purchased it without the aid of the Freedmen's Bureau.

Quite a few freedmen had a little money—including hundreds in Holmes County—by the time of the 1870 Census. Enslaved people acquired cash if they managed to plant an acre or two of cotton or raised chickens or other livestock they sold at market. Enslaved people with specialized skills, like blacksmiths, were sometimes hired out by the slaveholder and often received partial compensation for their hire.[53]

The 1870 Census lists twenty-six Black families in Holmes County who owned real estate valued at a total of $25,900, or about a half a million in today's dollars.[54] Hundreds of Black families are listed as having personal property—totaling $188,495 in value—but only twenty-six owned real estate.[55] A few Black farmers were granted land by those who had enslaved them, and a couple may have received government help. Most often, Black farmers appear to have simply purchased land on their own.[56]

I tried to match the twenty-six African Americans who owned land to records of land purchases in Holmes County. There was a certain match to only some of the Black farmers who owned land by 1870, meaning the name of the purchaser matched the name in apposite Census records and is unique in the county. For example, there might be a purchase by someone named "John Smith" and the Census may show that a Black man named John Smith owned real estate. But there might also be a white "John Smith" who owned land, so it is uncertain which John Smith was the purchaser of that particular property. Still, there are some unambiguous transactions that serve as examples of how recently enslaved people acquired land.

Only one bought his land from the State of Mississippi, suggesting it may have been confiscated land. Virgil Dulany bought land on October 28, 1869, during the period the bureau was active in the county, although I could find no reference to Dulany in Freedmen's Bureau records. Others bought from individual white farmers—J. R. Boyett bought from R. T. Jordan in November of 1868, the earliest purchase for which there is a clear match.[57] Similarly, Jacob Byrd bought from John Falls in May of 1869 and Willis Falls from W. G. Falls in November of 1869. The Falls family may have transferred land to those they had held as slaves, which seems to have also occurred in the Sproles family.

Land records include a contract with a marginal note that it is an "agreement between W. Jenkins and negroes." It is a land contract signed by Jenkins, Prince Safford (or Saffold), and Henry Walton. Jenkins agrees to furnish land and mules sufficient to cultivate the land, and a wagon free of charge and new nails to repair fencing. Saffold and Walton agree to turn over two-thirds of the crop and return the mules. They would retain rights to the land. The agreement was filed in June of 1869.[58]

At least some of the families who owned land in 1870—including the Saffold, Dulany, and Boyette families—still farmed in Holmes County in the twentieth and twenty-first centuries. Several bought early in the Reconstruction period, and most without any apparent help in purchasing property. They gained a level of independence, however, that allowed their descendants to remain in the county and, in several cases, become active in the civil rights movement of the 1960s.

RADICAL RECONSTRUCTION BEGINS

After two chaotic years of President Johnson's lenient Reconstruction policies, Congress passed the Reconstruction Acts of 1867 over a presidential veto. The acts created military districts headed by officials who could remove other state officials and appoint new ones. To be readmitted to the Union, states were to ratify the Fourteenth Amendment to the US Constitution providing equal protection under the law and were to provide voting rights to Black men. In 1868, Congress disbanded the Mississippi legislature, removed Governor Humphreys, and installed Adelbert Ames as a military governor. The period known as "Radical Reconstruction" had begun.

For six years, Republicans—both white and African American—would govern Holmes County. The county would have a brand-new system of public education, spurred in part by the Freedmen's Bureau but also by local churches and volunteers. The six years of so-called Radical Reconstruction brought real progress for African Americans—both politically and economically. For the white conservative Democrats, it was a time of heightened resistance to change. In a memoir written much later, Mrs. Samuel Donnell Gwin of Holmes County wrote:

> I have lived through three periods of war—the Civil, the Cuban and the World War. Their ravages can hardly compare with the Reconstruction period. For in those years the oppression of our Northern enemies became so unbearable Southern indignation was aroused to throw off carpetbag rule in our Southland. For a time the safety of our beloved protectors was agonizing. I now rejoice that my heroic husband risked life itself in the successful issue. On one occasion when ready to leave me for a night of investigation he [her husband] bade me good-bye saying, "Here is a double barreled shot gun, be very brave and use it if necessary." . . . He returned a victor at the dawn of a new day.

The memoir is not explicit about the "night of investigation." Mississippi writer and Pastor Will D. Campbell, who quotes the memoir, writes, "Anyone familiar with the way the defeated whites resisted the iron fist of Reconstruction can fill in the blanks."[59] During the six years of Reconstruction, African Americans and outsiders worked to forge a new social order. While they did so, white conservative Democrats were preparing to reestablish the old one.

But before anything else could proceed, Mississippi needed a new Constitution for readmission to the Union. It would be written by delegates to a convention in 1868. The election of delegates to the 1868 convention was the first election in which Black men could vote in Mississippi. Statewide, seventy-eight white men and sixteen Black men were elected as convention delegates. The whites included twenty-one northern white Republicans and thirty-five white moderates as well as fifty-four white conservative Democrats. The Holmes County delegates were white Republicans: Freedmen's Bureau agent Henry W. Barry was one; he was joined by D. McA Williams, also a white Republican. R. H. Montgomery, who was more conservative, and had been a delegate to the first constitutional convention, returned to represent Holmes and Madison Counties at Large.[60]

The constitution of 1868 included a bill of rights that provided property rights to married women and granted the right to freedom of assembly and speech. It also offered a framework for universal public education with no specification that the schools be segregated by race. It provided voting rights for all Black men as required by Congress and gave citizenship with full voting rights to men who had been in Mississippi for six months. It also barred from political office those who had voluntarily aided the Confederacy, exempting non-officers who had been conscripted into the army. Thus, it fully enfranchised Black men and newcomers and put limitations on the rights of former Confederate officers.[61]

In anticipation that this constitution might be voted down—whether through fraud or opposition—Republicans at the 1868 convention established a "Committee of Five" to take next steps if—and anticipating when—the constitution might fail. Two of Holmes County's delegates opposed or abstained, but Henry Barry played a significant role in the formation of the Committee of Five.[62]

The progressive 1868 constitution did indeed fail on its first try in June of 1868. It failed through a combination of white rage and, in some places, outright fraud. An editorial in the *Clarion-Ledger* gives a sense of the white conservative outrage: "The Scallawagerie have finally (we suppose) determined upon the twenty second of June as the day of commencing the election on the question of ratifying the proposed bastard and mongrel constitution. The week commencing that day will be fraught with momentous consequences for the people of Mississippi. Prepare for the work before you. The scheme must be defeated! It can be defeated if the white people whose all is at stake, will go to work now, and work until the election closes with all their might."[63]

At the time, the Mississippi electorate was 56 percent African American, and similarly progressive constitutions had been victorious in other states with significant African American populations. The Committee of Five, including Barry, argued that Congress should declare the constitution ratified despite the popular vote against it. The allegations of fraud had considerable justification, but overturning the electoral result was controversial even among Republicans. Instead, the constitution was back on the ballot in 1869 without the clause prohibiting Confederate officers from holding public office, which was considered as a separate question. The constitution itself passed on this second try while the section limiting former Confederate participation was defeated.

The Committee of Five was likely right that there was fraud. A quantitative analysis of the election result found that the percent of registered voters who were African American was a strong predictor of the vote on the new constitution—except in a handful of counties. Holmes County was not an outlier—its majority African American voting base supported the constitution in 1868 and 1869. Neighboring Carroll County was one of the outliers. Carroll had 3,730 registered voters and the population was 58 percent Black. In 1868, there were only 276 votes for the constitution and 2,727 against. Either Black voters in Carroll had quite different views than those in Holmes and elsewhere, or there was vote manipulation.[64] "Glorious news from Carroll," J. Z. George declared in sending Carroll County's returns to the *Clarion-Ledger*.

Following passage of the new constitution in 1869, Mississippi was readmitted to the Union. The 1869 constitution remains the most progressive of the four such documents that have governed Mississippi. It would be replaced later, but it is the only one written with significant African American participation, and the only one ratified by the voters.[65]

The Constitution outlines a structure for implementing the mandate of "a uniform system of free public schools" by assigning responsibility to a state superintendent of schools and establishing superintendents in each county as well. For the prior two years, the Freedmen's Bureau had responsibility for building public schools with Henry K. Pease as superintendent of education. After the constitution passed, Pease was elected as superintendent and continued in the position until 1874, providing considerable stability. A public school system had to be built virtually from scratch, particularly in a rural county like Holmes, which had no public schools before the Civil War.[66]

The State of Mississippi's public education history had begun in the 1840s when Governor Albert Gallatin Brown appealed unsuccessfully to the state legislature to develop a unified public school system in the state. Instead, the state legislature established boards of school commissioners and allowed special school levies. The participation of townships was voluntary, and the tax levies required local approval. As a result, as a nineteenth-century historian recounts, "The schools drifted along to the period of the Civil War, doing some good, more in some localities than others, of course, but in all crippled, in many paralyzed, by the want of a uniform and vigorous policy."[67]

In Holmes County, a surge of interest in education in the 1840s had produced in-town private schools for white students. The Lexington Male and Female Academies were founded in 1844, with two teachers who came from Vermont and Connecticut to teach. The schools grew in the 1850s after they were purchased by the Yazoo Baptist Association and had more than one hundred students by the second year thereafter.[68] Holmes County's historic Little Red Schoolhouse opened in 1848, first as the Richland Literary Institute and then as Eureka Masonic College with Robert Morris, founder of the Order of the Eastern Star, as its principal.[69] Still, there were no schools in the more rural areas and no schools at all for Black children.

The Freedmen's Bureau had money to build schools, although communities were left largely on their own in staffing them. Staffing was a challenge. Few white Mississippians were willing to instruct Black children, and few Black people were able to teach as it had been against the law for enslaved people to acquire an education. Black people who were free before the war often had an education, but free Black people generally lived in Natchez and Vicksburg. Holmes County was home to only ten free Black people in 1860. The American Missionary Association and other church groups sent volunteer teachers, but many were uncomfortable in rural areas like Holmes.[70]

The first of ten semiannual Freedmen's Bureau reports on education in Mississippi begins, "There is a mixture of good and evil to report from this state. . . . There is everywhere the usual eagerness to learn; but in some sections inveterate opposition from the whites."[71] The report tells of teachers who were threatened if they stayed in an assigned town and freedmen who paid their own money for a schoolroom who were forbidden by whites to use it. White opposition lessened over the years as some plantation owners found they could attract and retain labor by promising a schoolhouse. Still, incidents continued in other places with teachers harassed, and at least one schoolhouse burned down. The Freedmen's Bureau made some progress, but when their jurisdiction ended, only one in fifteen Black children in Mississippi were in school, the lowest proportion of any state.[72]

Holmes County had an effective superintendent of education from 1870 to 1873 in Marcus Morton Holmes. Holmes was white and originally from New Hampshire. He volunteered for the Union army right after his graduation from high school and was promoted to first lieutenant. After the war, he attended Dartmouth College, then came to Mississippi in 1869.[73] Dartmouth College had admitted Black students from its inception and provided Mississippi with several prominent figures—Black and white—during the Reconstruction period.

Superintendent Holmes avoided empty promises. He explained that he "would sign no warrant drawn on an empty treasury" so people needed to provide schoolhouses at their own cost. That happened largely by absorbing private schools into the public domain, but schools were also built or rented as needed as the county took baby steps toward a public school system for all children with help from African American churches.

The Union Methodist Episcopal Church in Lexington had opened a school shortly after the end of the war. Mount Olive Missionary Baptist Church taught school in its sanctuary in 1870. The Freedmen's Bureau provided a school building next to the church in 1871. The bureau renovated Lexington Male Academy as Lexington Colored School in 1870. It was the county's first non-church public school. The Little Red Schoolhouse, where the Order of the Eastern Star had been founded, became the first freedmen's school in the county in 1870 as the Richland Colored School.[74]

Finding teachers remained a challenge, with some teachers barely ahead of their students in scholastic achievement. One exception was Robert Augustus Simmons, the lead teacher at the Richland Colored School. Simmons was born in 1844 on the island of St. Barthelemy and is described in US Census and other documents as "mulatto." Slavery ended on St. Bart's in 1847, so Simmons was not enslaved as a child. He was a notable teacher, leading children on a celebration march through Goodman, and later became an important leader in Holmes County.[75] Interviews with older residents in the 1930s say that he, like Superintendent Holmes, attended Dartmouth College, although a census of nineteenth-century African American students at Dartmouth does not include him.[76]

In 1871, Superintendent Holmes reported that the county had sixty schools and sixty-seven teachers, with the first public school commencing on January 9, 1871. His report says, "Schools have been established within reach of all the children, except in a portion of the Yazoo bottom, in the western part of the county. Here, on account both of lack of buildings and scarcity of teachers, but four schools have been started where ten or twelve are needed. These will be supplied during the coming year."[77] Instead, the growth of public education would sputter and then stop.

AFRICAN AMERICAN POLITICAL EMERGENCE

During the period of Radical Reconstruction, Holmes County had African American state legislators, supervisors, and sheriffs. Some were from outside Mississippi, but others had been enslaved there. They were a remarkable group of leaders who began organizing themselves immediately after the war with the help of African Americans from the North, mostly sponsored by the African Methodist Episcopal Church. There were also white Republicans, mostly from outside the county, and ultimately tension between the white Republicans and African Americans.

African American Methodist ministers were especially active on issues of freedmen's rights after the war. Bishop Henry McNeal Turner, who had been a state legislator in Georgia, worked to establish African Methodist Episcopal churches in the South. Turner became the bishop for the region that included Mississippi. For Turner, the Holy Spirit was an agent of empowerment even more than of moral reform.[78] Baptist churches were also active but, in the 1860s, most were small, independent churches without a network of northern connections until the General Missionary Baptist Association was organized in the 1870s. Baptist churches in Holmes County were early members of that association.[79]

During Reconstruction, Holmes County had an active Loyal League. The Loyal Leagues—also known as the Union Leagues—were formed in the North before and during the war by free Black people and white abolitionists who wanted to advance freedom and equal rights for Black people. Several of the African American men who would shortly be elected to the state legislature were part of the Holmes County League.[80]

The principal Mississippi leader of the Loyal Leagues was James D. Lynch. Lynch was an African Methodist Episcopal minister, born in Baltimore and educated in New Hampshire (at Kimball Union Academy, not Dartmouth), who had led congregations in Illinois and Indiana. He was part of what became a seminal meeting with General William Tecumseh Sherman in Savannah during the war that led Sherman to grant a few African Americans there forty acres and a mule.[81] Lynch was the more moderate of two African American ministers with statewide influence in the 1870s. The other was Thomas W. Stringer. Unlike Stringer, Lynch allied with white Republicans, and sometimes even white Democrats, and he opposed the constitutional provision barring former Confederates from holding public office. Lynch would defeat Stringer to become secretary of state.

The Leagues began as local movements among freedmen. The Leagues had significant white participation in other states but not in Mississippi and certainly not in Holmes County. Ministers were a plurality of Loyal League members, with schoolteachers as the second-largest category.[82] Despite their moderate orientation, the Leagues were excoriated by the Democratic press. On the eve of the 1868 election, the *Grenada Sentinel* issued a warning: "We advise the negroes of this city to think well before they vote. If their league is not already a thing of the past it will be in the course of a few days, and then there will be no one found but will be ashamed to acknowledge he ever belonged to such a monstrous iniquity. Colored men beware how you vote to proscribe the whites, that yourselves may not be proscribed."[83]

An April 1869 Holmes County meeting of the Holmes County Loyal League drew gunfire in an apparent attempt to assassinate Lynch. Conservative white newspapers minimized the incident: "Several young gentlemen of Holmes County have been arrested by military order and brought to this city charged with complicity in the affair of the explosion of fire-crackers to the disturbance of the Lynch meeting in Lexington a short time ago," the *Clarion-Ledger* reported, adding that the men were arrested without warrant and innocent of wrongdoing.[84]

Lynch reported that the shots, fired at a rally attended by hundreds, hit two inches above his head. He left the area under protection of a group from the meeting: "Seventeen strong, valiant men, were immediately armed, ready to die in my defense." Lynch contacted the sheriff, then an appointee named Weston, who acknowledged that shots were fired. Lynch wrote, "Free speech and religious toleration does not exist in Mississippi. A man is not secure in his person, on a highway . . . if he is known to be an active preacher of the Methodist Episcopal Church of the United States, or a Radical of public influence."[85]

A sarcastic article posted from Lexington in the Meridian *Tri-Weekly Clarion* notes, "Since a number of our boys were taken on a pleasure trip (?) to Jackson at the instance of Parson Lynch, we have been almost frightened at our shadows and the quietest people up here at Lexington that you could imagine. . . . Parson Lynch may take due notice thereof, and govern himself accordingly." It ends, "Our people are hopeful that things will turn out well yet. We will have a constitutional government after awhile [sic], we trust, that will at least be tolerable."[86]

The election of 1869 in Holmes County chose three new state legislators. Two were African American, Cicero Mitchell and Edmund Scarborough. The third was a white Republican, William A. Williams, whom the *Lexington Advertiser* termed a "radical," meaning he supported Radical Reconstruction, including Black voting rights.

Edmond Scarborough was a Loyal League member. He was a minister and a farmer who had been born a slave in Greene County, Alabama, in 1835 and obtained his freedom in 1863. He was an active organizer in Holmes County. He had extended the invitation for James Lynch to speak at the 1869 Loyal League meeting in which shots were fired. Scarborough was still living in Holmes County at the time of the 1910 Census with his wife Martha, and he owned considerable property. His daughter married a man, John B. Scott, who had been born enslaved in Pickens, graduated from Tougaloo College, and came to own one of the largest farms in Holmes County.[87]

Mitchell was a blacksmith who was brought to Holmes County from North Carolina before the war. In 1870, Mitchell owned $300 in real estate at a time when land in Holmes County was selling for around $12 an acre. Mitchell was the subject of rumormongering the spring after his election. The rumor falsely alleged that he had brought a prostitute to a celebration of the passage of the Fifteenth Amendment to the US Constitution, which guaranteed the right to vote. In fact, the young woman in question was his daughter, and "the pride and light of my home," as he wrote eloquently at the time. The *Brandon Republican*, which had originally printed the story, retracted it, and other newspapers criticized the *Brandon Republican* for printing the unsubstantiated and damaging rumor.[88]

In the 1872 state legislative session, all three Holmes County representatives were African American: Harrison H. Truehart, Frederick Stewart, and Perry Howard. Based on a look at House journals for the period, Truehart, from Lexington, was an especially active legislator. Truehart was a blacksmith by profession and educated. By the time of the 1870 Census, he owned $400 in real estate and $200 in other personal property. Truehart's $600 would be worth $12,000 today.[89]

A 1930s interview with Mrs. Baxter Wilson tells a little of Truehart's history. Her father, Dr. Sutton, was a planter from Virginia who moved to Holmes County around 1840 and brought Truehart with him as an enslaved child, then called "Buck." According to the interview, "this little boy proved to be a very faithful servant and in return his master had him educated. Because of his education, his personality, and his level head, Buck became a leader among the Negroes."[90] Truehart served in the state legislature from 1872 to 1875 and was the county Republican Party chairman for a time.

More from Mrs. Baxter Wilson:

Buck never lost respect for Dr. Sutton and the rest of the white people; and at their request, he ran for state senator and was elected. He introduced the county farm bill which was passed; and if not for him the county seat would have been taken from Lexington. He fought the bill that provided for a consolidation of Attala and Holmes County with Durant the County seat. They soon found they would have to pass the bill during Buck's absence, so a message was sent to him stating that his wife was very ill. The Negro statesman seeing the trick, merely said, "I am no doctor," and finished his speech which defeated the bill.[91]

Truehart remained in Holmes County until at least 1910, with family there still.

Perry Howard, from Ebenezer, was also a blacksmith. He had been born a slave in 1843 or 1844 in South Carolina and was brought to Mississippi before the Civil War. The Census lists him as being literate in 1870 and as owner of $2,500 in real estate and $800 in additional personal property. He served on the County Board of Supervisors before his two terms in the state legislature.

The Howards were an extraordinary family. At least six of Perry and his wife Sarah's children graduated from college. Perry Wilbon Howard became an attorney in 1905 and later was a Republican National Committeeman from Mississippi and served in the Justice Department in Washington in three Republican administrations. Sons Elmer Elsworth Howard and Wesley Howard became doctors, and Andrew Jackson Howard was a math professor and interim president at Alcorn State University. Daughters Sarah and Eva became teachers. Perry Howard remained in Holmes County through the turn of the century. His wife, Sarah, is listed as a widow there in the 1910 Census.[92]

Finally, Frederick Stewart had been born in Virginia in 1831. He, too, was a blacksmith. He served only one term in the statehouse, although he still lived in Durant at the time of the 1880 Census. Like Scarborough, he was active with Lynch and the Loyal Leagues and was present at the 1869 organizing meeting.[93]

Holmes County's first African American sheriff, in 1872, was James H. "Jeems" Sumner. Sumner had come to Holmes County from Tennessee, where he served as doorkeeper of the Tennessee House of Representatives from 1867 to 1869 during military occupation of that state's capital.[94]

After Sumner died in 1874—a death we will discuss in the next section— Robert Augustus Simmons, the schoolteacher from Richland, was Holmes County's second African American sheriff. Simmons won election in 1874 by six hundred votes, but when he was refused certification, he was appointed sheriff by Governor Adelbert Ames.[95]

REDEMPTION AND CONSERVATIVE CONQUEST

White Democrats in Mississippi fought Reconstruction from its inception. They wanted "redemption" not Reconstruction, meaning a resumption of the power and authority they enjoyed before the war. They were unwilling to accept Black people as full citizens and were certainly unwilling to embrace their equality. During Reconstruction, violence toward African Americans continued unabated—from Heggie's Scouts immediately after the war to the emergence of the Ku Klux Klan a year or so later, to voter intimidation from the Red Shirts—and mysterious "nights of investigation."

The political stakes of Black voting rights were greatest in counties like Holmes with an African American majority. If that majority participated electorally, white conservative Democrats were not going to win. Tactics of voter intimidation included threats, shows of white force, and economic reprisals. In the 1930s, a then ninety-two-year-old former Confederate soldier explained, "During Reconstruction days, they mounted a cannon on a little knoll in front of the Eulogy ballot box and did not allow any negroes to vote, thus regaining white supremacy in the South over the carpetbaggers, scalawags, and negroes." The interviewer added, "He told us how it used to humiliate them because of having a negro sheriff named J. H. Sumner."[96]

Political violence built to a crescendo in Mississippi as the 1875 election approached. That year would end with the election of a conservative Democratic legislature, the forced resignation of Governor Adelbert Ames, and the departure from Mississippi of many of the northern Republicans who had been part of its governance. The brief progressive period of Reconstruction was to end and, with it, African American political representation (after a whimper in the 1880s) until the late 1960s.

Around the state, a white mob killed as many as three hundred Black citizens in Vicksburg in December of 1874, in what became known as the Vicksburg massacre. In September of 1875, white vigilantes shot into a picnic and rally in Clinton, Mississippi, organized by an African American state senator there.[97] In 1874 and 1875, Holmes County saw both the dissolution of the coalition between African Americans and white Republicans and violence by white Democrats.

Sheriff Sumner—Holmes County's first African American sheriff—died suddenly in 1874. Sumner was still alive on April 2, 1874, and present at a citizens' meeting that served as the nominating convention for Lexington's next mayor, although leaders of the meeting claimed it was not political in nature. Sumner reportedly asked the "political *color* of the convention; he was informed that it was a citizens' meeting and that politics would be laid aside for a time." That same day, Sumner published announcement of a reward for the apprehension of two escapees from the county jail—one Black and one white—who had been fugitives for six months.[98] Four days later, the *Clarion-Ledger* wrote that "I. H. [sic] Sumner (colored) Sheriff of Holmes County is dead, and our excellent confere [sic] of the *Lexington Advertiser* is announced as a candidate for the office."[99] There is no extant mention of Sumner's death in Holmes County newspapers.

It is possible that he died of natural causes, but the silence and the context of violence against elected officials that year make that explanation unlikely. I spent time exploring what happened to James Sumner. Few people in Holmes County had heard anything about a Black sheriff in the 1870s, and Sumner had no family in the area. Those who had heard anything about a Black sheriff had heard about Sheriff Simmons, who died in Holmes County fifty years later. Few African American graveyards have legible monuments, and there seemed no record of his burial. I could find no information on what happened to him. Given that he was a young man, and given the spate of violence at the time, it is highly probable that James H. Sumner, Holmes County's first African American sheriff, was assassinated.

Sheriffs were a frequent target of harassment, particularly the twelve Black sheriffs elected during Reconstruction. Sheriff Brown of Coahoma County was driven out by a violent mob in 1875. He escaped but later wrote that "a perfect state of terror reign supreme throughout the county." Hinds County's Sheriff Harney was charged with defaulting on his bond, although he had capital, and lost his business. Sherriff Wood of Adams County was elected in 1875 but allowed to serve only two months before he was removed, although he was elected again later.[100] The election of Sheriff Crosby in Warren County was the precipitating event of the Vicksburg massacre, which required federal troops to restore the peace and reinstate Crosby, although a year later, his white deputy shot him in the head. Crosby never recovered, and the deputy sheriff was never prosecuted.[101] Sheriff Sumner should likely be a part of this litany.

Meanwhile, disputes among Holmes County Republicans led to an August 1875 killing at the courthouse. The victims were Holmes County tax assessor Wiley Hill, who was Black, along with another African American man, Tom Ballard. Many at the courthouse heard the shots and saw Hill's body afterward. He was shot in the face and in the chest and died at the scene of at least two mortal wounds. Ballard was shot in the spine, paralyzing him, and he died shortly afterward.[102]

There was a lot of shooting that day, and the identity of who fired the fatal shots was never fully resolved. Among the most likely is J. G. Mills, the white editor of the *Holmes County Republican* newspaper. Captain O. S. Lee, an associate of Governor Ames and the white deputy treasurer of the county, also fired shots and was accused of firing fatal ones.

The shooting followed a fractious meeting of the Holmes County Republican Committee, which had adjourned because of allegedly "unparliamentary conduct" by Harrison Truehart. Following the meeting, Hill accused Mills of being a "liar and a thief" and for inciting violence against Black people during the Vicksburg massacre. Mills and his Republican newspaper had been vilified in the Vicksburg Democratic press, which called the paper an "organ of Radicalism." The Vicksburg press recounted a fight between Mills and a Black man named Charley Jackson, reputedly over a woman, "Miss Laura Olive, a dusky damsel." The story suggests Jackson was trying to protect Olive from Mills. The article closes with the statement that Mills is "a putrifying [sic] sore on the body of the editorial fraternity."[103]

Lee, a favorite of Governor Ames, was certainly present at the shooting of Hill and Ballard and acknowledged firing his gun. At one point he said he had fired in the air but in his sworn testimony he said he fired after Hill in self-defense, stating, "I returned the fire, but cannot say for certain whether I hit him or not."[104] No other available testimony says Hill fired shots.

Sheriff Simmons's testimony suggested that Hill had at least as much concern about Lee's behavior as Mills's. Simmons testified that Lee understood Hill had charged him with having colored men killed at Vicksburg. Simmons's testimony has Hill responding, "I did not say that, Captain, but I said this: That the N.O. *Picayune* and *Vicksburg Herald* stated that the Governor sent you and Packer to Vicksburg to quell the disturbance, but you compromised with the rioters and got Peter Crosby [the sheriff] to resign, and that you had a special train to take you and your friends away. On returning to Jackson, the Governor disapproved of your action and sent you back." Simmons reports that Lee countered by noting that the *Picayune* and *Herald* were Democratic papers. Hill said he was not commenting on the politics of the papers, only what they said.[105]

Governor Ames at least initially believed Hill was shot by the Klan. Ames writes of the incident in letters to his wife, Blanche Butler Ames, the daughter of Union general and later Massachusetts governor Benjamin Butler. She accompanied her husband to Mississippi but returned periodically to their home in Lowell, Massachusetts, in part to keep their children away during the yellow fever epidemic, and because she quite clearly did not enjoy Mississippi. Adelbert and Blanche Ames wrote almost daily during her frequent trips back north. On August 5, 1875, Adelbert Ames writes:

> I am somewhat disgusted today. Last evening I had a telegram from Warren, who is in Holmes Co. (the second county above us on the railroad), asking me to receive a person bringing me a letter at one o'clock this morning. I went to bed at twelve and between one and two was awakened to receive a messenger. The message was that Col. Lee and his friends in Holmes County had made an attack on their own party friends, and killed one and mortally wounded another. There has been

a feud in our own party there and has resulted as above stated. The persons killed (the second has since died) were both colored—the cause was "you lie" and "you are another."[106]

In subsequent letters, Ames adds:

Lee is here—he came on the last train. I have not seen him, but I have had a talk with Packer who went up there yesterday, and from him I judge it was a clear case of Ku Kluxism. I understand Lee was backed by the Democrats. I know not what the end will be, but it is easily forseen that such deadly feuds in our own ranks can but result injuriously.

The poor dead Negroes are to be buried today. Those who killed are at liberty, but are to be examined before a magistrate's court next Monday. Never before has the strife among our own friends been so bitter. What I have described above is being enacted in all directions only with not such violence—such deadly results. Do you wonder that I am disgusted?

Later in the same letter, Ames adds, "I am beginning to be much alone." On September 11, 1875, Governor Ames referred to the matter again: "Col. Lee who has been on trial before a committing court for murder up in Holmes Co., has been bound over to appear before the next circuit court in the sum of $2,000. He confidently hoped to escape without further action. He has no fears, but will be somewhat annoyed by being compelled to dance attendance on the courts."

Ames apparently continued to believe that Lee, if not Mills, was innocent. Reports are inconsistent but much of both the testimony and the coverage indicate Lee and Mills did shoot at Hill. It is feasible that Mills and Lee were the innocent subjects of vitriol from conservative Democrats. It is also quite likely that one or both at least behaved badly surrounding the deaths of Hill and Ballard. In either case, the Republican coalition of white northerners and African Americans in Holmes County had disintegrated.

Regardless of who did the shooting, proto-Klan groups took "credit" for the killing. A notice was printed in multiple newspapers across the state afterward signed "Several Democrats and Conservatives" declaring: "WANTED IMMEDIATELY: Colored men who desire to advance the interest of the Republican Party. An easy death guaranteed. Good pay is certain. Wiley Hill, of Holmes County, was the first to come forward to be sacrificed." It closed, "No applications considered if they are not fat and full of blood, or if they be more white than a mulatto. Full blood Blacks preferred."[107]

After the 1875 election in which conservative Democrats triumphed, Lee and Mills left the state. At least one of them headed to the Black Hills of South Dakota.[108] Lee was accused of absconding with $57,000 in public funds on his

way out of Holmes County,[109] although false accusations against departing outsiders were rampant and often unsubstantiated. South Dakota was a common
destination for those leaving Mississippi. Its Indian lands had just opened for
settlement, and gold was found there in 1874. Former state superintendent of
education Henry Pease ended up there, and former Holmes County superintendent Marcus Morton Holmes passed through before settling in Washington
State. Notably, more of the African Americans who came into leadership positions in Holmes County during Reconstruction remained in the county. Lynch
had died of natural causes in 1872. Both Scarborough and Simmons remained.

Still, Reconstruction had ended. The Freedmen's Bureau was shut down.
In 1877, congressional leaders and others negotiated what was known as the
Hayes-Tilden compromise. After the 1876 election, Democrat Samuel J. Tilden
was one short in the number of an electoral vote majority while Republican
Rutherford B. Hayes was twenty votes short. The remainder were disputed,
including disputed slates of electors in three southern states still under Republican control. The compromise was that Hayes became president of the United
States in exchange for all federal troops leaving the South. Twelve years after the
end of the Civil War, the African American community was again on its own.

UNEQUAL ALLIANCES

Conservative white Democrats had returned to power, but their dominance
was not yet complete in a place like Holmes County, which was two-thirds
Black, although most were no longer voting. Divisions also arose within the
Democratic Party between the wealthy landowners of what was called its
Bourbon wing and the small farmers. The Bourbon wing had mercantile
interests and close ties to the railroads while the small farmers saw agrarian
interests as paramount and sought support. Some joined a third party, the
Greenback Party. African American leaders, in turn, wanted to preserve some
voice and were open to coalitions since their constituency was no longer
voting. Two such coalitions elected Holmes County's final two nineteenth-
century Black state legislators.

One Black state legislator was a "fusion" candidate—an African American
candidate selected by white Democrats and running with their support, who
presumably could also attract the support of those Blacks who were still voting.
James G. Marshall, elected for the 1878–1879 term, was a farmer and a teacher
who was born in Louisiana. The *Yazoo Herald* wrote of him in 1876: "Among
the speakers who addressed the crowd at Lexington . . . was a young colored
man named James Marshall who lives on Bee Lake. He is a graduate of Oberlin
College and as a speaker he has few superiors. His services in behalf of the

reform movement, which has just been crowned with succes [sic] are highly appreciated by those who have heard him speak and seen him in action."[110]

As a fusion candidate, Marshall spoke at a rally in Lexington that included the rifle clubs and "Red Shirts" who were responsible for voter intimidation tactics. Immediately opposite the short story on Marshall, the *Vicksburg Herald* published "A Big Day in Lexington" about the Democratic and "Red Shirt" demonstration at which Marshall spoke: "There were twenty-six hundred men on horseback in the procession that moved in regular order through the town under the efficient leadership of that excellent gentleman and true-hearted patriot, Col. McBee. . . . The fair daughters of that good old county were out in full force, and their presence, as one may suppose, had a most inspiring effect upon each wearer of the "Red Shirt." The article then enumerated the "Rifle Clubs" present, including one headed by Captain Gwin. The closing paragraph noted that General W. R. Miles and General A. M. West addressed the "great multitude." It concluded by saying, "The demonstration in Lexington on Sat-urday was a grand success, and it squelched the spirit of Radicalism in that quarter so effectively that it will never, never rise again to vex the community with its baleful presence, roguish practices and villainous precept."[111] Marshall served one term and then left Holmes for Washington County in 1879 when he was appointed circuit clerk there by the Democratic governor.[112]

The final African American state legislator, Tenant Weatherly, ran as a member of the Greenback Party. Weatherly, born in Mississippi, was former Representative Edmund Scarborough's brother-in-law. He had helped Scarborough organize the Loyal League, and Weatherly, too, was active in the Methodist Church.[113] He had served as a Republican in 1874–1875 but ran as a Greenbacker for the 1880–1881 term.

The Greenback Party was itself something of a coalition. It included former Whigs, small farmers, and some African Americans, all of whom had issues with the conservative Democrats. Greenbacks were pro-agrarian and favored economic interventions to increase deflated farm prices. The conservative Democrats were, in their view, too aligned with railroad and merchant interests. To raise farm prices and exert more economic control over farm prices, they opposed the gold standard then operative and favored US currency, or "greenbacks." With a gold standard, banks set the value of gold and therefore of money. Without a gold standard, governments can control inflation and deflation by the amount of paper money they put into the economy.[114]

The leading Greenbacker from Holmes County was Absolom Madden West. West had deep roots in Holmes County. West's father, Anderson West, moved to Holmes County as a federal land grant holder in the 1830s.[115] Absolom West had been a Whig state senator and an officer of the Mississippi Central Railroad before the war. He was elected to Congress as a Democrat in

1868 as part of the delegation from Mississippi that was never seated. He lost confidence in the Democrats and became a Greenbacker and, after moving to Holly Springs in Marshall County, established a branch of the National Labor Union in Mississippi. West was far more supportive of African American advancement than most Holmes County whites of that period. He served on the biracial board of trustees of the Mount Hermon Seminary, a school for African American girls founded in 1875 in Clinton, in Hinds County. Charles Caldwell, the African American state senator from Clinton who was assassinated, had also served on the board.[116]

West became a leading Greenbacker nationally. He ran for vice president of the United States on the Greenback/Anti-monopoly Party ticket in 1884. The candidate for president on the same ticket was Benjamin Butler, former Union general and father-in-law of deposed governor Adelbert Ames. The Butler-West ticket received only 2 percent of the vote nationally. In Holmes, the size of the populist group was a little larger but hardly dominant, even in the eastern part of the county.[117]

Weatherly's 1879 election as a Greenbacker was contested. The three Holmes County representatives elected that year were seated only after an investigation. The investigation determined that the Acona ballot box and poll books were lost or destroyed, and those votes were not counted. There were five candidates within three hundred votes of each other, including H. J. Reid, who had been captain of the Black Hawk Rifles, and one of two candidates named McGehee, and the three who were declared the winners: Tenant Weatherly, Greenbacker; Henry Christmas, Democrat of Lexington; and Charles Murphy, a Republican from Durant.[118] Seating one member from each party looks more like a fusion-compromise than an electoral result. Still, Tenant Weatherly served until 1881 and was the last African American state representative from Holmes County until 1967.

The Greenbacker efforts in Holmes County ended abruptly on Election Day 1880 after the white Democratic sheriff, J. E. Ashcraft, and the white Greenback chancery clerk, J. T. Lockhart, shot and killed each other, bringing the sudden deaths of countywide elected officials to four between 1874 and 1880. The Lockharts and the Wests were related by marriage, and both were part of Greenbacker and Democratic-populist politics around Durant.

On election night 1880, Lockhart "made some general charges of Democratic swindling" that offended the twenty-six-year-old sheriff's father, prominent planter J. W. Ashcraft. Lockhart struck the elder Ashcraft and blinded him, then drew his pistol but was held back from using it at that point by Lexington mayor W. F. Cross.

Sheriff Ashcraft then arrived. According to the *Comet* newspaper from Jackson, "Lockhart and J. E. Ashcraft fired almost simultaneously, each receiving a mortal wound, the former in the groin and the latter in the neck. Ashcraft dropped back against the rope stretched around the polls, straightened himself, fired another shot, walked off a few steps and fell. After murmuring a word or two about his wife and children, he died. After his death he was found to have also received a mortal wound in the back. After being wounded, Lockhart walked around until his strength gave way and he fell, and was carried off by his friends."[119]

The shooting was widely covered as a tragedy. The coverage was markedly different from the silence at the death of Sheriff Sumner, or the focus on the perpetrators at the time of Hill's death. In this case, the two young men "belonged to the same church, the same Masonic Lodge, to the same Knights of Pythias lodge, to the same Knights of Honor lodge . . . the strongest ties that could under any circumstances, bind man to man, and heart to heart," wrote a paper on the Mississippi coast.[120] The lodges of which both men were members offered insurance and paid several thousand dollars to each of their families. Ashcraft's chief deputy was Baxter Wilson, whose father-in-law had enslaved Harrison Truehart. He became the next sheriff.[121]

THE UNEASY FARMERS' ALLIANCE

One more interracial alliance had an impact on Holmes County in the nineteenth century. For a brief time, the all-white Southern Alliance and the Colored Farmers' Alliance shared cooperative stores to help small farms across the county. That effort, too, would end violently when most leaders of the Colored Farmers' Alliance were killed.

In the 1880s, falling cotton prices and the rise of crop liens made it increasingly difficult for small farmers to turn a profit. Future crops were mortgaged, and declining crop prices made payments impossible. The financial squeeze on farmers sparked farm revolts across the country, including the formation of the Greenback Party. Another effort to fight back against traps in the system began in Texas with what became the National Farmers' Alliance and Industrial Union, known in the South as the Southern Alliance. The Southern Alliance allowed only white farmers to join, but one of its leaders formed the Colored Farmers' Alliance in 1886 to broaden and enlarge the farm coalition.[122]

The Colored Farmers' Alliance organized extensively in the 1880s in Central Mississippi. It published a newspaper in Vaiden, just north of Holmes County, and lodged a boycott on merchants who were charging unaffordable prices or interest rates. Two co-ops in Holmes County—one in Tchula and another in Durant—provided alternatives to usurious farm merchants on either side of the county.

The Tchula Cooperative store was doing business in Holmes and nearby Delta counties with Black farm owners (although not with tenants or share-croppers). It helped farmers keep their land out of the credit spiral because, while it charged slightly higher prices to those who did not have cash, it did not charge or compound interest.[123]

Another co-op, the Durant Commercial Company, was formed by the Southern Alliance and located near the Durant railroad station. It sold to farmers of both races. An advertisement for the Durant Commercial Company Alliance House in the Winona New Farmer in 1888 listed an array of merchandise and promised "Lowest prices ever offerd [sic] to the Farmers of this section."[124]

The leader of the Colored Farmers' Alliance in Mississippi was a man named Oliver Cromwell. The name itself is intriguing. Some speculate that he was named for—or chose the name of—an African American Revolutionary War hero who fought with George Washington.[125] In 1863, in Mississippi, a man named Oliver Cromwell from Wilkinson County signed up with the Fifth Regiment of USCT, staying in the military until 1872 when he was court-martialed and his pay suspended for violation of military discipline.[126] It's not certain that the Wilkinson County man and the leader of the Colored Farmers' Alliance in central Mississippi are the same, but there are reasons to think they may be.

In any event, the Oliver Cromwell who became a leader of the Colored Farmers' Alliance appears in 1875 as an organizer in Clinton, in Hinds County, to encourage freedmen to vote. The white attack on a Republican barbecue there, in which vigilantes fired into a largely Black crowd, became known as the Clinton Massacre. Cromwell rode a horse in a parade before the barbecue and wore an extravagantly plumed hat. Describing his role at the Clinton massacre, the conservative New Mississippian newspaper called Cromwell a "notoriously bad negro" who was a leader in the Clinton "riot." It added that after the Clinton massacre, Cromwell was "head of a band of thieves and outlaws operating between Brownsville [in Hinds County] and the Yazoo River, for which he was sentenced to the penitentiary for ten years, but, as per usual, was pardoned out at the expiration of five to renew his nefarious practices."[127]

By 1889, Cromwell was actively organizing in at least Holmes, Carroll, Leflore, and Tallahatchie Counties. He traveled the area, spoke to individual Black farmers, and distributed the Colored Farmers' Alliance newspaper. Cromwell argued that cooperative purchasing power would reduce reliance on white creditors and uncoil spiraling debt for small farmers. He criticized the practices of larger white merchants and suggested that Black farmers would find a better deal at the alliance store. In response, white landowners began circulating negative information about Cromwell as a criminal and suggesting he had a personal financial interest in the Durant Commercial Company. Sufficient Black farmers were concerned by the information to force a meeting on his leadership. In the end, the alliance members stood by Cromwell and retained him as their leader.[128]

Next, Cromwell received threats to his life. As described in the Jackson *Clarion-Ledger*, "He received notice to leave the county, accompanied by a cartoon representing a negro hanging from the end of a rope. This greatly enraged Cromwell, and he organized a mob, marched into Shell Mound [in Leflore County], paraded around the streets, made insulting speeches and defied the white people. He massed his forces near Minter City and defied arrest. The white people armed themselves, but were unequal to cope with Cromwell's band, which numbered 300."[129] Other reports portray a peaceful—although armed—protest of 75 alliance members.

Minter City is in Leflore County, and Sheriff T. L. Baskett there requested support from Governor Lowry and the state militia. According to the *New Mississippian*, Baskett's telegram to Lowry said, "Negroes congregated 500 strong at Minter City. Can't be persuaded to desist, and swear the fight has to come, and won't disband. Send us aid." Lowry called up three militia units, the Governor's Light Guards, the Winona Rifles, and the Durant Grays, and he showed up personally. The train stopped to pick up the Yazoo City Rifles and twenty citizens who were eager to join the fight. They met up with the Durant and Winona units on the afternoon of September 2, 1889.

Other calls to arms went out less formally. The *Grenada Sentinel*, in an article entitled "Race Troubles in Leflore County," wrote that the manager of a large plantation near Minter City contacted the plantation owner in Grenada to "come at once and bring all the white men he could" with the result that "about 35 men succeeded in getting needle and shot-guns and volunteered to go to the scene of the trouble." These Grenada volunteers joined up later with the Winona Rifles.

The massing of armed and ready white men was a little much even for Governor Lowry, who sent some of them back, although they were "somewhat disappointed at the turn matters had taken." The governor made "a sensible and law abiding speech to the crowd." Some of the press apparently left and reported that is all that occurred. But, yes, shooting began, as was inevitable.[130]

Reports on the number of deaths range between twenty and two hundred. Local papers reported that Colored Alliance leaders Adolphus Horton, Scott and M. J. Morris, and Jack Dial were shot, and that Cromwell associate George Allen was killed. Local press also reports that "160 negroes, well-armed with Winchester rifles" were camped about eight miles from Minter City and that a party of fifty men "was organized to interview the belligerent Blacks." The militia reportedly turned over approximately seventy prisoners to Sheriff Baskett two days later.

The northern and African American press report up to two hundred were killed. The *St. Louis Post-Dispatch* wrote that, after the militia withdrew, an armed posse of some two hundred whites combed the countryside for days and shot or hung more than twenty Black men. A story in the *New Haven Register* at that time listed eight additional names of men who were killed. The Indianapolis *World Letter* says there were forty to sixty killed. There is no knowing how many died, but shooting by an armed white posse went on for days. There are no reports of white people killed, but it seems that dozens—at least—of Black farmers were arrested—and shot or hung. The Durant Commercial Company was ordered closed and the Colored Farmers' Alliance newspaper was shut down. The Colored Farmers' Alliance was effectively squelched.

I became a bit obsessed with the question of what happened to Oliver Cromwell. Here was a significant statewide leader, and it was frustrating not to know what happened to him or, for that matter, where he came from. I did a deeper dive into the US Census and a more expansive newspaper search on the name. I spoke to a woman referenced as a descendant and tracked down relatives by marriage after finding that their family pastor and I had a mutual friend.

I believe Oliver Cromwell may have survived into the twentieth century, although it remains debatable. A man named Oliver Cromwell appears in later Census records from Wilkinson County, farming with his wife, named Tennessee. She died in 1921, and Oliver, in his eighties, married a woman forty years his junior, Hannah Levinson. He died in 1923. Hannah, according to her descendants, kept a picture of him on her mantel in his USCT uniform.[131]

The likelihood that the two Oliver Cromwells—the leader of the Colored Farmers' Alliance and the farmer and USCT veteran in Wilkinson County—are one and the same runs through another well-known scandal of late nineteenth-century Mississippi and may be another demonstration of an unlikely alliance: Colonel Jones Hamilton was accused of harboring Cromwell after the Leflore County massacre, although he denied it.[132]

Hamilton had been born into a prominent South Mississippi and Louisiana family and became the Wilkinson County sheriff. Later, he was a progenitor of Mississippi's notorious convict-leasing program. It leased convicts to rebuild railroads after the Civil War—and to private plantations—a practice that brutalized convicts who were unpaid for hard labor. Hamilton's leasing of convicts, and his opposition to prohibition, were the pillars of a feud with Roderick Dhu Gambrell, editor of the *Sword and Shield* newspaper.[133] Gambrell was a leader of the 1880s "reform" movement and the son of a prominent Baptist minister and prohibitionist. Reformers favored prohibition and agrarianism rather than industrialization, and they were leading voices for a new state constitution that would reduce the influence of Black voters. Hamilton was accused of shooting the younger Gambrell in 1887 but was found not guilty, in part because witnesses heard multiple shots.[134] Two of the exculpatory witnesses were Oliver Cromwell and a man named McNeil who was with him. In coverage of the trial, Cromwell is variously described as a "gambler" and "a very intelligent looking negro."[135] In any case, Hamilton seems to have been indebted to Cromwell.

Regardless of what happened to Oliver Cromwell, the story highlights elements that carry forward in Holmes County. First, it demonstrates the deep roots of African American–led cooperative purchasing and collective enterprise that continues in Holmes County through the twentieth century and to the present day.[136] It is also an early story of shooting back in self-defense, which did not happen before the Civil War but happens again in the twentieth century. Finally, it shows the establishment of purposeful alliances, even among the proverbial strange bedfellows of politics. That, too, would recur.

MINORITY RULE

After the election of 1875, few Black people participated in elections. Coalitions—like the two farmers' alliances—and fusion candidacies had held promise of a continued Black voice. But both of those had failed by 1881. The state—and Holmes County—had effectively reinstituted white minority rule. In 1890, it codified minority rule by rewriting its constitution to exclude Black voter participation. The constitution was written by elected convention delegates but was never ratified by the voters.

Conservative Democrats had long wanted to replace the 1869 constitution, which had in their view taken the unacceptable step of granting freedmen the right to vote. As one newspaper wrote in urging a new constitution, the 1869 constitution "was framed by a convention composed of carpetbaggers and negroes, was not fit for the state then and is unsuited now" and "it was accepted by the people under duress, with no thought of continuing it permanently."[137]

It took another fifteen years after Democrats won control of the state to rewrite the constitution because of continued division between two wings of the Democratic Party. The populist wing was centered in Mississippi's majority white counties and dominated by small farmers. It had absorbed the white remnants of the Greenback Party, which had fizzled nationally after its electoral failures in 1884. The populists generally wanted more help for small farms, less political clout for Delta counties, and no government funds to support the railroads. They opposed the convict leasing program in part because the convicts were rebuilding the railroads. They were also allied with the growing temperance movement. The other wing of the Democratic Party, the so-called Bourbon wing, was made up of the large planters in the Delta who had mercantile as well as agricultural interests. It had successfully squelched Black voter participation and so supported the post-1875 status quo.[138]

The impetus for uniting the two factions to rewrite the constitution was renewed concern that the federal government would act to protect Black voting rights, still on paper as part of the 1869 constitution. President Benjamin Harrison, a Republican and former Union army officer, had been elected in 1888. He favored strengthening African American voting rights. Harrison supported a bill sponsored by Representative Henry Cabot Lodge of Massachusetts that would have prevented poll taxes and literacy tests.[139]

Unlike most counties, Holmes County was divided internally between the two Democratic factions, with white owners of small farms and populists around Durant and West, and larger planters dominating in the western part of the county with its large plantations. The divisions had produced violence in the county just a few years before. The Holmes County delegates to the 1890 convention straddled the divide. Typifying the Bourbon wing was Walter Leake Keirn, who had been a Holmes delegate to the succession convention and organized the Holmes Volunteers at the start of the war. He was sixty years old when he participated in the 1890 convention.

Joel George Hamilton was the second delegate. Hamilton, age fifty-six, was a farmer in Durant and related by marriage to the West family. He was a follower of J. Z. George, active in the Southern Farmers' Alliance, and the Fifth Congressional District Democratic chair. George was a voice of the agrarian populist wing at the convention, although he did not push the interests of farmers as hard as the Southern Farmers' Alliance chair, Frank Burkitt.[140]

The third Holmes County delegate, Henry Hooker, was a thirty-nine-year-old lawyer from Lexington with a foot in both camps. Later, his daughter Hattie married into the Witty family from Winona. Fred Witty, who lionized Heggie's Scouts, was her nephew. The Hooker family would remain active in Holmes County politics through the twentieth century.[141]

The principal focus of the convention debate was how to write the constitution to exclude Black voters without violating the Fifteenth Amendment to the US Constitution, ratified in 1870—that the right of citizens of the United States to vote shall not be denied or abridged by the United States or by any state on account of race, color, or previous condition of servitude. Yet as the convention president declared, "Let's tell the truth if it bursts the bottom of the universe. We came here to exclude the negro. Nothing short of this will answer."[142]

The convention debated a variety of schemes. One was a suggestion to expand the vote to educated, property-owning women. Another would have adjusted the number of votes per person based on education or landownership. Such plural voting was unconstitutional and, according to some, would be insufficient to protect white interests in Holmes County. The *Pickens Enterprise* editorialized, "For plural voting to give whites control of Holmes County, every white man would have to vote 12 times. Why not just give one man 14 thousand votes, to overcome the 16 thousand negro voters?"[143]

In the end, the convention established poll taxes and literacy tests through the registrar of voters, an appointed position and presumptively a white Democrat, to determine whether the prospective voter could adequately read or interpret a section of the constitution read to them. The state still had a majority Black population, but after two years under the new constitution, only 11 percent of registered voters were Black. In Holmes County, the total number of registered voters fell from about 5,800 at the time of the convention to 1,243 in 1892, of whom 220 were Black. Eight whites and 10 Blacks were added to the rolls by registrars for passing the "understanding clause," meaning they had adequately interpreted a clause of the constitution read to them. The electorate was a fifth the size it had been, and virtually all white.[144]

The period of white minority rule—the Jim Crow period—was to last another seventy-five years.

Big Black River Station, Miss. Wagons and sheds. United States Mississippi Vicksburg Big Black River Station, February 1864. Photograph by Wm. R. Pywell. https://www.loc.gov/item/2018666956/. Library of Congress, Prints & Photographs Division, Civil War Photographs, LC-DIG-cwpb-01013.

Provost Marshal's Guard House, Vicksburg, Miss. United States Mississippi Vicksburg [photographed between 1861 and 1865, printed between 1880 and 1889]. https://www.loc.gov/item/2013649017/. Library of Congress, Prints & Photographs Division, Civil War Photographs, LC-DIG-ppmsca-35292.

Franklin Church, where a skirmish was fought between the Third Colored Cavalry, US Troops, and the Thirty-Eighth Confederate Infantry, with soldiers from Holmes County on both sides. Photo by the author, 2022.

Survivors of the Twenty-Second Mississippi Regiment, Confederate States Army, originally printed in *Confederate Veteran*, September 1899. Isaac Ramsey Heggie is seated on the right.

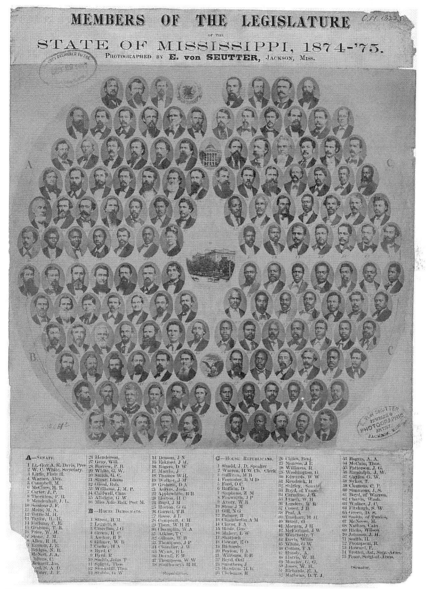

Members of the Legislature, State of Mississippi, 1874–'75. The photograph includes Harrison Truehart (#39) and Tenant Weatherly (#43). Photograph by E. von Seutter, Jackson, MS, circa 1877. https://www.loc.gov/item/2006687066/. Library of Congress, Prints & Photographs Division, LC-DIG-ppmsca-12860.

Chapter 3

A NEW CENTURY—1900 TO 1950

Don't rejoice against me, my enemy. When I fall, I will arise.
When I sit in darkness, Yahweh will be a light to me.
—MICAH 7:8 (WORLD ENGLISH BIBLE)

If we, the colored citizens of America, ever get anywhere, we must organize
on an economic basis. . . . The economic foundation—the "dollars and cents"
foundation must be laid. That is your job, you colored farmers of America.
—INAUGURAL ISSUE OF *MODERN FARMER* 1, NO. 1, MARCH 1, 1929

TURN OF THE CENTURY

Life in Holmes County under Jim Crow was much like it had been before the
Civil War. Most African Americans were sharecroppers and lived on plantations. The owners of those plantations made decisions about their workers'
economic lives, including what, if anything, they would be paid for their labor
and whether they could use a patch of land to plant food for their families.
There were new freedoms for sure—to marry, to stay together as a family, and
to worship as they chose. But sharecroppers did not have much more control over their economic realities than they had during enslavement. Douglas
Blackmon, who grew up in the Mississippi Delta, argues that the Jim Crow
period should be known as the "Age of Neoslavery" as Black people—whether
sharecroppers or industrial workers—were still fundamentally in a situation of
forced labor.[1] As we shall see, however, a remarkable number found their way
out of neoslavery to land ownership and self-sufficiency.

The violence did not stop. Across the country, lynchings and violence were
particularly frequent early in the twentieth century. Holmes County was no

exception. In March of 1909, a Black man named Joe Gordon reportedly shot at an overseer at the Shotwell plantation near Cruger. "A posse was at once organized for the apprehension of the would-be-assassin. Hundreds of men partook in the chase which was eventually crowned with success in his capture, about five miles from Yazoo City, yesterday evening. Further 'deponent sayeth not,'" reported the *Lexington Advertiser*.[2]

On June 17, 1910, the *Lexington Advertiser* reported a "Tragedy at Durant": "Frenzied by cocaine, a hitherto peaceable negro named Otho Mitchell went on a rampage at Durant about noon Wednesday, armed with a double-barreled shot gun. His eyes were bulging out and he had every appearance of being stark mad." A bystander "got his gun into play, shooting the negro through the head and through the body." The story adds: "To make 'assurance doubly sure' of his death the negro was hoisted by his neck to a nearby telephone poll where he remained for about an hour."[3]

Membership in the Ku Klux Klan rose in the early part of the twentieth century as its role in Reconstruction was romanticized. A novel called *The Clansman, an Historical Romance of the Ku Klux Klan* was published in 1905 and became a play of the same name and the basis for the film *The Birth of a Nation*. The play was performed all over Mississippi, drawing praise as "a simple story of a brave, proud people, humiliated to the bitter dregs, rising victorious over the desolation of war; the gross stupidity and deviltry of military despotism and the barbarism of the Black terror."[4] The *Lexington Advertiser* praised the Klan itself as "a potent factor in restoring order out of chaos in the dark days of Reconstruction."[5]

Mississippi's governor from 1908 to 1912 was Edmond Favor Noel, who was from Holmes County. He was grounded in the Bourbon rather than populist wing of his party with the added reform credential of opposition to alcohol. Noel opposed lynching, but he put little force behind his opposition. He sent the state militia to protect a prisoner from a lynch mob in Brookhaven, but the militia did not succeed. The mob waited for the arrival of prisoner Eli Pigot at the train station in Brookhaven and readily overwhelmed the Light Guards and the county sheriff ostensibly sent for Pigot's protection. "Pigot was dragged about 50 yards away, a member of the mob secured a rope, and he was quickly swung aloft from the arm of a telegraph pole. The mob then riddled his body with bullets, several hundred shots being fired."[6]

Noel's statement on the lynching closed with a pledge: "I shall see to it that when lynchings are threatened a sufficient number of soldiers will be sent along to furnish ample protection." Despite his expression of that sentiment, an additional forty-five people are recorded as lynched in the state during his term, and there were likely many more.[7]

The African American community had three fundamental responses to the forced labor and continued violence during minority rule. The first was to stay away from white people to the extent possible, advice African American parents have repeated to their children for generations. The second response was to leave. The Great Migration in which millions of Black people left the South began with the rise of violence. Changes in the South were accompanied by employment demand in the North at the start of World War I. The Black population of Chicago grew from four thousand in 1870 to fifteen thousand in 1890 and forty thousand by 1910.[8] In Holmes County the population dropped for the first time ever. The exodus included many who had been leaders in the African American community during Reconstruction, including the Weatherly family and most of the Howard family. The Great Migration would continue through the 1970s.

The third response was the building and strengthening of Black institutions. Nationally, the National Association for the Advancement of Colored People (NAACP) was founded in 1909. The Urban League was founded in 1910. The United Negro Improvement Association was founded in 1914. The Mississippi NAACP was first chartered in Vicksburg in 1918. The early part of the twentieth century also witnessed growth of African American newspapers. The *Chicago Defender* was founded in 1905, the *Pittsburgh Courier* in 1907, the *Amsterdam News* in 1909. Each had a national audience and covered national news, as African Americans became an expanding market across the country with outmigration from the South.

In Holmes County and elsewhere many African Americans chose instead to stay and to strive for self-sufficiency locally. Before learning about Holmes County, I was far more aware of the violence and neoslavery, as Blackmon called it, than I was of those leaders who with strategic focus and determination stayed and moved their communities forward. The first half of the twentieth century is not only a story of oppression but also of courage in Black agency and activism, sometimes aided by national organizations and philanthropy, but consistently reliant on local initiative and leadership. In Holmes County, African Americans founded a church that was to reach worldwide renown. The community financed their own schools, built their own businesses, and played a seminal role in a national organization of African American farmers. Nothing was easy—and the threat of violence was sustained—but so was a refusal to be victimized by the strictures placed on the Black community. Understanding the Jim Crow period in Holmes County—beyond the violence and neoslavery—helped teach me the continuity of struggle from slavery to Reconstruction and on to the civil rights era.

I SHALL SURELY RISE[9]

The most consequential development within Holmes County at the turn of the century was the founding of the Church of God in Christ (COGIC) in Lexington, Mississippi in 1897 by Bishop Charles Harrison Mason.[10] It now has millions of members globally with congregations across the country and around the world.[11] It is not the sole or even the dominant church in Holmes County now—there are more Baptists—but its history is integral to that of the county and, in some ways, to the civil rights movement. It has roots in the religious practices of slavery and in the practice of spiritual gifts that "offered ordinary people a new source of power in their efforts to confront evil in the world."[12] St. Paul Church of God in Christ is the Mother Church of the denomination, located in Lexington. Its brick building constructed in 1906 continues to serve its congregation today.[13]

The Church of God in Christ was born out of the Holiness movement of the nineteenth century, the Gospel of St. Paul, and practices that enslaved people brought with them from Africa.[14] Holiness was a biracial Christian movement characterized by a belief in sanctification: that as a vessel for the Holy Spirit a worshiper could be saved and live a life free of sin thereafter, adhering to standards of dress and personal behavior. The Holiness movement rejected religious formalism and stressed charismatic leadership, spiritual experience, and emotional worship. The movement was an alternative to institutionalized hierarchical churches—white and Black—that stressed biblical text with less spiritual emotionalism, emphasizing instead a personal relationship with God.[15]

Sanctification requires a strict code of moral behavior but also embraces joy. Many Protestant churches outside the Holiness movement did not use instruments like drums and guitars and favored an a cappella chorus and a serious mien. Holiness churches always had music and a theology that put the Holy Spirit at the center of salvation. Black Holiness churches then, and COGIC churches now, have guitars and percussion instruments in addition to keyboard, brass, and woodwind instruments. The music is not somber, but jubilant. Blues legend B.B. King, who was raised in the COGIC church, recalls in his autobiography how "Sunday is special. Sunday means church . . . a sanctified church . . . that's a Church of God in Christ, and that means they will be doing whatever it takes to praise the Lord, making a joyful noise, even talking in tongues. That's the church where I wanna go, where you exit happier than when you enter."[16]

The COGIC reliance on practices brought from Africa derived from the COGIC founder's own history and less directly from the teachings of a former slave named Amanda Berry Smith. The founder, Charles Harrison Mason, was born on the Prior Farm just north of Memphis in 1866.[17] His parents—Jerry and Eliza Mason—were devout Christians, who had been enslaved until just two years earlier. Prior Lee, the white farm owner, had property in Tennessee and Mississippi and was a member of the First Baptist Church in Jackson, Mississippi, which was founded in 1834. Prior Lee apparently not only allowed but encouraged Christian worship by the people he enslaved, some of whom laid the first bricks for Mt. Helm, now the oldest Black church in Jackson.[18]

The Mason family moved to Plumerville, Arkansas, in 1878 to escape the yellow fever epidemic. They became tenant farmers there, but they did not succeed in outrunning the epidemic. Jerry Mason died of yellow fever, and Charles Mason, the future bishop, became gravely ill with the disease two years later. He became delirious and nearly died. During the illness, Mason and his mother went to the nearby Baptist church where Mason's half brother was the pastor. Mason was baptized there, and his recovery began immediately afterward. Mason became a lay preacher, telling the story of his healing at meetings in Arkansas.

Mason was licensed and ordained to preach in 1891, but his first wife, Alice Saxton, did not want him to be a preacher. Conflict over his preaching resulted in her leaving him after two years. Mason was deeply distraught by the divorce and did not marry again while his first wife lived. During the period of his first marriage, Mason preached his first service on sanctification. It was during this period as well that Mason may have read the work of Amanda Berry Smith. Smith was important to the Holiness movement and widely read. She makes a direct connection between the receiving of the Holy Spirit and freedom from slavery and, indeed, freedom from race.[19]

Smith was born enslaved in Maryland in 1837 and published her autobiography in 1893. It recounts the religious conversion of the daughter of the family that enslaved her when Smith was a child. Miss Celie "converted in the old fashioned way; the shouting hallelujah way." Smith's father, Samuel Berry, at the urging of Miss Celie, was allowed to purchase his family's freedom when Smith was a young girl. Smith writes of her own experience of sanctification as a young woman in Pennsylvania:

> Somehow I always had a fear of white people—that is, I was not afraid of them in the sense of doing me harm, or anything of that kind—but a kind of fear because they were white, and were there, and I was black and was here! But that morning on Green Street, as I stood on my feet trembling, I heard these words distinctly. They seemed to come from the northeast corner of the church, slowly but clearly: "There is neither Jew nor Greek, there is neither bond nor free, there is neither male nor female, for ye are all one in Christ Jesus" (Galatians 3:28) I never understood that text before. But now the Holy Ghost had made it clear to me.

And as I looked at white people that I had always seemed to be afraid of, now they looked so small. The great mountain had become a mole-hill.[20]

Smith had formal education only to the third grade but studied in England and went on to preach in Britain, India, and Africa before returning to the United States. She was prominent in Wesleyan-Holiness circles, founded an orphanage, and was active in the temperance movement. Her autobiography was widely read in the late nineteenth and early twentieth centuries. In a fundamental way, it is about Christianity as a liberating force from slavery and of the value of "old fashioned" religion as practiced by enslaved people in the nineteenth century. Mason, too, has been described "as a race-transcending prophet—someone who never forgot the significance of race but refused to be confined to race."[21]

Mason had entered Arkansas Baptist College in November of 1893 but stayed less than three months. Arkansas Baptist was not part of the Holiness movement but rather aimed to raise the formal educational level of the Baptist ministry with a philosophy and curriculum that would make African American preaching grounded more in the text, and less in an appeal to charismatic experience. As Mason's biographer, Bishop Ithiel C. Clemmons, explained: "Mason decided that the college would be of no help in preventing the loss of Slave Religion's vitality because of its assimilation into the culture at large."[22] Mason committed to the Holiness movement and to sanctification.

In 1895, Mason met Charles Price Jones, pastor of Mt. Helm Baptist Church in Jackson, Mississippi. Jones was a graduate of Arkansas Baptist College, both a scholar and a powerful preacher. Together, Jones and Mason were preaching Holiness within the Baptist churches in Mississippi, advocating for an interdenominational, spiritual, and charismatic emotional doctrine.

In 1896, Jones was asked to preach about sanctification at Asia Missionary Baptist Church in Lexington, a church that had grown out of brush harbor meetings during enslavement and still serves the Holmes County community. Toward the end of that year, when Jones was unable to return to Asia Missionary Baptist, Mason went in his stead, but controversy around sanctification and the termination of Reverend Young, who had proffered the invitation, meant Mason preached from the steps of the Holmes County Courthouse, in people's homes, and at outdoor revival meetings. Mason was seen as a healer and drew both white and Black people to his services.

Meanwhile, in a desire for a nondenominational Christian approach, Jones and Mason wanted to change the name of Mt. Helm. Part of the congregation fought the change in court, and shortly thereafter Mason established the first Church of God in Christ "in an old [cotton] gin on the bank of a little creek in Lexington, Mississippi," with permission of its owner, John Watson, and then on a lot on Yazoo Street purchased from Mrs. John Ashcraft.[23]

Disagreements between Jones and Mason and the mainstream Baptist church were inevitable, as was, perhaps, the eventual separation between Mason and Jones. Their approaches were different. While Jones embraced Holiness, he was more rooted in European traditions and Mason more interested in the practice of religion during slavery. Each, however, had a major impact on the Holiness movement and, through it, on global Pentecostal movements.

In the United States, Pentecostal religious growth—white and Black—is traced to the Azuza Street Mission Revival in Los Angeles, led by William J. Seymour. Before Azuza Street, Seymour had visited Mason and Jones in 1905. Seymour was traveling the South and Midwest from his then home in Houston, Texas, and meeting with Holiness leaders. He went by "special revelation to Jackson, Mississippi, to receive spiritual advice from a well-known colored clergyman."[24]

Mason traveled to Los Angeles to join Seymour at the Azuza Street Mission Revival. Seymour, like Mason, was the son of enslaved people, but the Azuza Street movement was initially biracial. Charles Parham, a white Pentecostal preacher, had been teaching the importance of glossolalia as evidence of Baptism by the Holy Spirit. Parham had refused Seymour admittance to his Bible classes and made him stand at the door instead. Parham came to Azuza Street and Seymour invited him to speak from the pulpit. Parham took that as an opportunity to be harshly critical of the gathering,[25] perhaps because of his own racial attitudes, or from a sense of competition with Seymour. Parham's response was an impetus for racial division within the Pentecostal movement. The movement split along racial lines a few years after Azuza Street. Whites formed the Assemblies of God, while the Church of God in Christ grew as a principally African American Church.

Azuza Street—and Pentecostalism—embraces the teachings of Paul in Acts of the Apostles. St. Paul taught the importance of living a life separated from sin and the concept that Christians in accepting Christ accept responsibility to serve those who are less fortunate. Service to the poor and preaching the gospel to the poor remain critical parts of COGIC doctrine and part of a sanctified life. Worshippers can experience the in-dwelling of the Holy Spirit. A baptism of the Holy Spirit can include speaking in tongues, or glossolalia, although it is not necessary to receive the gift of tongues to be saved or sanctified. Mason's first experience with glossolalia was at Azuza Street. His second wife, Elsie Mason, later summarized his experience, referencing his own words: "The Holy Ghost had come! Finally, Elder Charles Mason had received 'the promise' which he had so heartily sought. And his personal baptism had been quite reminiscent of the First Day of Pentecost when the 'sound' came from heaven 'like as a rushing mighty wind' and 'cloven tongues like as of fire' sat upon each of the 120 waiting disciples as they spoke in 'other tongues as the Spirit gave them utterance.' He had experienced all three operations of divine grace: regeneration, sanctification, and spiritual baptism."[26]

Mason remained at Azuza Street for five weeks after this experience and then returned to Lexington, where the practice of glossolalia was controversial. Several of Mason's congregants took him to court with the aim of ousting him from St. Paul Church of God in Christ as his practice of religion had changed. The *Lexington Advertiser* wrote of the "unintelligible words" uttered by Mason and said of the suit that "the object of it is to oust Mason and his alleged heretic followers from the church and allow it once more to resume its normal functions as a religious organization." It suggested that, according to the suit, "Mason and his strange and heretical actions and antics has diverted the church property from its regular faith and is now using it for the service of the devil instead of the worship of God."[27] The divisions were not, at that point, racial. Whites, including local Jewish people, joined Mason's church at that stage and Mason ordained over three hundred white ministers into the church.[28] In 1914, white ministers would begin to split off from COGIC. They would eventually become part of the Worldwide Assemblies of God, which, as a Pentecostal church, shares with COGIC the centrality of baptism by the Holy Spirit with evidence of speaking in tongues.

Speaking in tongues was not new. The first letter of Paul to the Corinthians speaks of the gift of tongues, and there are multiple other biblical references. The practice of speaking in tongues has European Christian theological references dating back hundreds of years. The process of receiving a spirit has parallels in West Africa too,[29] and glossolalia is part of the West African–derived Santeria religion practiced in the Caribbean today.[30] Henry Louis Gates writes in the concluding section to his book accompanying his Public Broadcasting Service (PBS) series on the Black Church, "Possession by the Holy Ghost, which I so feared as a boy, is perhaps the most vibrant, complex, and mysterious vestige of the African cultural past retained by African Americans."[31]

Mason's opponents lost the suit against him that followed his experience on Azuza Street. They lost for purely secular reasons. The ruling said that the church had no established rules that had been violated but had acted congregationally and only the congregation could oust Mason. Mason retained support from the majority.

Jones and Mason, however, separated their partnership. Jones remained affiliated with both the Holiness movement and the Baptist church. Mt. Helm is now the oldest African American church in Jackson, Mississippi. Mason founded the national Church of God in Christ in Memphis in 1907, although he continued as the pastor at St. Paul Church of God in Christ in Lexington until 1949.[32]

Mason hit a greater bump of controversy in 1918. On April 1 of that year, the *Jackson Daily News* featured a banner headline that read, "Hun Money Used In Holmes County to Arouse Negroes Against Draft."[33] No part of the headline was true. It was true, however, that Mason was arrested, nearly lynched, and kept in the county jail and then moved to a federal jail in Jackson for his own safety.[34]

The backdrop was that some in the Black community were reluctant to fight in World War I as they lived under Jim Crow laws they did not wish to defend. Mason supported the purpose of the war and had urged his congregation to buy Liberty Bonds as he himself had done. He also urged congregants to seek conscientious objector status or noncombatant roles as those who were sanctified could not kill and needed to remain separate from those who would kill. The COGIC was not the only denomination to urge conscientious objector status—it was routine for Quakers, for example. But as a predominantly African American church, and a relatively new one, the COGIC belief in adhering to the Ten Commandments drew suspicion.

Federal agents quickly concluded that the COGIC leadership were not German sympathizers—the whites who came to the COGIC services or served as pastors in other states had no "Hun" ties. Under political pressure, the agents did bring evidence against Mason and two white COGIC leaders from California to a grand jury, but the grand jury did not indict them.[35]

The Church of God in Christ took a giant leap in renown nearly fifty years later following the murder of Emmett Till. On August 28, 1955, fourteen-year-old Emmet Till was abducted in Money, in Leflore County, about thirty-five miles due north of Tchula, then lynched at a barn in nearby Sunflower County. Till had reportedly whistled at a white woman, Carolyn Bryant, whose husband, Roy Bryant, and brother-in-law, J. W. Milam, took Till from his cousin's home in the night, beat him savagely and gouged out his eye, shot him in the head, and sank his naked body in the Tallahatchie River tied with barbed wire to a cotton gin wheel. Till's family were members of the COGIC, and his funeral was held at their church in Chicago, Roberts Temple Church of God in Christ.[36]

Young Emmett's body was returned to his home church in Chicago through intervention of his pastor and the mayor of Chicago, who also called on help from President Eisenhower. His body was displayed in an open-casket funeral attended by 2,500, with as many as 10,000 more people attending the viewing. Photographs of the body were broadcast worldwide.

At the funeral, an emotional eulogy was delivered by the family pastor, Bishop Louis Henry Ford. The title of the eulogy was "Vengeance Is Mine," taken from Romans 12:19: "Never avenge yourselves, but leave it to the wrath of

God, for it is written, 'Vengeance is mine, I will repay,' saith the Lord." Bishop
Ford quoted also from Matthew 25:40: "For as much as ye have done unto one of
these, my little ones, ye have also done unto me."[37] Bishop Ford, like his church,
had roots in Lexington, where he went to school and preached as a young man.

Till's funeral raised the COGIC's national standing as the first Christian
denomination founded and, by the 1950s, entirely led by African Americans.
The Reverend Martin Luther King preached his final sermon, "I Have Been
to the Mountaintop," at Mason Temple, the COGIC world headquarters in
Memphis, Tennessee. Pastors from the COGIC were involved in the sanitation
workers' strike that had brought King to Memphis. The funeral of Malcolm
X was at a COGIC church in Harlem, as the mosque was not big enough.
Several civil rights leaders, including Mississippi NAACP leader Medgar
Evers and the Rev. Al Sharpton, had early roots in the COGIC.[38] Many of the
student activists of the 1960s speak of the death of Emmett Till as a seminal
moment in their own commitment to equality. Emmett Till, born in 1941,
would have turned twenty years old in 1960. He was of the same generation
as the students who later came to work in Mississippi in the early 1960s to
organize for voting rights.

Bishop Mason died on November 17, 1961, at age ninety-five. He was succeeded as senior bishop by his close friend Bishop Orzo Thurston Jones, who
in turn was succeeded by Bishop J. O. Patterson, who was married to Mason's
daughter. In 1990, the General Assembly of the Church elected Bishop Louis
Henry Ford, who had preached the Till eulogy, as presiding bishop of the
Church of God in Christ. Bishop Ford believed the church should be involved
in secular events without compromising its core beliefs in sanctification. Bishop
Ford served as presiding bishop for less than five years before his death but left
a deep legacy on Holmes County and on the church.

Over time, African American Baptist and other churches, particularly in the
South, have embraced the teachings of the Holiness movement and become
more like the COGIC in their music and spirit. The style of services at the
Arkansas Baptist College, which Bishop Mason rejected as a young pastor,
with emphasis on textual analysis, is far less common. Charismatic services,
the use of full musical instrumentation, and speaking in tongues are practiced
in some Methodist and Baptist as well as COGIC churches in Holmes County.
The Church of God in Christ continues to be distinguished by its commitment
to sanctification: to living one's life as Jesus preached, separate from worldly
temptation and with deep commitment to the poor and the needy in the community.[39] Today in Holmes County, while there are more non-COGIC than
COGIC churches, the spirit of the Holiness movement and Bishop Mason's
influence continue to be broadly felt.

LIVE IN DIGNITY

From the beginning, Bishop Mason and the Church of God in Christ demonstrated a commitment to improving education. Education in Holmes County in the early years of the twentieth century was nearly exclusively for white children except for the efforts of African American churches, private individuals, and scattered public elementary schools. The COGIC played a significant role with the founding and later expansion of Saints School, which for a time was the only opportunity for Black children in Holmes County to complete secondary education.

The 1890 Mississippi State Constitution had left funding allocations up to county superintendents. Many of those county superintendents opposed Negro education entirely—including the superintendent in Holmes County.[40] Lack of support for Black education meant African American schools and schoolteachers received far less than their share. White and Black teachers statewide were paid the same monthly salary in 1883—$32.68 each, falling to $28.74 each in 1885. But at that point, the salary for white teachers began to climb while the salary of Black teachers continued to drop.[41] The monthly salary in 1910 was estimated to be $42.38 for white teachers and $20.52 for Black teachers.

Holmes County began discussion of a new public "negro school" in 1906. The president of the board of supervisors was authorized to deed a lot to the City of Lexington for which the city "will erect a suitable building for the negro school children" at a place selected by the mayor and board of aldermen," noting, "this order was authorized by an act of the legislature of 1906."[42] Subsequent board meetings over the next two years discussed the awarding of contracts to build the school, with support for a final contract awarded in August of 1908.[43] There was far more discussion on who would erect the building than on what or whom would be taught in it. The school appears to have been built in 1909 and was ready for occupancy in 1910, but it provided only a single year of secondary education.

Meanwhile, by 1914 Sister Pinkie Duncan was teaching school in her home across the street from St. Paul Church of God in Christ. Bishop Mason provided coal for heat and later invited Duncan to teach in the basement of the church. In 1918, Saints Industrial and Literary School was founded with its own campus adjacent to St. Paul Church of God in Christ. The school struggled in its early years, with little money and few supplies, and with erratic leadership. It would begin to thrive after Dr. Arenia Mallory, who arrived in the 1920s and later headed the school, became a significant force—for the school, within COGIC, and among African American women nationally. Over twenty thousand students attended Saints as an industrial school, a high school, or, later, as an accredited college.[44] The school remained open until 1983 and reopened again for a few years in the early 1990s. The school's motto was, "Walk in dignity, talk in dignity, live in dignity." For decades, it was the sole source of complete secondary education for Black children in Holmes County.

Bishop Mason supported elevated roles for women in the church. His recruitment of Mallory was the beginning of that effort. In the first part of the twentieth century, Black women were the source of the COGIC's rapid growth, and the COGIC held sewing circles and literacy classes. Women in the COGIC taught purity classes to young people and raised funds for the church and for expansion of its missions in Africa and the Caribbean. Women could not be ordained as pastors, but the COGIC had a Women's Department that provided an institutional, formal, and formidable role.[45] Initially, the Women's Department under Mother Lizzie Woods Robinson focused internally. Later, the Women's Department became a critical connection between the COGIC and the Black community nationally.[46] Mallory became an important voice in the church, as part of national African American women's movements, and in Holmes County, as her influence and that of Saints School grew.

Arenia Conelia Mallory was born in Jacksonville, Illinois, in 1904, and raised in a middle-class home. She was the daughter of musicians. Her mother hoped she would be a concert pianist. In high school, she went to a revival meeting and thereafter dedicated herself to religious work, with the plan of becoming a missionary in Africa. Instead, she was recruited by Bishop Mason to teach music at Saints School. He apparently thought that she had the skills to suc-ceed the current principal, who was aging. A woman school principal would be unusual, but so was Mallory, who arrived in Lexington in 1926.[47]

Mallory's longtime secretary, Dovie Marie Simmons, recounts that rural Mississippi was a shock to the northern-raised Mallory. Mallory experienced the realities of segregation for the first time on the train south as the train stopped so cars could be segregated. On arrival, she was taken aback by the roughness of the school's physical plant with its lack of running water or electricity, the poverty of the children, and the darkness of rural Mississippi at night.

Mallory was an imposing presence. She was tall, always impeccably dressed, with "a commanding proficiency of language and the ability to project," and she carried herself with pride and dignity. She was "demanding" in her very demeanor.[48] People in Lexington, both Black and white, did not know quite what to make of her, and she went through an adjustment period. During that time, she made a mistake and married outside the church. Apparently, she had also been married before. She went through a two-year period of public repentance and was then forgiven and taken back into the COGIC family.[49]

When Mallory became the head of the school, she put in a central heating system, running water, electrical appliances, and plank walks to cover the mud-died paths. The campus began to cultivate its own food instead of soliciting food for students, and she recruited nationally for a teaching staff. The staff included white teachers, which brought threats and harassment to the school and to Mallory personally.[50]

Mallory and Mason traveled throughout the Delta to other COGIC churches and communities to speak about the church, the school, and their work. In Clarksdale, around 1927, they met a young boy whose mother, a devout member of the local COGIC church, had recently died. The child continued to attend church. He borrowed shoes from his non-churchgoing father to do so, although his father took his shoes back during the service. That child was Louis Henry Ford, who nearly thirty years later would give the eulogy at the funeral of Emmett Till and later still would become the presiding bishop of COGIC. Ford was "practically raised" at Saints School and remained close to both Bishop Mason and Dr. Mallory.[51] He became the presiding bishop of the national Church of God in Christ in 1990 and served in that role until his death in 1995.

Mallory began to raise money for the school nationally. She brought students from the school choir, the Jubilee Harmonizers, to large churches like Abyssinia Baptist Church in Harlem, pastored by the Reverend Adam Clayton Powell Sr. There they sang and told their stories, and the story of Saints School, to its eight thousand members. With Powell's help, the Jubilee Harmonizers also sang at Riverside Church, an integrated church on Manhattan's upper west side, and later toured California.

In California, Mallory met Ida L. Jackson, a prominent woman in the Alpha Kappa Alpha (AKA) sorority, the oldest Black sorority in the country. Jackson came from Oakland to visit the school and then helped raise funds—and the school's profile—nationally through the AKA newspaper, the *Ivy Leaf*. The sorority not only helped build the school through significant funding, but sorority sisters visited and came for periods of time as teachers. Ida Jackson helped recruit Dr. Dorothy Boulding Ferebee, a prominent physician at the Howard University Medical School in Washington, DC, to direct the local health care program, as the county had no hospital beds and minimal health care for African Americans.[52] The AKAs remain proud of their role providing health care in Holmes County. It is featured in a film of their history and on their website as "the most widely known expression of social responsibility."[53]

Outside help did not sit well with white leadership in Mississippi in the 1930s and 1940s. They forbade sharecroppers to attend health care clinics, which led to a mobile health unit. The school continued to expand its role in the larger Holmes County community and throughout the Delta, offering night school for veterans after World War II and receiving a federal grant to teach migrant farmworkers.

Mallory's most important outside relationship was likely her friendship with Mary McLeod Bethune. Bethune, born in 1875 in South Carolina, was the daughter of enslaved people. By age nine, she could pick 250 pounds of cotton a day. She was educated at Dwight Moody's Institute for Home and Foreign Missions, and while she intended, like Mallory, to become an African missionary, she became an educator instead when she could not find a church sponsor for missionary work. Bethune opened a boarding school that later became Bethune-Cookman College in Daytona Beach, Florida. As founding president of the National Council of Negro Women (NCNW), she became acquainted with First Lady Eleanor Roosevelt. She worked closely with the Roosevelt administration and became vice president of the NAACP. She was also part of the group who founded the Women's Army Corps during World War II.[54]

Bethune shared Mallory's commitment to sanctification and the Holiness movement. She was not a part of the COGIC, but she had been heavily influenced by Amanda Berry Smith, who saw Bethune as her mentee. Bethune visited Saints School in the 1930s and brought Mallory into the Roosevelts' circle and the NCNW leadership, and she doubtless played a role in featuring Mallory on the cover of the NAACP magazine, *The Crisis*.[55]

Mallory's relationship with Bethune raised her profile and prominence and that of Saints School; it also led to changes in the school, which became more national, more middle class, and less local in its focus. The higher profile for Mallory did not always include the COGIC, which was not mentioned at all in the cover story in *The Crisis*.

The role of women in the COGIC was changing with a new generation in its Women's Department. In her book on women in the COGIC, Anthea Butler argues that Mallory was a connector, and the Women's Department's increasing involvement in public affairs not only raised their profiles but changed the meaning of sanctification within the COGIC. Butler writes, "The earlier emphasis on sanctification solely for the purpose of cleansing oneself before God and belonging to the COGIC community was beginning to shift to a broader focus, a focus that would alter COGIC women's goals from promoting self-sanctification to taking the message of sanctification into the world."[56]

Mallory remained at Saints School until shortly before her death in 1977 and remained active in education and civic matters in Holmes County. She became the county's first African American elected to the Holmes County School Board and was joined on the board by William Dean, now the bishop of the Mississippi Northern Ecclesiastical Jurisdiction Church of God in Christ. Mallory won on her reputation without mounting a political campaign. Others who served on the school board with her tell of her absolute dedication to children.[57] She was not political, but she would intervene—forcefully if judiciously—at several points in more modern Holmes County history.

THE GILDED AGE COMES SOUTH

Saints School was the most prominent effort to educate African American children in Holmes County in the first part of the twentieth century, but by the 1920s it was not the only one. Nationally, the early part of the twentieth century, leading up to World War I, was marked by scientific discovery and a new wave of industrial growth. It has been dubbed the Progressive Era for the commitment during that period to both reform and philanthropy. Mississippi did not fully participate in either the industrial revolution or the wave of progressivism—it remained agricultural and conservative. It was, however, the beneficiary of significant investment in African American schools by outsiders who were part of the period of progressivism.

"Nothing connected with the educational program of Mississippi during the past several years has had a more wholesome and stimulating effect upon the minds of the negro people and the general public than the Rosenwald Schoolhouse Building Campaign," declared Bura Hilbun, the state supervisor of negro schools in the 1920s. "This agency was made possible through the generosity of Mr. Julius Rosenwald, of Chicago, cooperating with the State Department of Education."[58]

The Rosenwald Schools were initially a collaboration between Booker T. Washington, head of the Tuskegee Institute, and Julius Rosenwald, a founder of the Sears Roebuck Company. The two men met in Chicago at a YMCA dinner in May of 1911. On his fiftieth birthday, in August of 1912, Rosenwald gave his first $25,000 for the establishment of Negro schools. By 1932, when the program ended, Rosenwald had helped build nearly five thousand school buildings throughout the South—over six hundred in Mississippi, including thirty-four in Holmes County.[59]

Booker T. Washington's focus was on "industrial" education for Black children. He believed Black children needed to acquire skills that would help them work in farms and factories and that through hard work and patience they would earn the respect of white people. Washington's focus on industrial education put him in conflict with W. E. B. Du Bois, who devotes an essay in his famous 1903 book, *The Souls of Black Folk*, to his differences with Washington. Du Bois quotes Washington as saying in a speech in Atlanta, "In all things purely social we can be as separate as the five fingers, and yet one as the hand in all things essential to mutual progress." Du Bois asserts that, especially in the South, Washington's suggested compromise was subject to varied interpretations as "the radicals received it as a complete surrender of the demand for civil and political equality; the conservatives as a generously conceived working for mutual understanding." Du Bois presents a nuanced analysis of Washington's work, but his fundamental view was that industrial education helps "money-makers" use Black people as laborers. Du Bois forcefully advocated for the "ambition of our brightest minds" and concludes that those who believe in full equality must oppose Washington when he is willing to accept anything less.[60]

Saints Industrial and Literary School straddled the philosophical divide between Du Bois and Washington with a curriculum that spanned practical and academic education. The Rosenwald Schools in Holmes County focused on workforce training. Dr. Sylvia Reedy Gist, who attended the Rosenwald School in Poplar Springs as a child and has written extensively on the history of Holmes County schools, acknowledges the limitations of the Rosenwald curriculum but asserts the community was "glad to get any type of education."[61]

Rosenwald Schools were built with a combination of public funds and private donations, supplemented by grants from the Rosenwald Foundation. In Holmes County, a quarter of the funds came from Rosenwald with another 15 percent from public tax dollars and 10 percent from individual white donors. The remaining half—almost $50,000—came from the local Black community.[62]

I could not find a record of how the Black community in Holmes County raised funds—the effort received no coverage that I could find in the *Lexington Advertiser*—but there are records in other communities: African American churches took up collections dedicated to new schools, Black farmers pledged the proceeds from an acre of cotton a year for a seven-year mortgage on school buildings, and in some places the Black community contributed material and labor as in-kind contributions. In other communities, whites cooperated fully, but white cooperation seems limited in Holmes, given both the comparatively small dollar amounts provided by them and the lack of local press coverage of the Rosenwald Schools. Given the views of the recent Holmes County superintendent, who opposed Black education, some whites may have felt their tax dollars already constituted excessive support for Black schools.[63]

In most places in Mississippi, whites welcomed the Rosenwald Schools if for no other reason than Rosenwald funds allowed public funds allocated for educating Black children to be spent on schools for white children instead. According to the Southern Education Foundation, Hilbun's successor as the state supervisor of Negro schools acknowledged in 1939 that the state appropriated nineteen cents per Black pupil for every dollar it spent on a white child and that most counties spent no money on Negro schools. Even then, more than a third of rural Black schools were privately owned, as individuals or churches—not the government—provided education for Black children.[64]

Statewide, the Rosenwald program in Mississippi was marred by Hilbun's diversion of funds. Hilbun was a personal friend of Governor Theodore Bilbo, a white supremacist and Ku Klux Klan member who was the state's governor from 1916 to 1920 and again from 1928 to 1932. Hilbun diverted funds by reporting to Rosenwald that schools had been built that never existed. Hilbun's successor—who was no friend of Bilbo's—uncovered a total of seven "ghost schools" that had never been built, although Rosenwald had contributed grant monies for them. Hilbun had also allegedly embezzled funds from other programs designed for "negro schools" and in 1931 was sentenced to five years in prison.[65]

The Rosenwald program erected school buildings. Teachers were still paid by the community or supported by philanthropy. Teachers were recruited from the Holmes County Training Center in Durant, which went through the tenth grade, or from the historically Black colleges: Tougaloo, Rust, Alcorn, and Jackson State. The number of teachers available to instruct Black children remained in short supply, especially given their low pay. One retired teacher said she was sometimes without a salary for up to six months and relied on community donations of food and cash. In 1941, 104 teachers taught 2,610 white children in Holmes County while 202 teachers taught 14,700 Black students.[66]

Holmes County had at least one longtime teacher-supervisor, Ruby Ross Smith, who was a "Jeanes teacher."[67] Jeanes teachers were paid by the Jeanes Foundation, founded by Anna T. Jeanes. Anna Jeanes was the last survivor of ten children in a Quaker family in Philadelphia, Pennsylvania, none of whom had children. Anna Jeanes inherited from all nine of her siblings and left the bulk of her inheritance, around $1 million, to "the benefit of elementary negro schools in the South, and to develop improved means of education for the negroes . . . with particular interest in the little country schools."[68]

Other philanthropists also supported Black education in Holmes County early in the twentieth century, adopting the training school model. The Slater Fund, supported by wealthy Rhode Island textile mill owner John F. Slater, replaced the Lexington Colored School, which had burned down in 1910, with the Ambrose Vocational School. John D. Rockefeller's General Education Board constructed the Holmes County Training School in Durant and renovated the Mount Olive Colored School, changing the name to Mount Olive County Training School. The training schools taught farming and domestic service to students in grades 1 through 8. Those who completed grades 9 and 10 taught younger students.[69]

Philanthropic investments in African American schools in Holmes County and elsewhere were to end with the Great Depression. Julius Rosenwald had died in 1930, and the building program ended in 1932, although several of the schools it built were used until the middle of the 1960s. The Jeanes Foundation continued to pay teachers in the rural South until 1968.[70]

HAND OVER THE LAND[71]

Even before the Great Depression began in 1929, Holmes County was strug-gling economically. The early years of the twentieth century had been prosper-ous. The 1910 cotton crop was the most valuable the South had ever produced, and the value of the land itself had doubled in a decade.[72] Lexington, as the county seat, was evolving as a commercial center, with new stores and other businesses as the county population reached thirty-nine thousand in 1910, double the population of 1870.

The most prominent white families early in the twentieth century were often descendants of those who came before the Civil War. Walter Leake Keirn died in 1901, but his son, Claude Leake Keirn, kept the family plantation operational for many years and was a member of the Holmes County Board of Supervisors at the time of his death in 1955.[73] Members of the Gwin family owned a grocery store and a hardware store, and a family member ran for county sheriff, while the next generation of Hookers and Dyers practiced law.

The prosperity of the century's early years also produced economic growth in the Black community. In 1910, there were just under 1,400 farms in Holmes County and nearly 800 were Black owned. Black-owned farms were smaller, on average, so whites still owned most of the land, but most farm owners were African American.[74] The number of Black-owned businesses also expanded. Yazoo Street in Lexington became a Black commercial center with shops, a photography studio, a restaurant—and a blacksmith shop operated by the Truehart family.[75]

After a prosperous start to the twentieth century, a series of disasters, both natural and man-made, would upend the county's economic progress over the next twenty years. The price of cotton would drop at the start of World War I, although it would recover. Even before the price drop, a threat to cotton was creeping its way to Holmes County. In an apparent first of many references to come, the *Lexington Advertiser* wrote on June 4, 1903, that planters in Mississippi were becoming alarmed at the arrival of the Mexican cotton boll weevil, a bug that had already decimated crops in Texas. It would take another decade to invade with full force, but the boll weevil was coming. Between the weevil itself and reactions to the weevil, Mississippi's cotton dominance would never fully recover.

Initially, some asserted that the exceptional circumstances of the Delta would make the weevil less of a threat to cotton there. Greenville planters Alfred Stone and Julian Fort, with help from the First National Bank, published a monograph, *The Truth about the Boll Weevil*, arguing that the Delta would be immune. Stone and Fort's real purpose may have been to keep the labor force, largely African American sharecroppers and tenant farmers, from leaving the Delta as thousands of farmworkers had left Texas in the weevil's wake.[76]

Holmes County leaders did not buy into the notion that the Delta was protected. The *Lexington Advertiser* published a *Boll Weevil Bulletin* written by state etymologist Glenn W. Herrick that proclaimed, "This is the most serious insect pest that has ever attacked the cotton plant in America." Herrick added that the weevil was "spreading over the cotton growing area of the United States with alarming ease and rapidity." The damage in Texas had totaled over $15 million in 1903, and the weevil was now in Louisiana. Inevitably, the weevil arrived, first in southern Mississippi, then crawling its way north. In July of 1910, farmer J. M. Roach discovered boll weevils in his cotton field four miles south of Lexington. They were reported to be multiplying rapidly.[77]

The weevil infestation reached its peak in 1913 as the *Advertiser* warned that "six hundred thousand weevils may be produced in ninety days from one Pair of weevils."[78] The weevil was especially hard to see—and to eradicate—because it spent much of its life "in the square"—encased on the series of nodes of the main stem that grow before the cotton plant first blooms. Similar-looking snouted bugs could also be found in cotton fields, so identifying a boll weevil took some skill.

Between 1903 and 1919, the *Lexington Advertiser* was to reference the weevil over 700 times, peaking at 136 references in 1913, at which time the boll weevil "seems today to be the chief concern of all the people in our county," and "It is 'boll weevils, boll weevils,' these days. You can't hear anything but boll weevils and starvation."[79] A third of the cotton was lost to the weevil that year. In part as a reaction to the devastation brought by the weevil, the federal government expanded its investment in cotton production in California, where arid conditions were unappealing to the boll weevil. Western cotton would provide new competition to southern cotton thereafter.[80]

Mississippi farm practices in the nineteenth and twentieth centuries were destructive of the land and encouraged the weevil. Experts bemoaned the cotton monoculture in the state. A 1909 USDA report on Holmes County wrote that "not enough corn and hay have been grown to supply the local demand. Cotton has been the money crop and success in farming has depended on this one staple," adding later in the same report, "Too much dependence is placed on a single crop, cotton;" and "the system of cultivation practiced at the present time tends to 'wear out' the soil rather than build it up, and the number of livestock is far below what it should be." Cotton monoculture encouraged the weevil's rapid spread since the insects could readily spread to the next field, which was, "almost invariably, planted in cotton."[81] If the adjacent field had been another crop, less appealing to the weevil, the spread would have slowed.

The same monograph decried the degree of soil erosion, again recommend-
ing the need for crop rotation, as well as deeper and level plowing. "A systematic
crop rotation should be followed, deeper plowing practiced, and, especially
in the hills, ridge cultivation abandoned. More attention should be given to
dairying and the raising of beef cattle and hogs. Winter forage crops such as
rye, barley, oats, and vetch should be grown more extensively. Cowpeas, alfalfa,
and other legumes may be used to increase the fertility of the soil as well as to
furnish an abundance of nutritious feed. The washing of the soil may be greatly
checked by deep cultivation and the incorporation of more organic matter in
the surface soil." Some land under cultivation "should never have been cleared"
because it was so subject to erosion.[82] Much of the land most subject to erosion was in the hills, north of Lexington, where there were a disproportionate
number of small Black-owned farms.

Farm tenancy and sharecropping also contributed to cotton monoculture.
Owners required sharecroppers to plant cotton, allowing them only a small
plot for food or other produce. Cash tenants needed to pay the landowner,
which required planting more acres in cotton, as it was still the most profitable
cash crop.

Just one year after the weevil infestation peaked, Europe entered World War
I, which put a sudden brake on cotton exports. Cotton prices plummeted, falling in a single year from 10.6 cents a pound to 6.6 cents a pound. Prices would
recover and briefly reach a new peak when the United States joined the war
and domestic demand increased. Meanwhile, there were lean years for cotton
farmers even while the weevil infestation slowed.[83]

As the cotton crop recovered, the Delta was forever changed by the Great
Flood of 1927, which remains one of the worst natural disasters in American
history. Twenty-three thousand square miles flooded from Illinois to Louisiana.
The waters did not fully recede for four months. The human costs in the Mississippi Delta were catastrophic as thousands lost their homes. Holmes County
suffered far less than its neighbors, some of whom took refuge in Holmes, but
the impact was long-lasting.

President Coolidge put his secretary of commerce, Herbert Hoover, in
charge of the response to the flood, and the Red Cross launched a major media
campaign to raise money to help people affected by the flood. Both Hoover
and the Red Cross had formidable media operations to promote their efforts.
The reality on the ground—told later in African American newspapers—is
that while white people were evacuated and housed in hotels in the wake of
the flood, Black people were forced into camps and not allowed to leave. In
some camps, they slept on wet ground, were restrained from leaving, and were
forced into labor rebuilding the levees along the river.[84]

The Mississippi River has flooded throughout its existence, but human intervention at times made the problem worse. Forests absorb water and hold the land. Draining wetlands causes worse flooding farther downstream as wetlands effectively store water and slow its course. Levees, too, may direct flow in the short term but can concentrate flooding in the long term. Oxbow lakes form from the river's meander, which levees prevent, helping store water. Land reports on the Delta from before the 1830s list flood-intolerant varieties of trees showing that before that time, sections of the Delta had remained dry even during serious flooding.[85]

Much of Holmes County is protected from flooding by Dogwood Ridge—the highest part of the loess hills—but part of the Delta portion of Holmes County shared in the devastation of the 1927 flood. Total property damage in Holmes totaled $65,025. That compared, however, to over $4 million in neighboring Humphreys County and more than $22 million in Washington County, where a one-hundred-foot crevasse in the levee, which ran almost a half a mile deep, devastated Greenville.[86]

The weevil and the flood created new insecurities about the cotton economy and accelerated outmigration from much of the Delta to the North. It also brought migration from parts of the Delta to counties, like Holmes, where the flooding was less severe. The Holmes County population fell between 1910 and 1920, but then grew 12 percent from 1920 to 1930.

NOT SOME MORE CONVENIENT SEASON[87]

The 1920s were not the best of times in Holmes County, as the economy was still reeling from the weevil and was about to face the flood. The county also experienced rising violence against its Black citizens following World War I and into the century's third decade. But despite the inopportune times, African American economic leadership grew, with expanded support for Black-owned farms and businesses.

A wave of racial violence came in the wake of World War I. Uniformed Black soldiers had been a target across the South. In Pickens, a soldier was killed for writing an "inappropriate note." The soldier in uniform and a Black woman "accomplice" were found hung after the soldier allegedly paid a woman twelve dollars to write a note to another woman on his behalf.[88]

Holmes County had a highly active Klan chapter in the 1920s. It had a Klavern in Owen Mills—between Lexington and Durant—that had thirty rooms. The Klan advertised regular meetings in the local newspaper. The 1920s Klan took pains to say it did "not countenance lawlessness" and that "it is not a 'negro whipping' order" and "it is not intolerant in its attitudes." On the other hand, the grand dragon of the realm of Mississippi asserted "that this country was built by and for the white, Anglo-Saxon, protestant people, is the cardinal principle actuating the Ku Klux Klan." He added that "alien people" already controlled New York and Chicago and half the country's elected and appointed leaders were "alien." Such alien people "are unfitted by tradition, by racial characteristics, and by environment for type of government." While "only in the South can the pure and undefiled stock of our forebears be found."[89]

Against the backdrop of such unreconstructed attitudes, the African American community organized themselves. They built not only churches and schools, but hospitals and support systems for the purchase of land and for farming it profitably. There was no waiting for times to get better but active intervention to make them so.

The Black fraternal organization Afro-American Sons and Daughters was founded in nearby Yazoo City by Black entrepreneur Thomas Jefferson Huddleston, owner of Century Funeral Homes. Huddleston organized branches of the organization throughout the region, including Holmes County—in Lexington, Pickens, and an especially active lodge in Tchula. The branches raised money to build the Afro-American Sons and Daughters Hospital, which was completed in 1928. Huddleston also published the *Afro-American Courier*, beginning in 1926, which functioned as a community newspaper, reporting on activities of the local lodges, listing those who were treated at the hospital, and reporting deaths. Huddleston was a follower of Booker T. Washington, who had helped found the Rosenwald Schools, and believed that through self-help African Americans could attain acceptance and respect.

Holmes County also had a division of Marcus Garvey's Universal Negro Improvement Association (UNIA). Garvey, born in Jamaica, was a Black separatist and a proponent of Black Nationalism, who founded the UNIA in 1914. The UNIA faded in the mid-1920s through internal strife following the arrest, imprisonment, and eventual deportation of its leader, although Black Nationalism remained. Garveyism resonated in Mississippi, particularly as even in the 1920s, the state still had formerly enslaved people who had been born in Africa. There were a cluster of UNIA divisions in the Delta—and one in Holmes County—drawing membership disproportionately from Black landowners.[90] The Holmes County unit was in the community of Wyatt, a town that no longer exists but was then located just north of Tchula.[91]

Among farmers, the goal of independence and self-reliance was taken up by the National Federation of Colored Farmers (NFCF). The federation was founded in 1922 by four African American leaders who had attended Tuskegee Institute. The NFCF advocated and assisted Black land ownership and nurtured land purchases and cooperative marketing with a foundational belief in self-sufficiency. There were philosophical differences between the UNIA and the

NFCF, especially later in the 1920s, but the UNIA newspaper, the *Negro World*, frequently covered NFCF efforts, and in some places, including Mound Bayou, the UNIA and NFCF units met together.[92]

The very first local unit of the NFCF anywhere in the country was founded in Howard Bottom, in Holmes County, in 1929. The initial membership was about thirty farmers, mostly tenants and sharecroppers. They had previously bought monthly supplies from the plantation store with "limit money" received from the plantation owner. Instead, by pooling their resources, they began buying supplies at just above wholesale prices—about half the price—from a store in Memphis. There was, unsurprisingly, pushback from plantation owners, just as there had been to similar co-ops in the 1880s. The Howard Bottom effort flourished, however, and was joined by Holmes County units in at least Tchula, Cruger, Lexington, and Mt. Olive. The Baldwin unit in Cruger received unusual welcome by white planters there as a mechanism to help sharecroppers become better farmers.[93]

Several units helped Black farmers purchase land and equipment. The Federal Farm Loan Act of 1916 created regional banks with local associations to help lower interest rates and help farmers pay off their principal as well as interest. At the time, most farmers who borrowed money to buy land paid interest in regular monthly installments and then owed the principal at the end of the loan term, generally requiring them to refinance. The Land Bank loans were amortized so that farmers paid principal and interest on loans over a longer period. Interest rates were also lower than on loans from commercial banks and more available to disadvantaged farmers. Loans could be paid off in full after the fifth year.

In 1927, with support from the Rosenwald Foundation, Black farmers formed the Holmes County Agriculture, Livestock, and Industrial Association to expand Black-owned acreage and productivity. The board of directors included African American farmers who owned more than one hundred acres.[94] Some of the same individuals were active in the NFCF. The *Modern Farmer*, the NFCF newspaper, reported that the Lexington unit in Holmes County "secured over a quarter of a million dollars in Federal land bank loans" for 154 Black farmers. During 1929, four farmers had paid off their loans in full. The *Modern Farmer* commended the officers of the association—C. C. Richardson, the owner of a two-hundred-acre farm, and Ulysses S. Donelson—for their work.[95]

The same issue of the *Modern Farmer* reports that the Mt. Olive unit was purchasing twenty-one tons of nitrate of soda, a fertilizer, saving its members six dollars a ton, and buying twelve dozen pairs of overalls. One member, Isaac Randall, had purchased a tractor secured through the NFCF offices and was sawing ten thousand board feet of lumber a day. Another member, Robert Booker, had built a modern poultry house for one hundred hens.

In 1930, the Howard unit hosted the state convention of the NFCF, "the first convention of organized Negro farmers ever held in America," wrote the *Modern Farmer*. More than five thousand farmers attended, representing twenty-seven units from ten Mississippi counties. The following year, the convention was held at Mound Bayou, but Tchula won the prize for the largest delegation, and Isaac Randall won a prize as the marketing agent for the unit that had bought and sold the most merchandise.[96]

A few years later, during the depression, the Howard unit bought a big truck and took livestock directly to Memphis for sale. Leon Harris, one of the founders of the NFCF, said in an interview in 1940, "Ten years ago a vast majority of members in this Unit were tenants and sharecroppers. Today, nearly all of them are farm owners. And they have depended less on the government for relief and loans than any group I know of anywhere in the United States."[97] Another founder of the NFCF, James P. Davis, would soon become part of President Franklin Roosevelt's Federal Council of Negro Affairs. The impact of the Roosevelt administration on Holmes County would be mixed, however, particularly in the administration's early years.

THE CRASH

On October 29, 1929, a day that came to be known as Black Tuesday, the stock market crashed, and the Great Depression began. It didn't happen all at once, and certainly not on a single day. The crash started in September, showed its power in October, but like a reverse flood did not bottom out for a while.

The Great Depression hit the South especially hard given its dependence on agriculture, and Mississippi perhaps hardest of all given its dependence on cotton. The US government had encouraged farm production after entering World War I. Elevated levels of agricultural production meant lower prices for agricultural products as demand receded. In the Delta, when the crash came, farmers and planters were still recovering from the back-to-back scourges of the weevil, price drops, the flood of 1927, and a season of drought. By 1933, farm income was only a third of what it had been in 1929.[98]

Herbert Hoover, who became president in 1929, did little to address the poverty of the Great Depression. He believed the economy would self-correct, but the situation for cotton was so bad he made a special effort to raise cotton prices. In 1930, his Farm Board urged a voluntary reduction in cotton planting given the oversupply. Few complied, as they wanted the income from whatever cotton they could harvest even while prices continued to drop. In the spring of 1930, the Farm Board established a cotton stabilization corporation, one of only three crop-specific efforts (with the other two for wheat and grapes).

But the corporation stopped buying in the summer of 1930 as cotton piled up in warehouses. The price of cotton fell to seven cents a pound at the end of 1930.[99] In 1932, to no one's surprise, Hoover was resoundingly defeated for reelection, carrying only a handful of northeastern states. Mississippi was Franklin Delano Roosevelt's second-strongest state, as he won it with nearly 96 percent of the vote.[100]

Roosevelt's initial New Deal efforts to restore farm prosperity brought better cotton prices to landowners but hurt tenant farmers and sharecroppers even more deeply than Hoover's laissez-faire approach. While well-intentioned, Roosevelt's top agriculture advisors were not familiar with the practicalities of sharecropping. Roosevelt's secretary at the Department of Agriculture was Henry A. Wallace, who would become Roosevelt's vice president in his third term and the Progressive Party candidate for president after Roosevelt's death. Another major voice on agriculture policy in Roosevelt's first term was Rexford G. Tugwell. Tugwell was an original member of Roosevelt's "brain trust," recruited in 1932, when Tugwell was a professor of economics at Columbia University in New York. Tugwell had strong beliefs about economic management and what he called "the power of the collective will," but he had no firsthand experience with farming and neither he nor Wallace had ever lived in the South.[101]

Roosevelt's Agricultural Adjustment Administration (AAA), headed by Tugwell, paid planters and farmers to produce less, which was far more effective than Hoover's brief voluntary approach. But the AAA paid landowners, not cash tenants or sharecroppers. After the act passed in May of 1933—when the year's cotton was already planted—many plantation owners ploughed under their tenants' cotton and evicted the tenants while farming the land they had not rented out. If the plantation owner needed labor, he would hire back former sharecroppers as day laborers at lower wages than he would have paid for their cotton.

A quarter of the southern population were sharecroppers or tenant farmers. In Mississippi, 75 percent of the cash tenant farmers and sharecroppers were Black. As one historian asserts, "Black people suffered a disproportionate share of the burden."[102] In Holmes County, over 90 percent of all tenant farmers were Black—70 percent of the cash tenants and 94 percent of the sharecroppers.

Recollections of sharecropping in Holmes County during the depression were collected in the late 1980s by the youth of the Rural Organizing and Cultural Center. ROCC was a countywide organization created to address poverty. For two summers, seventh, eighth, and ninth graders from ROCC's summer program interviewed older people to explore their own heritage and printed interviews in a publication called *Bloodlines*. Mrs. Catherine Jefferson told the young people that she was one of eleven children in a sharecropping family. She worked in the fields from the time she was ten years old. In 1930, the family was evicted with nothing: "At the end of that year, we didn't clear anything, and they broke us up. They took our wagon, mule, cow, horses, corn, potatoes and peas, and put us outdoors . . . we was put off in November. November and December was rough . . . when we got through picking cotton, my mama took the sacks and made my brothers some jumpers so they would have something through the winter." The family stayed with relatives, six to a bed, with only cornbread to eat all winter.[103]

The desperation of southern sharecroppers drew national attention on the political left. Well-known socialist Norman Thomas published a pamphlet in 1934, *The Plight of the Share-Cropper*, which began,

> Sooner or later any search among the millions of exploited Americans for those most truly forgotten, to whom the advance of the machine age has meant the least, will bring you to the country where cotton is still king, who rewards his subjects and his most loyal workers with poverty, pellagra, and illiteracy. I have seen much of the misery of city slums and something of the poverty of mountain farmers and the dreary little towns which coal barons or textile manufacturers own. In none of them is life on the average so completely without comfort for the present or hope for the future as among the share-croppers of the South.[104]

Tenant farmers in the South fought back. The NFCF continued until the mid-1940s, but its tenet of growing Black land ownership faltered during the Depression, and the economic burdens of tenant farmers reached a breaking point. In 1934, two white tenant farmers in Poinsett County, Arkansas, formed the interracial, avowedly socialist, Southern Tenant Farmers Union (STFU). Arkansas tenant farmers were better positioned to take on the status quo, as a majority were white; they had voting rights and political clout, and the sympathy of white merchants.[105] Black sharecroppers and cash tenants had none of these. At its peak, the STFU had about thirty thousand members, concentrated in Arkansas. Its impact, however, was broader as the union organized a tenant farmers' strike in Arkansas that succeeded in raising farm wages and drew national attention with a march on Washington, DC, for higher farm wages.

The STFU had some limited success organizing in Mississippi. The Greenwood Commonwealth published a story under the all-caps headline "AGITATOR HERE BOTHERS LABOR" with the subhead "Southern Tenant Farmers Union Operating Around Greenwood."[106] The story reported the circulation of fliers urging farmworkers to refuse to work for less than $1.50 for a ten-hour day. The police chief in Greenwood took the position that distributing fliers violated a city anti-trash ordinance and offered a $10 reward for the arrest of anyone distributing them.[107]

There was STFU activity in Howard Bottom, where the NFCF had been active. Sharecropper Walter Jones attended meetings in Dyersville, Arkansas, where the STFU was founded, and returned to Howard Bottom for a time before moving to the Missouri Bootheel, a center of STFU organizing.[108] The STFU relied heavily on religious rhetoric and inspirational hymns in their organizing—as did the later civil rights movement. The leaders of the STFU believed Pentecostalism and their union had a shared premise in the empowerment of ordinary people to bring change for themselves whether through communalism or the power of the Holy Spirit.[109] Later, there would be STFU activity, too, at Holmes County's interracial enterprise, Providence Farm.

The STFU drew the attention of the Roosevelt administration, where the next wave of policies was both sympathetic and helpful to tenant farmers. The Agriculture Adjustment Administration in its original form ended in 1936 when the US Supreme Court found the corporate tax that funded it unconstitutional. Some of its functions were replaced by the Resettlement Administration, which Tugwell also headed until it was liquidated in 1938. The process of assigning cotton allotments, the number of acres each farmer could plant, was taken over by a modified 1938 AAA law without tax financing and, from 1961 to 1994, assigned to the Agricultural Stabilization and Conservation Service (ASCS). (In those years, it would discriminate against African American farmers, as recounted in a later chapter.)

Meanwhile, in 1937, Congress passed the Bankhead-Jones Farm Tenant Act, designed to aid tenant farmers in purchasing land and providing low-cost loans to other farmers. The mechanisms in the act were not specific and left a great deal of latitude in its administration. It was the basis for the Farm Security Administration (FSA), which, along with the remnants of the Resettlement Administration, created considerable material benefit to tenant farmers—particularly in Holmes County, where it was responsible for founding the Mileston Co-op, which was to play a significant role in the 1960s civil rights movement.

A PRACTICAL MAN

On July 28, 1939, the following notice appeared in the *Greenwood Commonwealth*: "The Farm Security Administration has secured an option on the properties of the Mileston Planting Company and the W. E. Jones estate, with the exception of the homestead at Goodhope plantation, it is announced. The tract is on Highway 49 East and contains 9,350 acres. Information is that the FSA intends to establish a negro community on the property providing an opportunity for the rehabilitotion [sic] for selected negro families, including many now living on the properties acquired in the purchase."

The *Clarion-Ledger* reported a few days later that the option was accepted and added, "The response of leading citizens of Holmes and adjoining counties to the announcement of the FSA's plan for the new development assures the full support from the persons involved for the project. Resolutions of approval of the Farm Security's acquisition of the land in Holmes County have been passed by leading civic organizations in the county."[110]

The "new development" was Mileston Farms, which became the Mileston Co-op. There were multiple resettlement communities, but Mileston was the only community for which Region VI of the FSA was directly and entirely responsible. It was developed with multiple sources of funds, including funds from the Resettlement Administration when it was liquidated in 1938. On one level, it was a practical demonstration by the regional office to the top brass and ideologues at the United States Department of Agriculture (USDA) on how to achieve Black farmer uplift in the South—with full participation of Black farmers, on top-quality land, with support for the broader needs of the community. On another level, it was a continuation of the collective and cooperative efforts of African American farmers that dated back to at least the 1880s.[111]

The head of Region VI, first for the Resettlement Administration and then FSA, was T. Roy Reid. While the FSA had its liberal leaders, Reid was reportedly not among them. He has been referred to as "a conservative man." He was the son of a "prosperous and substantial" South Carolina farmer, the grandson of a Confederate soldier, with family who immigrated to the South before the Revolutionary War. Reid had graduated from Clemson College and earned a master's degree from the University of Wisconsin. He married a woman from Mississippi, and they settled in Arkansas.[112]

Reid had long functioned within the southern agricultural bureaucracy and was not inclined to rock the boat unnecessarily. He did, however, believe small farmers needed public assistance, and he knew more about farming, and farming in the South, than many whose visions were more ideologically driven. He also showed considerable political skill in his management of the USDA bureaucracy and local politics in Mississippi.[113]

At the time of his appointment as FSA regional administrator, Reid headed the Agricultural Extension Service in Arkansas. One Arkansas newspaper noted Reid "has been the pride and despair of his associates in 18 years of extension duty in Arkansas because he never stops work." The article notes that Reid had just spent a week in Washington, "where he attended President Roosevelt's conference with resettlement directors and had several personal interviews with Dr. Rexford G. Tugwell, head of the Rural Resettlement Administration."[114] Reid's hands-on knowledge of agriculture and ingrained understanding of the South were important practical factors in developing

Mileston. The relationship between Reid and Tugwell was critical in gaining both the latitude and resources Tugwell granted to Region VI.

Reid did not confront the white status quo directly, but he hired Black staff, as was the agency's policy, and successfully shepherded all-Black cooperative farming projects. One illustrative example of Reid's handling racial cross-pressures comes from Adams County, where a group of citizens protested the hiring of a Black man as assistant supervisor of rural rehabilitation, noting that "young white ladies" were employed in the same office. Governor Bilbo added his voice to the protest, resulting in a letter to the governor from Reid designed to defuse the situation. Reid explained that the employee was needed for going into Negro homes and working "intimately" with them on farm operations. Reid added that the staffer was not working in the same office as white people and that it was not his intention to have Negro staff "where it is objectionable to white people."[115]

During his tenure as Region VI director, Reid spoke and wrote extensively about what the organization aimed to accomplish. He emphasized benefits to both tenants and landowners. Some of his words smack of paternalism, but his mission was clear to anyone paying attention. FSA's purpose, said Reid, was "the conservation of human resources in order to conserve, maintain, and perpetuate the physical resources at hand." He added that FSA looked to aid the lower third of the farm population whose failures were not "brought about by lack of native ability and initiative, for I have come into contact with many of them and I believe they are well supplied with those virtues, but it is caused by their environment that beats their resistance down and kills the desire to better themselves."[116] Based on a 1937 analysis of over twenty thousand tenant farmer FSA clients, Reid asserted that 75 percent could be ready to qualify for the responsibility of full farm ownership within five years.[117]

To be clear, FSA programs had evident biases in favor of white farmers. The Tenant Purchase Program only made loans to those they judged well-qualified to become owner-operators and able to repay loans. They used detailed criteria for the lands they would help purchase and the eligibility of the prospective purchaser, which included community input. In Mississippi, where 75 percent of tenant farmers were Black, only 26 percent of loans in the 1938 fiscal year were to Black tenant farmers. That rose to 35 percent in 1945 but was still less than half what would have been a proportional rate of loans. The loan criteria helped the program remain popular with conservative members of Congress, however, as the cautious approach resulted in a repayment rate of over 98 percent.[118]

While Reid was cautious, Tugwell became a lightning rod for controversy. He wanted the Resettlement Administration to build planned communities, including moving low-income people out of cities to communities in more rural areas. He had visited the Soviet Union in 1927, and that visit, his self-evident liberalism, and his ideas for land collectives made him the center of conservative ire, bringing him the nickname "Rex the Red." Because Congress did not support his efforts, Tugwell resigned, and the resettlement projects were liquidated in 1938.[119] On his way out, Tugwell allocated all remaining resettlement funds to Region VI, saying, "They've got land down there and they can make better use of it than any other region."[120]

The resettlement funds, combined with tenant purchase and community development monies, built what is now known as the Mileston Co-op. Land was owned individually—an effort at cooperative land ownership was rejected by the community—but other resources are cooperative. Between 1939 and 1945, Mileston benefited from a flood control project, workforce training, farm planning, a cooperative store and cotton gin, and the building of a school and a health center. On September 11, 1939, the *Greenwood Commonwealth* reported on flood abatement projects, deepening the channel in the Yazoo River and excavating "a cutoff opposite Mileston, thereby providing a by-pass around that section of the existing lake which has very little capacity." In August of 1940, FSA held its first of several "training days" with talks ranging from the FSA Resettlement program itself to farming practices, community facilities, landscaping, and immunization.[121]

Support for the whole community was critical to the Mileston effort. In 1940, newspaper reports stated that "the government will expend $500,000 in the construction and establishment of the FSA project at Mileston. . . . The program calls for the rehabilitation of 103 farm units, one ten-room school building, project auditorium and gymnasium, office building, store building, shop, warehouse and six personnel buildings. The station for the colony will be drained and a 14-mile highway . . . will be built."[122] A woodworking and crafts program was added in 1941.[123]

The Mileston School was the most modern school for Black children in Holmes County. While most schools for Black children were one room with a wood-burning stove and outhouses, Mileston had seven rooms, running water, inside bathrooms, and a cafeteria. FSA had to meet repeatedly with the school board to get them to accept the school and had to promise grants to fund it in lieu of taxes. The board balked at its offering more than eight grades of education but ultimately agreed that the school could offer a ninth-grade vocational year.[124]

FSA provided two nurses in 1940. Earless Hope was the first nurse. The chief medical officer at FSA, biases intact, described her as "an unusually capable negro nurse" when he described how impressed he was at her addressing health issues at Mileston. The Mileston Community contracted with two physicians in Tchula for health services and built their own clinic in 1942. Families paid fifteen dollars a year to join the Mileston Medical Association to receive home and office visits as needed and ordinary drugs.[125]

From the beginning, farmers participated in running the enterprise. They projected budgets and profits. "The whole corporation, in theory, is operated by the tenants. At first, much of the operation was acquiescent to the direction of the community manager and his staff, but officials report interested discussions now by the negroes at each meeting and a growing sense of initiative and responsibility. Only recently the family heads met and elected their own board of directors."[126] The FSA public press releases in the beginning stressed that "this association—officially known as Mileston Community, Inc., is 'management controlled,' that is, its affairs are administered by Farm Security Administration."[127] The FSA turned the project fully over to the community in 1945.

The *Jackson Advocate* reported the success of Black farmers in Holmes County in the 1950s: "Holmes is considered one of the most substantial Negro land owning counties in Mississippi. Figures secured from the Census Bureau in Washington, D.C. as of 1945 show there are 906 farm owners with 82,536 acres valued at $2,011,321 in this county. Shadrach Davis, R. 2, Tchula; Ceaser and Solomon LeFlore, Mileston, and Aaron Gatson, R. 1 Goodman were top-notch producers of cotton and grain last year."[128] The *Advocate* profiled the success of the Ralthus Hayes family in 1958 when they paid off their tenant purchase loan. The Hayeses are "former sharecroppers who 'graduated,' now own a 114-acre farm, two tractors, and a combine, and are grossing between $8,500 and $10,000 annually." Several of these farmers will reappear in later chapters as leaders in the civil rights movement of the 1960s; some of the Mileston farmers also have the same family names as those who bought land in the 1860s.

Mileston and the town of Howard, where the NFCF was so active, are ten miles apart on main roads and less than half that as the crow flies. I wondered whether the two were officially connected, especially as James Davis, cofounder of the NFCF, was part of the Roosevelt administration. I could not find a record of related correspondence. Region VI archives are at the National Archives in Fort Worth, but Mississippi files are missing. In any case, there could have been unrecorded conversations. It certainly may be that the deep history of African American cooperative farm efforts in Holmes County was foundational in its selection as a site for the Region VI effort.

THROUGH HAZEL EYES

The development of the Mileston Co-op was an important precursor to the civil rights movement in Holmes County. Mileston, with its more economically independent farmers, provided early leadership. The Holmes County civil rights movement was also to receive favorable and extensive press coverage in the 1960s because of the then publisher of the *Lexington Advertiser*, Hazel Brannon Smith.

Hazel Brannon arrived in Holmes County in 1936 as a twenty-two-year-old recent graduate of the University of Alabama. She convinced a local bank to loan her $3,000 to purchase the *Durant News*. It was twenty-five years later that Hazel Brannon Smith, as she was then known, won a Pulitzer Prize for editorial writing for her coverage of civil rights issues in the *Lexington Advertiser*, which she bought in 1943. She was the first woman to do so.

Holmes County went through many changes during the nearly fifty years Brannon Smith was a local newspaper publisher, and so did Brannon Smith herself. Through it all, Brannon Smith was consistent in her belief that journalism should serve the community and tell the truth. She believed passionately in the rule of law and that those in positions of authority should follow the law. She was not a liberal, although she is often portrayed that way. She was a reformer, rooted in a sense of journalistic integrity. She believed her job as a journalist was to uncover hypocrisy, corruption, and any disregard for the rule of law by those in power.

When Brannon Smith first arrived in Holmes County, she was by all accounts beautiful, aggressive, and full of zeal to tell her new community important truths. Jeffrey Howell, who grew up in Holmes County, tells the story in his 2017 biography of Brannon Smith of a very smart young woman from a middle-class family in Alabama City.

According to Howell, Brannon Smith was the oldest of five children. Her father taught wiring at the Republic Steel Mill while her mother taught Sunday school at their Baptist church. Brannon Smith graduated high school when she was only sixteen. Her parents thought she was too young to go to college, so she got a job at a local newspaper, the *Etowah Observer*. She sold advertising on commission until the size of her commissions became problematic. The newspaper put her on salary because it cost them less. She also edited the society page and was welcome to submit other stories for which she was paid one dollar apiece, with several of her efforts published on the front page. Brannon Smith had found her calling long before she arrived in Holmes County.[129]

Howell recounts that at the University of Alabama, Brannon was mentored by Professor Clarence Cason, who taught his students that journalism was a service to the community. He taught that they could make a difference, especially by remaining in the South. Cason was what then counted as a liberal on race. There is little evidence that Cason's liberalism transferred to his mentee at that point, although his enthusiasm for reform clearly did.

Brannon Smith devoted her early efforts to simply making the *Durant News* a success—more widely read and profitable. Howell tells of her greeting travelers who got off the train in Durant to ask about their visit to expand her coverage of social and business events in the *Durant News*. Readership grew from about 200 to 1,400 and advertising dollars with it, allowing

Brannon Smith to pay off her loan by the end of the decade and purchase the *Lexington Advertiser*.[130]

Brannon Smith's principal cause in the 1940s was opposition to the sale of bootleg liquor. Mississippi had outlawed liquor in 1908 under Governor Edmond Favor Noel, a Holmes County native, and statewide prohibition remained in place until 1966 (and only in 2020 did liquor possession become legal in every county). Prohibition did not stop Mississippians from drinking, however. Bootlegging grew as an industry during the Depression as other economic opportunities dried up. Willie Morris in his memoir *North toward Home* quotes his father saying the only difference between the drinking habits of Mississippi and neighboring Tennessee, with no prohibition, was that in Mississippi you could buy liquor on Sunday. Illegal liquor sales were so rampant, and so well acknowledged, that the state even passed a "black market tax" on liquor sales in 1944 and had county sheriffs collect it.[131]

In Holmes County, bootlegging was widespread. Juke joints, bars, and clubs were all over the county, particularly in Durant and Goodman with their easy accessibility along Highway 51 and proximate train stations. Janice Branch Tracy, with family roots in Holmes, collected information on more than two dozen drinking establishments along Highways 51 and Highway 12 dating back to the 1940s. The Rainbow Garden, upscale and catering to whites, was one of the largest. The Blue Flame Café, owned and operated by her cousin Tillman Branch, catered principally to Blacks. There were dozens of other clubs.[132]

When Brannon Smith first arrived in Holmes, she stayed at the Durant Hotel, right in the center of much of the bootleg liquor activity. As Howell writes, "Between 1944 and 1947, Holmes County Sheriff Walter Murtagh served as Brannon's main whipping boy." She repeatedly excoriated him for allowing clubs to stay open, for reneging on his campaign promise to go after illegal liquor, and for tolerating the slot machines and other illegal gambling at Holmes County clubs. Brannon Smith was not a teetotaler but an occasional social drinker. She believed nonetheless that the sheriff should uphold the law as written.[133]

Brannon Smith was more approving of the next sheriff, Ellis Wynn, who made at least a dent in Holmes County's illegal liquor activity. During his four years as sheriff, his officers arrested 242 people for the sale or possession of alcohol and destroyed 116 stills and 585 barrels of bootleg liquor—which is a considerable quantity for a county with, at that time, roughly 30,000 people. Toward the end of his term, he requested support from the governor, who sent in the State Guard, who raided 21 nightclubs across the county and seized $25,000 in cash, weapons, and gambling paraphernalia.[134]

During this period, Brannon Smith appeared oblivious to the ongoing violence against Black people. The 1940s saw a surge of violence across the country. Violence in Harlem began when a crowd heard of the killing of a

Black soldier by a white policeman and in Detroit with an interracial brawl in a park. Both cities had flammable tensions to which those incidents gave spark. As one commentator noted, "The most basic and general cause of the 1943 riots was the discrepancy between the promises of American democracy and the realities of Black life."[135]

In Holmes County, Brannon Smith was living in a white bubble. She outlined her views in a 1943 editorial entitled "The South's Racial Problem," which she proudly published twice in her newspaper, following the riots in Detroit: "America is a white man's country," Brannon Smith declares, and "the white man and the black man have dwelt together in peace and harmony in the south for many, many years, because each has known its place and kept it." The South, writes Brannon Smith, is especially a white man's country, and "that is why the so-called "negro problem" must be solved by southern white and negro people. . . . We must solve it ourselves because it is peculiarly our own. No amount of legislating in Washington however inspired can change that."

The "peace and harmony" Brannon Smith found is certainly not the Holmes County recollected by the Black community. Chalmers Archer, who grew up in Holmes County in the 1930s and 1940s, writes in his memoir, "Those were the days when fears and hatreds haunted a troubled land. It was a time when black people's lives and the lives of their families were always on the line. There was a pervasive feeling among black people that whatever they said or did about anything would make absolutely no difference."[136]

Brannon Smith praised the work of the Delta Council, the association of Delta plantation owners that, in the early 1940s, was trying to retain African American labor with some efforts toward better schools and health care. "Here in Holmes County," she continues, "we are blessed with some of the finest self-sustaining and self-respecting negro men and women in the state and in the south. . . . They work hard and most of them are well to do."[137]

Brannon Smith was clearly thinking of the most elite members of the Black community; the sharecroppers, who were a majority at that time, were certainly not well to do. She may have thought of Arenia Mallory, about whom she wrote at length in 1950 on the twenty-fifth anniversary of Saints Academy. Brannon Smith sounds as if Mallory did it all. Her story on Mallory does not mention Bishop Mason and barely mentions the COGIC. While Mallory had experienced her own difficulties with white attitudes in Holmes County, Brannon Smith writes only that "it is impossible to describe the heartaches and problems during the infancy of her venture. But today the white leaders of the community accept her and admire her."

Brannon Smith would have been considered moderate in the 1930s and 1940s. She reflected the common white misconception that Black people were satisfied with their second-class status and only complained in response to external agitation. She favored harmony and recognized value in "good" Negroes, while at least implicitly reflecting an attitude of white supremacy.

Brannon Smith's reporting of the 1946 lynching of Leon McAtee illustrates both her aggression in getting a story and her self-absorption when ostensibly pursuing justice. McAtee was accused of stealing a saddle from a white farmer named Dodd. After McAtee was jailed, Dodd arranged with the sheriff to have McAtee released into his custody after dropping the charges. Dodd, his son, and three other white men acknowledged whipping and beating McAtee but said he then ran away. McAtee's body was later found face down in a stream with no water in his lungs. The men were charged, but an all-white jury took only a few minutes to find them not guilty.

Here's what the article in the *Lexington Advertiser* says happened next: "Pretty young Hazel Brannon, crusading editor of Lexington's weekly newspaper, *The Lexington Advertiser*, was not satisfied. She waylaid McAtee's widow, Henrietta on her way out of the courtroom. Henrietta had been told not to talk to anyone about the case. But Miss Brannon got a story."[138] The widow had seen her husband, his hands bound and badly bruised, in the back of a pickup truck belonging to one of the men. Mrs. McAtee's testimony, which pointed to Dodd's culpability, had not been provided to the court. Brannon Smith was arrested and held briefly on charges of contempt of court for talking to the widow.

Brannon Smith did, indeed, get her story and drew praise for doing so in the African American press.[139] Dodd's stepson later confessed that he was the one who had stolen the saddle. The men who killed McAtee, having been found not guilty, still went free, a point Brannon Smith did not emphasize. Over time, she would become more cognizant of the racial injustices in the county but arguably remained more about the rule of law than the consequences of injustice.

PROVIDENCE LOST

In 1936, the same year Brannon Smith arrived in Holmes County and shortly before the founding of the Mileston Co-op, another group arrived in the Delta. They too founded a cooperative farm. Their motivation was less practical than T. Roy Reid's. Instead, they were avowedly ideological and new to farming. Their story would intersect with Brannon Smith's as both became victims of their views on desegregation in the 1950s. In the meantime, they made significant contributions to the Holmes County story.

The founders of Providence Farm were avowed Socialists and Christian Realists who believed deeply in a new collective and interracial southern order. The leaders of the farm were followers of Reinhold Niebuhr, a prominent Protestant author, theologian, and founder of American Christian Realism who at one point was president of the farm's board of trustees. Niebuhr advocated for democracy and justice as integral to the Christian faith. He is perhaps best known for writing the "serenity prayer" used by Alcoholics Anonymous and other human development groups.

Another founder of the enterprise, William Amberson, had worked with Norman Thomas on his pamphlet on the plight of sharecroppers and had alliances with leaders of the STFU, including union founder H. L. Mitchell and Reverend E. B. McKinney, its African American vice president.[140] The founders of Providence Farm also worked with Mack Rust, brother of the inventor of an early cotton picker, which he hoped could give relief to those who labored in the cotton fields.[141]

Neibuhr, Amberson, and Rust were on the board, while two of Niebuhr's followers, Sherwood Eddy and Sam H. Franklin, ran the farm day-to-day. Eddy was a Christian missionary and a man of independent wealth who provided initial financial backing. Franklin was also a Presbyterian missionary who had recently served his church in Japan. The theological basis of the enterprise was important to each of them. Franklin wrote, "The theological outlook which most of us found congenial was that of the 'Biblical realism' of the president of our Board of Trustees, Reinhold Niebuhr. We recognized that the iniquitous systems to which we were opposed had their origins in contradictions of the human heart which only the grace of God could finally change."[142] Eddy initially hired Gene Cox as a bookkeeper, although his role would expand. Cox had been a seminary student at Texas Christian University and shared the commitment to "practical Christianity." Cox stayed over twenty years—longer than anyone else—and toward the end of his tenure managed the farm.[143]

Before founding Providence Farm in Holmes County, the group tried a similar experiment in 1936 in Bolivar County called Delta Cooperative Farm. That effort began failing within two years because of racial tensions within farm leadership, isolation from the community, and a poor choice of land, as the soil there was a heavily clay variety known as buckshot, which retained water but dried to a hard-packed surface. A visitor to the Bolivar County farm observed that "the staff of the cooperative seemed to me like Robinson Crusoes washed up by good will on the Delta of Mississippi where they were applying their city brains and missionary Christian enthusiasm energetically and ingeniously to the hard problems of the isolated land," adding "none of those in the immediate direction of the Delta Cooperative are farmers."[144]

The group did better with their farm in Holmes County—it was better land, and they worked to engage with the broader community. The nearly three thousand acres they purchased just northeast of Tchula included five hundred acres of Delta land for row crops, a working dairy, and several outbuildings. It also included a Native American mound from the Woodland period.

Minister and civil rights leader Will D. Campbell authored a book on the history of the land that became Providence Farm. The land had been owned by Louis Leflore before it was platted and allocated in the Treaty of Dancing Rabbit Creek to Turner Breshears, a Choctaw who was related to the Leflores by marriage. Campbell writes that there was "some confusion" on the disposition of the land in the 1840s as Breshears was entitled to the land if he remained for five years. Instead, land records show a transfer from Breshears to Wiley Davis but also show that the land at that time was owned by William McKendree Gwin. It became the subject of lawsuits against Davis. As part of a settlement the land was owned briefly by Samuel McAllister, one of the plaintiffs, and then sold back to Gwin.[145] Campbell does not cite the machinations of the Chocchuma Land Company, but the land was evidently part of that company's purchases since Gwin and Davis were integrally involved with Chocchuma.

During the 1840s, a portion of the land was sold to William Pinchback, the father of P. B. S. Pinchback, but for the most part the land was held by members of the extended Gwin family until the 1930s. Campbell notes that the $6 an acre Providence Farm paid for the land in the wake of the Depression was almost exactly what William McKendree Gwin had paid a hundred years earlier, although the land had at one point commanded $750 an acre.

Providence Farm made several course corrections during its nearly twenty-year tenure, some planned and others forced by circumstance. It was never an economically practical effort, but it survived for nearly two decades as a more interracial and idealistic effort than most other Holmes County institutions of its time or since.

In addition to its core management staff, the farm had its own medical team headed by Dr. David Minter. Minter worked with the AKA sorority sisters, overlapping with the group at Saints Academy, to provide medical services for the community. Minter treated more than ten thousand Holmes County patients in 1942. He was drafted into the army at the end of the year, returning to Providence after the war.[146]

Fannye Thomas Booker, who joined the Providence community around 1941, proved a critical leader in connecting the farm and the Holmes County African American community. Booker was born and raised in Holmes County and attended the Clower School, one of the Rosenwald Schools built in the early 1920s. She finished her education at Durant Training School, Jackson State, and Mississippi Industrial College. She became a teacher for a time in Tallahatchie County but returned to Lexington when her employment was terminated after she attempted to register to vote.[147]

Booker began what she called a "camp school" at Providence for children from third grade through high school who had failed to advance to the next grade. The residential program lasted nine weeks over the summer. It was staffed by Booker and summer interns from Saints School and historically Black colleges. It was reportedly highly successful in getting children to the point where they could be promoted with the rest of their class.

Several of the children later became professionally successful and carried fond memories of Booker and what they learned from her at the camp school. One child was Odell Hampton Jr., whose mother cooked at the summer camp and who, much later, became a county supervisor. As an adult, he recalled: "I was a mean little rascal. And Mrs. Booker told me, she said, 'Son, if you're going to survive in this world, you're going to have to know how to treat people.' I took that seriously. After that I started treating people like I wanted to be treated. And that was one good thing she taught me. I learned from that, and I survived from that."[148]

Another child at the camp school was Phillip Rushing. Rushing had lost both his arms in a terrible accident in which he tried, without success, to save a friend struck by a fallen power line. Providence Farm was a place where he found solace, egalitarianism, and spiritual renewal. Rushing became a social worker and wrote a book about his spiritual growth at Providence and later at Saints School. Rushing loved Fannye Booker, whom he felt took a real interest in him, and he was much struck by the Cox family. "Mixed emotions warred within me as I stood in front of the Coxes' ranch house the last week of camp. There was pride—this was my first invitation to dine with a white family. And there was guilt—I had no business being in this place, as my Grandaddy Forty-Four would have been the first to tell me."[149]

Booker was sympathetic to the Southern Tenant Farmers Union, which shared Christian and socialist roots with the leaders of Providence Farm. Hearing that her union brethren were being denied bank loans to plant crops, she and Gene Cox formed the Providence Credit Union, so farmers had an alternative to the commercial banks. The credit union began in the 1940s, and Booker served as its first president—the only woman credit union president in the state and the only credit union run by both Black and white people. It began with around one hundred members from Providence and the nearby community and grew to around two hundred members in the early 1950s.[150]

Sociologist William Minter, Dr. David Minter's son, who spent his childhood at Providence Farm, stressed Booker's importance to the enterprise. William Minter acknowledged that the farm floundered, but that, in addition to his father's clinic, the camp school, the co-op store, and the Providence Credit Union, each of which Booker helped manage, were successful and left lasting positive legacies. His time at Providence Farm also gave Minter a lifelong commitment to civil rights, beginning with his joining the staff of the Student Nonviolent Coordinating Committee in southwest Georgia as a young adult and later as editor of the *AfricaFocus Bulletin*.[151]

Eugene Cox succeeded Sam Franklin as director of the enterprise. Franklin had been controversial at Delta Cooperative Farm, and some of the same issues carried over to Providence. Cox by all accounts created a happier and more democratic atmosphere. Franklin's formidable intellect and vision were accompanied by some arrogance. He cast aspersions on local religious practices, apparently alluding to the COGIC. Franklin was also concerned about offending the white power structure in the community. He had run-ins with Sam Checkver, a radical Harvard graduate who organized an STFU local at Providence in 1940. Franklin believed Checkver would draw white community opposition—and possibly violence—to Providence and convinced Eddy to ask him to leave the farm.[152]

The conflict between Franklin and Checkver appears to place Franklin on the side of pragmatism. It may also have been a conflict over grassroots organizing strategy compared to a more hierarchical view. In his own writing, Franklin praises Checkver's "brilliance" and "absolute moral idealism [that] drove him to identify with the suffering of the sharecroppers." Franklin adds that Checkver "became critical of what he regarded as departures from the socialist-cooperative ideal . . . in the degree of authority which the trustees imposed through me on the decisions of the people."[153]

Perhaps Franklin's most egregious violation of the professed spirit of Providence Farm was the result of economic pressure. Will Campbell, who admired Cox, Minter, and Booker, writes that under Franklin, workers at Delta Cooperative Farm were paid less than they were paid on nearby plantations. Workers were paid sixty-six cents a day for chopping cotton while traditional plantations were paying a dollar a day, and the STFU was urging its members to demand five dollars a day, which Franklin asserted would break the farm. Franklin punished Delta Farm residents who worked at other plantations by not allowing them credit at the co-op store or distributing clothing to them that was gifted to the co-op. When the crops suffered because of co-op residents working elsewhere, Franklin brought in day laborers from Clarksdale and paid them the going rate.[154] Franklin left for a commission as a US Navy chaplain at the start of World War II. After the war he returned to his missionary work in Japan.

The war hit Providence hard, with Minter, Franklin, and others leaving for the war effort. The farm was still relying on donations rather than sustaining itself economically, and donations dried up during the war. By the late 1940s, the farm's financial situation forced a reorganization. The original structure, headed still by Niebuhr, Rust, Eddy, and others who had served on the board for a decade, was liquidated and a new foundation formed. Minter and the Coxes—Gene Cox and his wife Lindsay Hail Cox, who came to Providence as a nurse at Minter's clinic—played expanded roles as officers of the foundation, so it was fully controlled by those who lived on the farm. The farm continued a commitment to community engagement and African American empowerment, until 1956. For nearly twenty years, it was an island of interracial respect and idealism that also served the broader community. A later chapter tells of its demise in the 1950s.

THE WAR BEGINS

Events stateside during World War II were important in creating opportunity for the coming civil rights movement to flourish. The war accelerated the Great Migration, which increased support for change in the North. When the Great Migration began in 1910, nine out of ten Black people in the United States lived in the South. By 1940, 1.6 million African Americans had moved north. Five million more would move north between 1940 and 1970 as industrial job opportunities expanded. As the Great Migration depleted the population of the South it brought a critical mass of African Americans north, where they had voting rights and thus a political voice, which led to more federal support for civil rights. The network of African American newspapers also grew with a larger northern market, creating a forum for demands for change.

The Double V campaign—for victory at home and abroad—launched from a letter by an individual to a prominent Black newspaper grew to a national cause. The impetus came after passage of the 1940 Selective Service Act, requiring all American men ages twenty-one to forty-five to register for the draft. James G. Thompson from Wichita, Kansas, wrote to the *Pittsburgh Courier*, one of the largest Black newspapers in the country with a circulation above two hundred thousand.[155] Thompson's letter began, "Like all true Americans, my greatest desire at this time, this crucial point in our history, is a desire for a complete victory over the forces of evil, which threaten our existence today." After continuing to write of his commitment to his country and to the war efforts, Thompson raised questions, leading with: "Should I sacrifice my life to live half American?" Thompson suggested a Double V campaign, "The first V for victory over our enemies from without, the second V for victories over our enemies within." Thompson concluded, "I love America and am willing to die for the America I know will someday become a reality."[156]

A week later, the *Pittsburgh Courier* launched an insignia proclaiming, "Democracy At Home Abroad" and ran it weekly through the war. The Double V campaign took off. It resonated broadly and was picked up by the NAACP. Entertainers and politicians joined the campaign, and Double V Clubs began across the country. In Mississippi, Double V events to raise war bonds were held in at least Jackson and Meridian.[157]

While the army remained segregated through World War II, it expanded roles for African Americans and enlarged officer training. The "Tuskegee Experiment," to see if Black Air Force personnel could be trained to fly, produced the much-heralded Tuskegee Airmen. The army also launched a propaganda program, originally aimed at African Americans. The low-budget film *Henry Browne, Farmer*, for example, showed a Black farmer—who owned his land and two mules—doing his best for the war effort by planting peanuts, while his son was a Tuskegee Airman.

Back in Holmes County, Hazel Brannon's *Durant News* picked up on the theme with an article on a Black farmer who "is a good example of what hard work and thrift can accomplish for a colored man and his family on a Southern farm." The Holmes County farmer's son was not a Tuskegee Airman but was posted overseas in England.[158] Hazel Brannon Smith's example of a hardworking farmer was Gus Courts, who would later play a significant role in the civil rights movement in the region.

A far more substantial effort from the War Department than the Henry Browne film was *The Negro Soldier*, a forty-three-minute film produced by a department headed by Frank Capra, who already had a series of films on democracy to his credit, including *Mr. Smith Goes to Washington*. *The Negro Soldier* was written by Black writer Carlton Moss, who also appears in it as a preacher and the lead narrator. The film shows Black achievement ranging from Joe Louis winning the heavyweight boxing title against German Max Schmeling to the settlement of the West and the building of the Panama Canal. It references the poetry of Langston Hughes and shows white men under the command of Black officers. It was initially intended only for Black audiences, but after some inevitable controversy it became mandatory viewing for all replacement soldiers between February of 1944 and August of 1945 and had civilian distribution of over 7.5 million.[159]

Black organizations in the South, too, grew during the 1940s in response to the mood for change. The Progressive Voter League was founded in 1936. The Mississippi Voter League—founded in 1947 and headquartered in Hattiesburg and Jackson—had a chapter in Holmes County. It promoted nonpartisan civic education but did not lead voter registration efforts. Its president, T. B. Wilson, proclaimed that its "moderate" posture appealed to its middle-class Black audience.[160]

NAACP organizer Ella Baker traveled south to help organize NAACP units in the 1940s, targeting the Mississippi Delta. Membership in the Mississippi NAACP grew from merely 129 members in six branches in 1929 to more than sixteen branches in 1947, most of which had the minimum of 50 members needed to send a delegate to the NAACP national convention. The NAACP founded the Legal Defense and Education Fund in 1940, with Thurgood Marshall at the helm, and expanded legal capabilities dedicated to expanding civil rights.[161]

In 1944, Thurgood Marshall argued successfully before the US Supreme Court that all-white primaries, like the Democratic primary in Mississippi, were illegal. In the next Mississippi gubernatorial election, a small percent of the state's Black population—about 2,500 Black people—managed to cast ballots, although more were turned away. More than 200 Black Mississippi voters registered to testify against the legitimacy of the Bilbo election in the United States Senate. They argued that Bilbo should be impeached since his election rested on fraudulent practices that denied African Americans their rights. The congressional committee was dominated by segregationists and impeachment efforts failed, but the effort drew the attention of the national press and presaged efforts to come.[162]

In September of 1945, the *Pittsburgh Courier* replaced the Double V with a Single V to indicate the need to combat racism at home now that victory abroad had been achieved. As African American veterans returned home, they became leaders for change.

Bishop Charles Harrison Mason portrait, circa 1920s. Mason was the founder and the first senior bishop of the Church of God in Christ. Credit: The Flower Pentecostal Heritage Center.

Group photograph of people at the COGIC Women's Convention in Boston, Massachusetts, 1955. Standing in the front (l-r): Bishop C. H. Mason, Mother Lillian Brooks Coffey, and Mother Retha Herndon. Standing behind them (l-r): Bishop Samuel Crouch, Bishop O. M. Kelly, and Bishop O. T. Jones Sr. Mother Mattie McGlothen is standing in the last row, far right, with a white hat and glasses. Credit: The Flower Pentecostal Heritage Center.

"In front of the Courthouse on Saturday afternoon, Lexington, Holmes County, Mississippi Delta, Mississippi." Photograph by Marion Post Wolcott, (November?) 1939. https://www.loc.gov/item/2017755198/. Library of Congress, Prints & Photographs Division, FSA/OWI Collection, LC-DIG-fsa-8a41490.

"Kitchen in Negro tenant home on Marcella Plantation." Mileston, Mississippi Delta, Mississippi. Photograph by Marion Post Wolcott, November 1939. https://www.loc.gov/item/2017801557/. Library of Congress, Prints & Photographs Division, FSA/OWI Collection, LC-USF34-052310-D.

"Picking cotton." Mileston Plantation, Mileston, Mississippi Delta, Mississippi. Photograph by Marion Post Wolcott, October 1939. https://www.loc.gov/item/2017801515/. Library of Congress, Prints & Photographs Division, FSA/OWI Collection, LC-USF34-052269-D.

"Negro day laborers brought in by truck from nearby towns, waiting to be paid off for cotton picking and buy supplies inside plantation store on Friday night." Marcella Plantation. Mississippi Delta. Mississippi. Photograph by Marion Post Wolcott, November 1939. https://www.loc.gov/item/2017801443/. Library of Congress, Prints & Photographs Division, FSA/OWI Collection, LC-DIG-fsa-8c30353.

"Negro tenants working in their garden of turnip greens." Good Hope Plantation, Mississippi Delta, Mississippi. Photograph by Marion Post Wolcott, October 1939. https://www.loc.gov/item/2017801537/. Library of Congress, Prints & Photographs Division, FSA/OWI Collection, LC-USF34-052291-D.

Farm Security Administration head Dillard Lasseter with Agriculture Department officials. T. Roy Reid is in the front row, wearing glasses, with his fist on the desk. June 17, 1946. Courtesy of the Harry S. Truman Library & Museum, Accession Number: 2014-3970.

Hazel Brannon Smith at a banquet, circa 1950. Brannon Smith is at the end of the table wearing a hat. Mississippi Press Association Papers, Manuscripts Division, Archives and Special Collections, Mississippi State University Libraries.

Mary McLeod Bethune, president of the National Council of Negro Women, presents awards to ten women chosen for their "devotion to the public good," March 15, 1946. Arenia Mallory is third from the right, in front of the flags, wearing a corsage. Reprinted with permission of the DC Public Library, Star Collection © Washington Post.

Chapter 4

DESEGREGATION AND VOTING RIGHTS—1950 TO 1980

Segregation of white and Negro children in the public schools of a State solely on the basis of race, pursuant to state laws permitting or requiring such segregation, denies to Negro children the equal protection of the laws guaranteed by the Fourteenth Amendment—even though the physical facilities and other "tangible" factors of white and Negro schools may be equal.

—US SUPREME COURT IN *BROWN V. BOARD OF EDUCATION OF TOPEKA, KANSAS*

SEC. 2. No voting qualification or prerequisite to voting, or standard, practice, or procedure shall be imposed or applied by any State or political subdivision to deny or abridge the right of any citizen of the United States to vote on account of race or color.

—VOTING RIGHTS ACT OF 1965

FIRE FIGHT

In early 1950s Mississippi, organizing and legal strategies for desegregation and voting rights were underway but not always publicly visible. It was a period of apparent calm with a storm just visible at the horizon. The storm would arrive in 1954 with the US Supreme Court decision on *Brown v. Board of Education*, ruling that separate school systems were inherently unequal. The decision by the US Supreme Court would spur both the Black community and white opposition into a prolonged battle over school desegregation and voting rights.

In Holmes County, however, 1954 did not begin quietly. It began with a shooting spree that is still talked about there as a Black man shot four white men and never went to jail for it. On the eve of the US Supreme Court decision on the Brown case, the shooting spree divided the county, bringing fear to whites and raising the ire of the African American community. The incident added to tensions just as the US Supreme Court decision came down. It was also a lesson to some that visibly fighting back was survivable.

The shooting spree began on January 9, 1954, when a Black man named Eddie Noel, whose name was by no coincidence much like that of the former governor from Holmes County, shot and killed a white man named Willie Ramon Dickard at the Dickard family store in southwestern Holmes County. Noel then shot four more white men, two of them dead, during the eighteen days he remained a fugitive.

The facts of what happened are well known. They were widely reported at the time throughout Mississippi. Later, Holmes County native Allie Povall, whose father was the mayor of Lexington in 1954, authored a book based on contemporaneous coverage and extensive interviews.[1] Still, the narrative surrounding the facts, and Eddie Noel's impact on the county, depend on who is doing the telling.

Dickard's was a general store during the day and a honky-tonk at night. It was one of dozens of such establishments but one of only a few that served both Black and white customers in the same space. Eddie Noel was an army veteran who did odd jobs for a living and made and sold moonshine on the side. Since the Noel family had arrived in Holmes County early in the nineteenth century, the surname was a common one by the 1950s. Povall traces Eddie Noel's lineage to former Governor Noel's brother, Leland Noel Jr.

Eddie Noel was by all accounts a crackerjack shot. He could, according to multiple sources and at least one eyewitness, strike a match with a bullet from his .22 rifle without destroying the match. He could shoot fast from either shoulder. When the right-handed Noel shot from his left shoulder, he could continually pump the bolt so his rifle fired repeatedly, like an automatic weapon would.

On the evening of January 9, Willie Ramon Dickard and Eddie Noel had a confrontation about Noel's wife, who had a job serving drinks at Dickard's. They ended up in a wrestling match, at the end of which Dickard literally threw Noel out of the store. Meanwhile, Willie Ramon's father, armed with a baseball bat, had a confrontation with Noel's cousin Percy Cobbins, who had brought his own liquor into the store to spike his Coke rather than purchasing liquor from the Dickards as required. Noel went to get his rifle out of the car and returned to the store. The elder Dickard grabbed the rifle and the younger Dickard slapped Noel across the face, and the two dragged him out of the store again. They threw his rifle out after him, so it lay on the ground. As both Dickards struggled to throw Cobbins out of the store, Noel picked his rifle up off the ground and shot Willie Ramon Dickard dead.

The sheriff at this time was Richard Byrd, who had won with Hazel Brannon Smith's support because he promised to clean up the illegal liquor business. He had not done so; rather, there were rumors that Byrd was being paid on the side by the Taylors, Dickard's cousins who were among the biggest bootleggers in the county. At one point, Brannon Smith had estimated that based on their black market liquor tax, the Taylors were drawing over $1 million a year from illegal liquor sales.[2]

The posse to find and capture Noel began the evening of Willie Ramon Dickard's death. The Dickard family and their friends set up a roadblock near the Noel home, and they were joined by Byrd and his deputy John Pat Malone. The roadblock succeeded in trapping the Noel family car, in which Noel's wife, her sister, and the sister's two young children were passengers. Noel escaped into the woods but not before a shootout that left Malone mortally wounded. The passengers in the car, including the two infant children, were taken to the Holmes County jail.

The posse grew to over four hundred men the next day as Sheriff Byrd sent a sound truck around the county with the message: "A colored man named Eddie Noel has killed two white men near Brozville. All able-bodied white men arm and assemble at the Antioch Baptist Church at noon. Manhunt. Posse. Dogs. Help bring in the killer of Willie Ramon Dickard and John Pat Malone. Killer. Colored. Two white men dead. We are going to catch him."[3] The civilians who joined the posse were supplemented by Mississippi highway patrolmen and local law enforcement from surrounding counties. The posse looking for Noel became the largest the state had seen, with more than five hundred men, hound dogs supplied by the state prison at Parchman, and a spotter plane.

In the early morning hours, the day after the shooting, Noel went to his own house, built a fire, barricaded himself in the bedroom, and went to sleep. That afternoon three highway patrolmen and several civilians showed up at the house and saw the smoke. Local civilian Joe Stewart said he knew Noel a bit and perhaps could coax him out. Stewart, armed with a pistol, entered the bedroom. Noel shot him dead. As the other men retreated, Noel came out to the porch shooting his bolt-action rifle like a machine gun from his left shoulder while he reloaded with his right hand. Two more men were wounded, Red Hocutt and Andrew Smith. (Smith would later succeed Byrd as sheriff.)

Noel remained a fugitive for nearly three weeks. White people were terrified. Povall reports widespread fears that a race war was beginning. White people were afraid to go out; schools closed. The mail was left undelivered. The media fed fears with high-drama headlines: "3 Men Shot Down as Lexington Negro Runs Wild with Gun," screamed an inch-high headline in the *Clarion-Ledger* on January 11. The next day the *Clarion-Ledger* showed the burned remains of the home of the "Negro triple-killer." "Crazed Rifleman Still at Large," proclaimed the *Biloxi Daily Herald* on January 13.

While whites were terrified, the Black community felt terrorized. The posse showed up at Black people's homes without warrants and searched their attics, closets, and outhouses. They arrested members of Noel's family and others they believed, often without reason, might help hide Noel. Farmer T. C. Johnson recounts, "They just harassed a lot of Black people. Catch 'em out on the road, sit 'em down, dog 'em around and call 'em names." Johnson recounts police shoving a gun in his face and dragging his cousin out of a car while asking about Eddie Noel. Johnson was acquainted with Noel but neither he nor his cousin had seen him, nor was there any particular reason to think they had.[4]

Hazel Brannon Smith blamed illegal liquor. Noel, the Dickards—and several members of the posse—all sold alcohol. Brannon Smith also blamed Sheriff Byrd, whose commitment to reducing the sale of liquor in Holmes County had been short-lived. In her view, the illegal liquor trade undergirded a pattern of lawlessness.[5]

In the end, Noel gave himself up. His family believed he was not safe in the Holmes County jail or with local law enforcement. The surrender was negotiated by Arenia Mallory, who spoke out against the violence and had publicly urged Noel's surrender, plus Noel's mother, Mayritta, and her brother Phillip Brooks. Noel surrendered to W. C. Grice of the State Livestock Sanitary Board, with whom Philip Brooks was acquainted and whom he apparently trusted.[6] The surrender was low-key and without surprises. The aftermath had unexpected twists.

Noel signed confessions acknowledging he had killed the men. He did not argue for self-defense but did assert he had only shot people who had attacked him. His mother hired a young attorney, David Williams, at the recommendation of the presiding judge. Williams requested the trial be moved out of Holmes County, and the judge ruled in his favor. The trial was initially set for April, then postponed until May 17, with the venue moved next door to Leflore County.

Meanwhile, Noel had been moved from the Hinds County jail to the state mental hospital at Whitfield for psychiatric evaluation. It turned out that Noel had been hospitalized while in the army after being found "mentally incompetent" with "homicidal tendencies." Four months later, the director of the state hospital at Whitfield wrote to the presiding judge that Noel was mentally incompetent and that he had been so since childhood. He was unfit to stand trial.

Eddie Noel remained at Whitfield from 1954 until he was released in 1972. His Holmes County case had become inactive, and his social worker said there was no reason to keep him incarcerated at the mental hospital.[7] He was freed and lived until his death in 1994 in Fort Wayne, Indiana, where he had relatives, reportedly visiting family and friends in Holmes County on occasion.

Over the years, people in Holmes County have speculated that someone well-connected helped Noel escape the electric chair. Of course, it may simply have been that he was insane and justice was served. It may have been that white members of the extended Noel family had a soft spot for Eddie and sought to save him, as is rumored in the county and hinted at in Povall's book. It may also have been that the anticipation and then reality of the US Supreme Court decision on *Brown v. Board of Education of Topeka, Kansas* meant the white establishment felt they faced a greater threat than Eddie Noel.

Noel's trial had originally been scheduled for May 17. That was the day the US Supreme Court announced its decision on *Brown v. Board of Education*. There had been fear Noel would cause a race war, but now he was safely out of the county. From the perspective of white leadership, a war had come—the war against school integration. Noel was a distraction from that fight.

Some Black people drew a different lesson: "It did give some of the Black peoples the idea that they didn't have to take the beatin' and runnin' and that abusement like they had been. I've heard a lot of 'em say it was good that somebody had the courage and the nerve to stand up like a man rather than be treated like an animal."[8] Regardless, the Eddie Noel story shows the depth of divisions in the county on the eve of the *Brown* decision.

THE CITIZENS' COUNCIL

The United States Supreme Court ruled on May 17, 1954, that separate schools for Black and white children were inherently unequal. Schools in the South were required to integrate, with a follow-up case in 1955 ruling they should do so "with all deliberate speed." It would be another sixteen years before Black children in Holmes County could enroll in white schools there, the result of a 1969 US Supreme Court case in which Black families from Holmes County were the lead plaintiffs. In 1954, instead of compliance, furor ensued—nationally, throughout Mississippi, and in Holmes County.

Nationally, Senator Harry Byrd of Virginia called for "massive resistance" to desegregation, and southern representatives in Congress—including every member from Mississippi—signed the Southern Manifesto, saying, "The unwarranted decision of the Supreme Court in the public school cases is now bearing the fruit always produced when men substitute naked power for established law."[9]

The national response took time to develop but the Mississippi response was immediate. States' Rights Party activist and circuit court judge Thomas P. Brady, who later sat on the state supreme court, spoke at a late May meeting of the Sons of the American Revolution in Greenwood, just up the road from

Holmes County. Brady's speech declared, "Whenever and wherever the white man has drunk the cup of Black hemlock, whenever and wherever his blood has been infused with blood of the Negro, the white man, his intellect, and his culture have died."[10] Brady put together his speeches and other writings into a ninety-two-page pamphlet titled *Black Monday*, which became a "handbook for segregationists" and argued for the abolition of public schools, a new and separate state for Black people, and the elimination of the NAACP.[11]

On July 11, 1954, fourteen white men in Indianola formed the first Citizens' Council to fight integration and African American voting rights. The second Citizens' Council in the nation was formed just a few days later in Holmes County. By the end of the year, Citizens' Councils had spread across Mississippi.[12]

From the perspective of the twenty-first century, an end to Jim Crow laws appears inexorable. It did not look that way in Mississippi at the time. Segregation was simply the way things were. The perception was that only a heavy-handed federal government wanted change. There was shockingly little understanding that African Americans wanted change too. The white establishment in Mississippi believed they could stop integration and maintain Jim Crowism if they stood firm and united against federal interference.

In 1956, the Mississippi State Legislature approved the formation of the Mississippi State Sovereignty Commission (MSSC). Governor J. P. Coleman wanted an organization to fight integration, over which the state had more control than it did over local Citizens' Councils. The reverse became true: The Citizens' Council remained in control while the MSSC functioned as a surveillance agency that collected and fed information to the Citizens' Council and even helped fund their activities.[13]

Citizens' Council members were established pillars of their local communities. They were particularly strong in counties like Holmes, with large Black majorities.[14] Some have suggested they were more middle class than the Ku Klux Klan, but many individuals were members of both groups.[15] Indeed, with dues at only five dollars a year and considerable pressure to join, most white men in the Delta were members of the Citizens' Council. Some towns in the South limited membership to Christians, but there was no discernable sign of anti-Semitism in Lexington with its substantial Jewish community, a community that remained ostensibly neutral on integration.[16] Perhaps the best evidence of the pervasiveness of Holmes County whites' opposition to integration is the 1954 vote on a constitutional amendment that would abolish public schools entirely should they be required to integrate: 2,393 voted for the measure with merely 70 votes against it.[17]

The MSSC files record which community leaders were the most active Citizens' Council members who provided information to the Sovereignty Commission. Active countywide leadership included the sheriffs—Byrd and his successor Andrew Smith—business leaders, and local and state elected officials, most prominently state legislators Ed White, J. P. Love, and Wilburn Hooker.[18] In Lexington, county attorney Pat Barrett was an early and active member. The Barretts were not a founding family of the county, but Pat Barrett's father had come to Holmes County in 1898, when he married a member of the Burwell family, which had lived in Holmes County since before the Civil War.[19]

The goal of the Citizens' Council was to erect an insurmountable wall of opposition to integration, without any gaps or holes of dissent. As one author described, "The right of free expression was one of the earliest casualties in the war to defend segregation," adding that "in this repressive atmosphere the moderate was vilified, and he who was found 'soft' on integration was adjudged treasonous."[20]

Hazel Brannon Smith was found soft. It was not her nature to conform. She had spent her professional life arguing for truth and for adherence to the law. She did not favor integration—either in 1954 or later—but she did favor following the Supreme Court ruling. Brannon Smith wrote about the Supreme Court decision:

> The unanimous Supreme Court decision may be morally right when it says that "separate educational facilities are inherently unequal." One does not have to be an educator or a genius to recognize that.
>
> But we know that for practical purposes for both races that the traditional separate educational facilities are desirable in the South and other regions where two or more races live and work together side by side . . .
>
> Our present situation has all the ingredients necessary for (literally) a bloody revolution—unless the leadership of both races keeps their heads and does better in the future than they have in the past.
>
> All around us we hear people saying "the Supreme Court is not the law of the land."
>
> And, "They can't force us to do something we do not want to do of our own free will."
>
> Well, I am here to tell you that the law of the land is what the US Supreme Court says it is until proven otherwise.[21]

The Citizens' Council allowed no dissent: There was renewed violence against Black people, and teachers, ministers, and other community leaders lost their livelihoods for speaking out against actions of the Citizens' Council. In Holmes County, the council launched a sustained battle against Brannon Smith and the *Lexington Advertiser* that would ultimately destroy the paper financially. And within three years, the twenty-year-old interracial experiment that was Providence Farm would come to an end. One violent incident spurred the Citizens' Council forays against both Brannon Smith and the leadership of Providence Farm.

On Saturday July 3, 1954, Sheriff Byrd stopped a group of young Black men standing outside a nightclub, who reportedly started "whooping" as Byrd and other law enforcement officials drove by. Byrd struck one young man, Henry Randle, and ordered him to move on. As Randle fled, Byrd drew a pistol and fired at him repeatedly, hitting him once in the back of the thigh. Randle went to Dr. David Minter at Providence Farm for treatment of the wound.[22]

Brannon Smith had already criticized Byrd for allowing liquor establishments to remain open and for the role illegal liquor played in the mayhem surrounding Eddie Noel. She had also questioned Byrd's brutality toward Black people and noted he had harassed two other Black men the night he shot Randle. She called for Byrd's resignation.[23]

Byrd sued her for libel, and the case went to court in October of 1954. Brannon Smith said she had been telling the truth, which was her job as a newspaperwoman. Dr. Minter testified on Brannon Smith's behalf as he had heard about the shooting from Randle when he treated him that night. The jury took very little time deliberating and ruled for Byrd, awarding him a $10,000 judgment (the equivalent of about $100,000 today). While the ruling was overturned on appeal, the Citizens' Council was not finished yet with either Brannon Smith or Minter.[24]

Once again, the leaders of Providence Farm were whispered to be Communists. The interracial nature of the enterprise made them suspect, not inaccurately, as integrationists. The leaders of Providence Farm called on prominent friends from around the state to write to Holmes County officials on their behalf. They even conferred with county attorney Pat Barrett for advice, either unaware at the time of his role with the Citizens' Council or believing a decade-long relationship would inoculate them. Barrett, however, responded with public criticism of Cox.[25]

Minter, the son of a Presbyterian minister and the brother of two Presbyterian missionaries, was expelled by his church, First Presbyterian Church of Tchula. He had served as a deacon and taught Sunday school there for seven years. The church had previously supported integrating the congregation but, in 1955, they reversed themselves. The church elders issued a statement that they would "pledge ourselves to retain segregation under the guidance of the Holy Spirit and for the Glory of God."[26]

Then, on September 26, 1955, just three days after Emmett Till's murderers were found not guilty a few miles away in Sumner, an alleged interracial flirtation occurred at a school bus stop near Tchula. It became the excuse the Citizens' Council had been seeking to expel the residents of Providence Farm, although the relationship of the matter to Providence Farm was oblique. In the incident, several white children were waiting at the school bus stop when a pickup truck carrying a young man named Curtis Freeman and three other Black children drove by. Freeman called out, "Hey sugar, you look good to me." One of the white children, Mary Ellen Henderson, who lived at Providence Farm, presumed the remark was meant for her and started to cry.[27]

Young Mary Ellen was still crying when she boarded the school bus. The driver reported the incident to Sheriff Byrd, who brought the four young men in for questioning by himself and county attorney Pat Barrett. Most of the questions concerned Providence Farm. The teenagers did not live there, but their families shopped at the cooperative store, and they had spent time on the property. The questions included whether Minter and Cox were registering Black people to vote, encouraging integration, or perhaps allowing interracial swimming.

Sheriff Byrd and Barrett called an emergency community meeting for the following evening at the auditorium in Tchula to discuss what was happening at Providence Farm. They were joined in convening the meeting by outgoing state representative Edwin White and representative elect J. P. Love. White was a virulent white supremacist who was especially focused on the danger of interracial sex and the threat of a single amalgamated mixed race in the South. Love was a member of the Tchula Citizens' Council who had introduced legislation to allow boards of supervisors to fund Citizens' Councils with tax dollars.[28]

The meeting did not go well for Cox and Minter, who were confronted with a hostile audience spewing questions and accusations about their ties to communism and integration, two concepts linked in the minds of the crowd. Three people did stand up for them, if only by leaving because they didn't want to be part of the mob. Samuel J. Foose, a prominent local planter, and Marsh Calloway, a white Presbyterian minister from Durant, spoke out in their favor. (After Brannon Smith praised Calloway in a column for being a "brave man," his congregation asked him to leave.) Love concluded that Cox and Minter were "following the Communist line" and called for a vote from the assemblage, which responded with little dissent by asking them to leave the county, which had been their home for nearly twenty years. Barrett said the move was not personal but an effort to avoid another Till case. Minter and Cox pushed back for a time but were gone before the following summer.[29]

The Citizens' Council was not done with Hazel Brannon Smith. After the sheriff sued her, Brannon Smith heard that her husband, Walter D. Smith, was about to be fired as the administrator of the Holmes County Hospital. Most of the staff signed a petition supporting him, but the hospital board fired him anyway. He went to work at the *Lexington Advertiser*, and Brannon Smith continued to write articles critical of the Citizens' Council and praising Black leadership. Then in 1958, a group of local businessmen launched the *Holmes County Herald*.[30]

William Moses, the titular head of the county Citizens' Council, chaired the meeting; Pat Barrett worked on the charter for the new newspaper; and Wilburn Hooker took on the task of selling stock in the new corporation. All were leaders in the Citizens' Council, and Hooker later served on the executive committee of the State Sovereignty Commission. Armed with their own newspaper, this group went after Brannon Smith's subscribers and advertisers to undermine the economic viability of the *Advertiser*. Sovereignty Commission files soon after declared that she no longer had any paid subscribers.[31] While that was not true, she had neither the subscription base nor advertising base to stay out of debt. An examination of early 1960s issues of the *Lexington Advertiser* found only ads from federal sources—like the National Park Service—and a handful of classified ads. At Christmastime, local businesses bought space, however, to wish readers the joy of the season.

In 1963, Brannon Smith won the Pulitzer Prize for editorial writing, the first woman to do so. One of her prize-winning editorials was entitled "The Free Press and the Citizens Council." She wrote, "The right to dissent from the Councils has already been lost by the average citizen of the state through whole-sale intimidation and fear. . . . Economic boycotts, unbelievable intimidations and inhuman pressures have been the lot of the few who have refused to bow down to the Councils. This has been especially evident in the last four years when the professional and top leadership of the Councils has worked closely with state government."[32] She called on Mississippians to support a free press.

Brannon Smith found support in the Black community in Mississippi, including economic support, but her attitudes held her back from finding common cause with African American leadership. A year after she won the Pulitzer Prize, the *New York Times* reported on a "fete" for Brannon Smith at Saints Junior College, as it was then, which was attended by "some 500 Negroes from this poor 'Black Belt' rural county." The gathering presented Brannon Smith with a check for $2,852.22 to help keep her newspaper alive. "Can you imagine this county without Hazel Brannon Smith and the *Lexington Advertiser*?" asked Arenia Mallory. Mallory recalled Brannon Smith's article on Sheriff Byrd shooting Henry Randle, declaring, "This story reduced her from a woman of almost wealth to a woman who has had to struggle like the rest of us. She defended a little boy who couldn't defend himself."[33]

Brannon Smith was a moderate and a reformer, but she never embraced integration. She had relationships in the African American community, but she also went her own way on a variety of issues. An essay in the Pulitzer Prize archives by Leonard Pitts, an African American and a Pulitzer Prize winner himself, notes the phrase "product of her times" is usually used as an excuse for self-evident prejudice. He concludes, "And yes, we *are* products of our times. But the life and legacy of Hazel Brannon Smith prove this is no excuse for failure to be brave. Because our times are also products of us."[34]

THE BLACK COMMUNITY GATHERS

While the Citizens' Councils were organizing in the 1950s, so was the African American community, although more quietly. A critical player during that decade was the Regional Council of Negro Leadership (RCNL), founded by Theodore Roosevelt Mason (T. R. M.) Howard. Howard was an entrepreneur and the chief surgeon at the hospital built by the International Order of Twelve Knights and Daughters of Tabor in Mound Bayou, which is about seventy miles northwest of Holmes in Bolivar County.

Mound Bayou was a center of activism historically. It was founded as an African American town shortly after the Civil War by Isaiah Montgomery and others from the Black-run Davis Bend plantation. In the late 1940s and 1950s it became a hub of economic activity as Howard started a company to build homes, opened a swimming pool for Black people, and purchased a controlling interest in the Magnolia Mutual Life Insurance Company.[35]

In 1951, Howard proposed the RCNL. His original intent was an economic development organization, parallel to the all-white Delta Council, which would work with that organization. Howard sent out letters inviting Black leaders from an array of sectors to an organizational meeting of the "Delta Council of Negro Leadership." The powerful white Delta Council was having none of it and disavowed any relationship, resulting in replacement of the word "Delta" with "Regional."[36]

The rejection by the Delta Council provided latitude for the Regional Council to become far more political than it might have been otherwise. It had committees on voter registration, separate but equal, and race relations. The leadership included *Jackson Advocate* publisher Percy Greene;[37] future state NAACP president Aaron Henry; Amzie Moore, president of the Cleveland, Mississippi branch of the NAACP; and Arenia Mallory, although she pulled back from the RCNL as it became more confrontational.[38]

Amzie Moore had met with Ella Baker when she was organizing in Mississippi in the 1940s. Baker, Moore, and Henry all emerged as important leaders in the 1950s and 1960s.[39] Baker would convene the conference at Shaw University in 1960 that led to the formation of the Student Nonviolent Coordinating Committee (SNCC), which she continued to mentor. Moore was the seminal source of SNCC's focus on voter registration. He and Henry would provide crucial advice and support to SNCC workers when they came to Mississippi in the 1960s.[40]

Howard hired Medgar Evers in 1952 at the Magnolia Life Insurance Company to go door-to-door throughout the Delta to encourage the purchase of life insurance. In 1955, Evers would become the first NAACP field secretary in Mississippi, a position he would hold until his murder in 1963. Evers used his canvassing for Magnolia as an organizing opportunity, urging Magnolia customers to join the NAACP and to attend RCNL rallies. He also organized the 1952 boycott of gas stations that had no Black restroom, distributing fifty thousand bumper stickers that read, "Don't Buy Gas Where You Can't Use the Rest Room."[41]

Several of those who would soon lead the movement in Holmes County attended meetings of the RCNL and the NAACP in the 1950s. Ralthus Hayes, the farmer who had been featured in the *Advocate* for paying off his FSA loan, was at an RCNL meeting in 1954 headlining Thurgood Marshall, just days before the US Supreme Court decision on the Brown case: "He [Marshall] was there then talking to us, telling all the lawsuits and things the NAACP had been doing and did and what all was going to be did—how all he was going to tell the President and Congress about us. He said he was going to take care of Ole Miss, meaning Mississippi, the state. And he told us about registering to vote." Hayes tried to register at that time without success. "When I went up to try to register, the Circuit Clerk gave me so much trouble with saying the books was closed and all that. But I didn't try to get others to go with me. See, it was different then."[42] Others from Holmes County who became important activists in the 1960s were also part of efforts in the 1950s—the Carnegies, the Mitchells, the Saffolds, Reverend C. L. Clark, and others—attended RCNL or NAACP meetings in the 1950s.

Two leaders with Holmes County connections were victims of violence during the 1950s. Reverend George Lee lived in Belzoni, seventeen miles west of Mileston in Humphreys County, and preached a circuit of Baptist churches, including churches in Tchula and Lexington. Gus Courts was from Pickens, where he farmed when Hazel Brannon Smith profiled him in 1943. A few years later he bought a grocery store in Belzoni. Lee and Courts had organized a Humphreys County branch of the NAACP by 1954, registering ninety-five Black voters there. Most of those registered were fired from their jobs after the list of who had registered was distributed to their white employers. Lee and Courts responded by redoubling their organizing efforts.[43]

Lee received national attention following his participation in the April 1954 Regional Council meeting, which had thirteen thousand in attendance. *Ebony* and *Jet* magazines had also sent a correspondent, who wrote that Lee's "down home dialogue and sense of political timing" had "electrified" the audience.[44] "Unlike his brethren, he preached well beyond the range of the Bible and Heaven and the Glory Road . . . he sermonized about voting and eventually electing a Negro congressman."[45]

On the evening of May 7, 1955, Lee was driving along Church Street in Belzoni when a convertible overtook him and pulled alongside his vehicle. Shots rang out, hitting Lee in the face and shattering his jaw. His car ran into a nearby home, awakening the occupant, who, along with two men who had heard the shots, drove Lee to the county hospital. He died before they arrived. The Humphreys County sheriff pronounced that Lee had died from a concussion due to a traffic accident.[46]

Lee's wife Rose reached out to Black doctors and a local undertaker who was an NAACP member to examine her husband's body. Telephone operators began telling Black customers that no long-distance lines were available, so one group of Lee family friends drove to Jackson to inform the president of the Mississippi NAACP of the murder while another drove to Mound Bayou to confer with T. R. M. Howard. Howard called Michigan Congressman Charles Diggs, who, in turn, contacted the national office of the NAACP and the White House. FBI agents came to Mississippi to investigate. In the end, the sheriff acknowledged Lee had been shot, although he spuriously suggested that Reverend Lee had been a lady's man shot by a romantic rival.[47]

Six months later, Courts was shot at a café in Belzoni. He survived after insisting he be taken sixty miles away to Taborian Hospital rather than to the county hospital.[48] In 1957, Courts moved his family to Chicago, where Howard also moved after threats on his life. In the 1950s, Chicago's Black population grew by 65 percent, with two thousand Black people a week moving there, many arriving on the Illinois Central or coming up Highway 51 from Mississippi.[49]

From its founding, the Sovereignty Commission tried to track NAACP activity in the state. They used informants, traced car tags at meetings, and followed up on rumors. They missed a lot. In January of 1959, Sovereignty Commission investigator Zack Van Landingham interviewed Holmes County sheriff Andrew P. Smith and Ed White, a prominent member of the Citizens' Council. Both reported there was no NAACP chapter in Holmes County and little racial tension, but "Mr. White stated that he understood that a Negro preacher by the name of Rev. Clark had been preaching for integration and taking up collections for the NAACP. He said he had heard this fact rumored and did not know it for a fact."[50]

Two months later, Van Landingham returned for more interviews and learned there was indeed an NAACP branch in Holmes. His memo named Robert Green, a man named Johnson, and Chester Hayes as part of it.[51] Even three years later, in May of 1962, investigator Tom Scarborough reported to the Sovereignty Commission that Sheriff Smith had reassured him that "no Negroes had paid poll tax for 1961," and that meant no Negroes could vote. "He further stated that racial conditions in Holmes County at this time were, in his thinking, in good condition."[52] That assessment would change in 1963.

THE FIRST FOURTEEN

Nineteen sixty-three was a consequential year for the country, the national civil rights movement, and in Holmes County. Nationally, it was a year of assassinations, church bombings, and mobilization for passage of the Civil Rights Act that would outlaw segregation. Organized efforts to register voters and integrate schools sprang up across Mississippi—in Hattiesburg and McComb in the southern part of the state and in the state capital in Jackson—but the Delta was proving a more difficult organizing target. Then on April 9, 1963, a group of Black people came to the Holmes County courthouse to register to vote. They did so as an organized unit under the watchful eye of the US Department of Justice. As one of the first such organized efforts in the Delta, they became known locally as the First Fourteen.

The First Fourteen were not a sudden spontaneous group. Several had been part of the RCNL meetings years before, and all had been participating in regular training sessions for months. Nearly all were African American farmers, and most were from the Mileston Co-op. At the courthouse, they were greeted by Sheriff Andrew P. Smith and a bevy of deputies. None were allowed to register to vote that day—nor were most able to register for nearly three more years—but the effort launched what became known as the Holmes County Movement. It helped give rise to the Freedom Democratic Party and to efforts to achieve Black voting rights that became a model of strength in the Delta region.

The First Fourteen and other local leaders who emerged in the early 1960s were confrontational. They directly challenged the existing power structure. Jodie Saffold, known as Preacher, owned land near Durant and was interviewed by his grandson, Marques Saffold, on early organizing in Holmes County: "It was the so-called dumb people. Up from the grassroots they call it. But now, the schoolteachers, the educated people, they ain't did a damn thang! The preachers ain't neither. See the table was set. Yeah, and when the table got set with cake and pie, and schoolteachers and everybody come in helping eat it up."[53] Local grassroots organizing became the central hallmark of the civil rights movement in Mississippi.

The Student Nonviolent Coordinating Committee provided training, support, inspiration, and coordination to local leaders. In the summer of 1962, SNCC had launched a voter education and registration project in Greenwood, the county seat of Leflore County, and about twenty-five miles due north from Tchula on Highway 49. Several of the First Fourteen who had been meeting on their own began attending the SNCC meetings in Greenwood on how to prepare people to register to vote.

Rosie Head, who became a core activist, was then a teenager. She was born in Holmes County, but the family lived for a time near Money, where she knew Carolyn Bryant, whose complaint about Emmett Till led to his murder. Head began attending the meetings in Greenwood in 1963. "We would just sit around and talk about the things that was unfair to Black people, like the segregated places. . . . We talked about how we were second-class citizens but we were having to pay taxes like first-class citizens . . . what we had to do to get registered to vote, and that's where the power was, that we could get some of the things we needed if we were first-class citizens, and that's what would make us first-class citizens."[54]

SNCC itself had been born from student sit-ins as college students organized to take direct action: to integrate stores and restaurants across the South, to participate in Freedom Rides to integrate public transportation. In February of 1960, Ella Baker, then the executive director of Martin Luther King's Southern Christian Leadership Conference (SCLC), persuaded King to help fund a student conference. The conference was held at Shaw University in North Carolina and attended by 126 student activists. SNCC was formed at that conference.[55]

Over the next two years, SNCC moved from direct action to a focus on voter registration work, as recommended by Amzie Moore. In Mississippi, SNCC helped found the Council of Federated Organizations, known as COFO, which included the NAACP, SNCC, the Congress of Racial Equality (CORE), and SCLC. SNCC contributed the largest number of staff members to COFO in the early 1960s, beginning with Robert Moses, who was recruited by Ella Baker. Baker suggested Amzie Moore as a key contact for Moses.[56]

Moses, a New York native, had been unaware of the denial of voting rights in Mississippi: "I was taught about the denial of the right to vote behind the Iron Curtain in Europe; I never knew that there was denial of the right to vote behind a Cotton Curtain here in the United States." Moses joined Moore in advocating for a voting rights project during a SNCC conference in Atlanta. Moore and Moses recruited Sam Block, who grew up in Cleveland, Mississippi, mentored by Moore, to run the voter registration project in Greenwood.[57]

John Ball, an organizer from Itta Bena, Mississippi, was assigned to work with the Holmes County group on voter registration training. The registration form included twenty-four questions. The process required answering questions from the county clerk to prove literacy and familiarity with the US Constitution. Any errors on the form—like misspellings—would provide an excuse to disallow registration. Questions were often absurd, like asking how many bubbles were in a bar of soap. People planning to register were also trained to expect physical intimidation as Sheriff Smith's dogs were legendary. T. C. Johnson tells of an earlier effort to register accompanied by Ed McGaw and Lucas Sims: "We were met by some German Shepherds and the sheriff, Andrew P. Smith, and some deputies. This kinda put a little fear in your mind."[58]

People who went to register knew that violence against them was an ever-present possibility. The memory of the shootings in Humphreys County was fresh. One of the SNCC organizers in Greenwood, Jimmy Travis, survived being shot in February of 1963. In the winter of 1962–1963, the Leflore County Board of Supervisors cut off the federal surplus commodities program, which thousands depended on for food, in retaliation for voter registration efforts in what became known as the Greenwood Food Blockade.

The denial of food was not a new phenomenon—some contracts with share-croppers during Reconstruction had limited planting to cotton, and food short-ages were common in the Great Depression. Most sharecroppers still bought groceries and household goods from plantation commissaries, putting what cash they had back in the plantation owner's pockets. Indeed, the blockade may have been inspired by the wholesale grocer who supplied most of the plantation commissaries. The Lewis Grocer Company, the largest grocery wholesaler in the state, was founded in Lexington after the Lewis-Herrman Company merged with the Barrett Grocery and the Gwin Grocer Company in the 1920s. Just days before the Greenwood Food Blockade, Morris Lewis Jr., owner of the Lewis Grocer Company by the early 1960s, wrote to his four hundred retail store customers complaining about the commodities program. The distribution of surplus food, he wrote, requires "the Federal Government to enter the food business in competition with tax paying food retailers and wholesalers in the state."[59]

The blockade was certainly designed to weaponize food. In this case, however, the denial of food backfired. SNCC organized across the country for one hundred thousand pounds of food to be delivered to the Delta after the Greenwood Food Blockade cut off access to commodities.[60] As Bob Moses wrote, "Blacks saw what hadn't been clear to them before: a connection between political participation and food on their table."[61] The power in political participation connected directly to the most basic level of self-sufficiency and independence.[62]

SNCC organizer John Ball met regularly with the Holmes County activists at New Jerusalem Church of God in Christ in Mileston. Another SNCC organizer, Hollis Watkins, who was born and raised in Mississippi, wrote that the lifestyle and spirit of the farmers was central to their effectiveness: "The lifestyle of farming made the notion of sacrifice relatively easy because sharing what one has with one's neighbor was not a new concept to farmers." They were used to pooling their resources as a collective. They drew an analogy to pooling resources to repair a church building and now pooled resources "to make sure that we get our freedom, get our rights, and we have to make the same kind of sacrifice. . . . They dug deep and came up with it. These people understood the importance of being sovereign."[63]

The day after the first group showed up at the courthouse to register, the *Holmes County Herald* listed the names and printed pictures of fourteen of them: Alma Mitchell Carnegie; Charlie Carnegie; Norman Clark and his wife, Rosebud Clark; Chester Hayes; Ralthus Hayes; Jack Louie; Annie Bell Mitchell and her brother Ozell Mitchell, who was a deacon of New Jerusalem church; Sam Redmond; Reverend Jesse James Russell; Reverend Nelson Trent; Hartman Turnbow; and John Daniel Wesley.[64] Some who were there counted twenty-one volunteers on the first day. Other volunteers came on subsequent days, and a few stayed home to take care of farm responsibilities if the others were arrested. Shadrach Davis, president of the Mileston Co-op in the early 1960s, and Hayes generally planted their crops together. Hayes asked Davis to stay home in case they needed someone to bond them out or to carry on the farmwork.[65]

Sherriff Andrew Smith was waiting on the courthouse steps with thirty men he had deputized that morning to assist him. Smith had heard about the registration effort from the Justice Department, which had naively thought that Mississippi law enforcement might offer protection. The sheriff and his deputies were an intimidating sight. Reverend Russell described the scene years later:

> The high Sheriff, deputies, and many other plain-clothed policemen was on duty. They challenged us. We told them we wanted to redishter. They said, for what? We said, to vote, and they was sounding off, talking and hollerin'. But we didn't get excited because we had men from Justice in Washington sittin' right there in front of the courthouse taking pictures, asking questions to see if anything had happened where they could report it back to Washington.
>
> In two days three of us got in: Mr. John Daniel Wesley, Mr. Turnbow second, and I was third. Well, that was unfair because you know what time the courthouse open in the mornin'. And we would stay there until it close in the evenin'.[66]

Reverend Russell returned five times, but neither his registration nor any of the others' was accepted by the county clerk, who said their forms contained errors.

About two weeks later, Hartman Turnbow's house was firebombed. Turnbow had been especially outspoken at the courthouse. The group had not chosen leaders, but Turnbow volunteered to be among the first. He spoke directly to the sheriff. Rosie Head describes Turnbow as "fearless" and said that "he would get people all stirred up and they would be ready to go."[67] Turnbow speculated later that the sheriff had asked who would be first to identify a leader and that having spoken up he was perceived as having a leadership role.[68] The

Sovereignty Commission files confirm that Turnbow was perceived as leader of the group, along with Sam Block from SNCC.

In fact, SNCC organizing was more communal than hierarchical, both as a culture and as a matter of strategy. Hollis Watkins gives an example from his own history when he was part of a group arrested in Greenwood for escorting people to register to vote: "We were housed on the county farm, and the jailer came to the door and said, 'I need to talk to the leader of the group.' A couple of us simply replied, which one? And, he said, 'I want to talk to the leader. Whoever the leader of the group is, that's who I want to talk to.' So, then we replied, 'All of us are the leaders of the group. So you choose which one you want to talk to.'"[69]

Turnbow's house was easy to find as it was right on Highway 49. Night riders threw firebombs and fired into the house where Turnbow, his wife, and young daughter were sleeping. Turnbow grabbed his .22 caliber rifle and shot back. In the morning, Sheriff Smith, whom some believe was one of the night riders, arrived and arrested Turnbow for arson in his own home. He also arrested Bob Moses, who was there taking pictures of the damage. The sheriff had ordered Moses to stop taking pictures and when, instead, he took the sheriff's picture, Smith arrested him for interfering with the investigation.[70]

The arrests around voter registration in Holmes and Leflore Counties brought John Doar from the Justice Department's Civil Rights Division to Mississippi. Doar managed the cases from that point. Turnbow was concerned about a murder charge as he believed he may have hit one of the night riders. Turnbow had been convicted of manslaughter in the death of his first wife in 1951. A Holmes County grand jury was convened but voted not to indict Turnbow on the arson charge, and no other charges were brought against him.

SNCC was committed to nonviolence, but many of those it organized were equally committed to self-defense. Rural people in Mississippi—Black and white—are gun owners. As Turnbow explained to SNCC organizers the morning after the firebombing, "I wasn't being non-nonviolent; I was just protecting my family." After a second attack on his home a year later, Turnbow recalled FBI agents who interviewed him imploring him, "Don't kill nobody." Turnbow responded that agents better keep anyone from attacking his home again because otherwise, "it's gonna be some trouble, 'cause I'm gonna git my gun and get busy and see who I can shoot."[71]

No one was shot at that point in Holmes County, but in June of 1963, a member of the Greenwood Ku Klux Klan and Citizens' Council assassinated Medgar Evers in front of the Evers family home in Jackson. The assassination of Medgar Evers drew a single paragraph in the *Herald*: "With reference to the murder of Medgar Evers, NAACP Field Secretary, the situation to say the least is a deplorable one. That any one person, of any race, would be presumptious

[sic] enough and downright fool enough to risk bringing chaos that this affair could cause to a whole State or a whole country, is unthinkable. What a mess!"[72] The Citizens' Council paid for the assassin's defense.

In contrast, the editorial on the murder of Medgar Evers in the *Lexington Advertiser* read in part, "It is imperative that each of us examine our own heart and conscience and determine what part we have played, either in things done or left undone, in acts of commission or omission, in creating a society which permits a man to be murdered because of his desire to be free and equal under the law—a man who fought Hitlerism in Germany for all our freedom."[73]

Nineteen sixty-three continued as a consequential year. In August, 250,000 people from across the United States marched on Washington, DC, calling for equal rights and urging Congress to pass the Civil Rights Act. In November, four little girls attending Sunday school were murdered in Birmingham. In Holmes County, Reverend Russell's church was burned to the ground. At the end of November, President Kennedy was assassinated.

As 1963 ended, almost no Black people had been allowed to register to vote in Holmes County. Statewide, only about twelve thousand African Americans were registered, with about ten individuals in Holmes County. It was increasingly clear that political enfranchisement would require federal action as well as local organizing.

THE FREEDOM VOTE AND FREEDOM SUMMER

The SNCC and COFO goal at the close of 1963 became demonstrating to the nation that Black Mississippians wanted to register to vote and to engage in the political process. Some whites in Mississippi—and some members of the national press—thought registration was slow because Black Mississippians did not care about it. To demonstrate the breadth of desire for political empowerment, civil rights organizers built a parallel political structure in which Black people could participate freely.

SNCC and COFO held a Freedom Vote in the fall of 1963. An October COFO convention chose candidates, after which an unofficial ticket ran a three-week campaign for public office. Mississippi NAACP president Aaron Henry was the candidate for governor, and Edwin King, the white chaplain at Tougaloo College, was the candidate for lieutenant governor. Balloting was at churches and Black-owned businesses over a two-day period. The intensity of the effort required outside volunteers to help inform and mobilize voters, especially as the effort was unusual—the vote did not count electorally—but anyone, Black or white, could participate in it.[74]

Over 83,000 Black Mississippians cast a ballot in the Freedom Vote, a remarkable showing given both the nature of the vote and the short timeline of the campaign. In Holmes County, 993 people participated in the Freedom Vote, at a time when closer to a dozen had been allowed to register for the regular election.[75]

Following the Freedom Vote, SNCC and COFO established the Mississippi Freedom Democratic Party, an ongoing effort in which all Mississippians could participate. The FDP would elect delegates to send to the Democratic National Convention in the summer of 1964. The success of the Freedom Vote also raised discussion of a summer project that would recruit volunteers from around the country to consolidate and further build the statewide organization launched through the Freedom Vote. The summer project became Freedom Summer.

Many of the SNCC staff were uncomfortable with the idea of Freedom Summer. They felt that the process of building local organizations could be disrupted by an influx of outsiders, especially outside white people. White students from elite universities would make local leaders with less education and less money feel embarrassed, some argued. "I came into SNCC and saw Negroes running the movement and I felt good," said one SNCC staffer, "and then the whites take over leadership. We're losing the one thing where the Negro can stand first." One argument for the summer project was that white America was ignoring the brutalization of Black people in Mississippi but would respond to violence against a white college student or, alternatively, the presence of such white college students would bring protection from violence.[76]

An estimated 650 volunteers participated in Freedom Summer. Some stayed just a few weeks. Others stayed for the whole summer, and a handful remained in Mississippi after the summer was over. Approximately 35 summer project workers were based in Holmes County. They taught in Freedom Schools for school-aged students, helped plan and build a Holmes County Community Center, and continued efforts to register Black citizens in the county to vote.[77]

Volunteers received thorough training before they arrived. They were taught how to protect themselves physically and to respect local leadership. Volunteers watched a film showing both an eccentric African American activist from the Delta and a stereotypical angry white circuit clerk hostile to Black registration. At least one group giggled nervously at the personalities and were chastised by a SNCC organizer for their laughter. The gap between the dedicated mostly Black staff who had been organizing in Mississippi for months and the often-privileged white students who came for the summer never fully closed. Many of the students said afterward that the experience contributed more to them than they contributed to it.[78]

In Holmes County, the Black community welcomed the volunteers into their homes. Volunteers stayed with the local activists and in an abandoned farmhouse in Mileston. Reverend Russell told *Bloodlines* that the volunteers did not have too much trouble adjusting "because we tol' them the role of Mississippi 'n' what they would run into when we went up there. A bus load of us went up [to the training in Oxford, Ohio] for about a week. And we tol' them what would happen when they be here and they were willin' to come. Because we told 'em that's a Black community, Mileston, down there that over 200 families just owning their own land. And we controls that. Black folks!"[79]

Summer volunteer Susan Nichols Roughton came from a rural background and asked to go to Holmes County, "not knowing the history but recognizing and appreciating a farming way of life." Her praise for the Mileston community mirrors Hollis Watkins's observation about farmers. Roughton said, "Farming your own land or working for another African American landowner contributed to the independence and strength I saw. The co-op and small farming in general promotes people working together creating the sense of community and personal efficacy that contributed to the high level of Movement activity in Holmes County."[80]

The Holmes County volunteers included several who became lifelong advocates, organizers, and civil rights activists. Stephen Bingham, a student at Yale University, originally came to Mississippi to help with the Freedom Vote and then helped recruit other volunteers for the summer. Bingham's grandfather had been a United States senator from Connecticut. The family was "absolutely quintessential old money WASP from New England. My direct ancestors came over on the Mayflower, and so, obviously, in my past, there are people who had slaves." Freedom Summer, he recalled, "changed our lives. . . . The peculiar institution of slavery created a people whose peculiar historical experience needed more attention than anything else. And that played out in my life," Bingham said in a 2019 interview. Bingham later became a civil rights attorney in California. "It was an amazing community experience of people in Mileston. And I just always remember that community as very special . . . we all got a whole lot more out of it than we put into it."[81]

Mario Savio and Marshall Ganz roomed together that summer at the abandoned farmhouse in Mileston. Savio, originally from New York, returned in the fall to the University of California, Berkeley, where he became the leader of the Berkeley Free Speech Movement. Its "sit-ins" became a model for campus protests later in the 1960s. He explained the origin of the protests: "I spent the summer in Mississippi. I witnessed tyranny. I saw groups of men in the minority working their wills over the majority. Then I came back here and found the university preventing us from collecting money for use there and even stopping us from getting people to go to Mississippi to help."[82]

Marshall Ganz, originally from California, left Harvard College to join the summer project and stayed until the fall of 1965 as a member of the SNCC staff. He then joined Cesar Chavez's effort to organize farmworkers in California's Central Valley. He returned to Harvard College twenty-eight years later and stayed to complete a PhD. He remains a senior lecturer at Harvard in leadership, organizing, and civil society and was instrumental in developing the grassroots organizing strategy for the 2008 Obama presidential campaign.[83]

Bingham, Savio, and Ganz were at least initially assigned to voter registration activity that included door-to-door canvassing and locally organized marches. As Bingham describes the canvassing script and the process, he introduced himself informally but was always addressed by those he was canvassing as "suh." He observed "the immediate fear that was apparent the minute I mentioned voting" and how in some towns "the sheriff, his deputies, or just carloads of whites, would constantly drive by the Negro homes where we were conversing." Bingham was beaten up by just such a carload of whites in Durant.

The summer project volunteers also participated in marches and mass meetings. Reverend Russell describes a march in Lexington during Freedom Summer: "There was 550 people, and you know by that, we were well organized. . . . We marched three hours around the courthouse, sang, prayed, then talked to the town. . . . White and Black together but it wasn't local whites. Those from up North—Chicago, Detroit, Ohio, and everywhere. They came in to help us. We all held hands together and marched around. . . . Following the march, we got more people to participate that was afraid . . . so the march was a success."[84]

As the summer continued, registration focused increasingly on "Freedom Registration," participation in precinct caucuses organized by the Freedom Democratic Party in anticipation of a challenge at the Democratic National Convention in Atlantic City. Statewide, volunteers had brought more than 17,000 people to officially register to vote but only 1,600—fewer than 1 in 10— had been allowed to do so. Only registered voters could participate in official caucuses to choose convention delegates. The Freedom Registration required a simple sign-up. Freedom Democratic Party precinct caucuses fed into county and congressional caucuses and, ultimately, a statewide convention in Jackson to select Mississippi Freedom Democratic Party delegates to the Democratic National Convention in Atlantic City.[85]

In Holmes County, volunteers who were not engaged with voter registration helped at the community center in Mileston, located across the road from the house where several volunteers were staying. Others taught at one of the three Freedom Schools in Holmes County: at Mileston, Mount Olive, and Pilgrim's Rest. One hundred and five students were in attendance by midsummer.

Freedom Schools had been the idea of SNCC staffer Charles Cobb. Staughton Lynd, a historian at Spelman College and, later, at Yale University, ran the program. A COFO background memo on the Freedom Schools noted that Mississippi still spent four times as much teaching white children as Black children and that the curriculum for Black children was limited and restrained discussion of controversial topics. The core curriculum of Freedom Schools was Negro history and citizenship in the mornings with special classes (with French and typing as examples) and special projects (like student newspapers) in the afternoon. Evening classes were held for adults and working teenagers.[86]

It was not long into Freedom Summer—on June 21—that three COFO workers—James Chaney, Andrew Goodman, and Mickey Schwerner—went missing in Philadelphia about fifty miles east of Holmes County. Everyone in the civil rights movement presumed right away that they had been killed. They had been, although the bodies were not found for forty-four days. During the six weeks the bodies of the three civil rights workers were missing, the national media followed the story and the reports of violence in Mississippi. That coverage, which I followed as a child in New York City, was my introduction to Mississippi and to its civil rights movement.

On August 4, the bodies were found buried in an earthen dam. The condition of the bodies after they were buried by a bulldozer and controversies surrounding the autopsy have left multiple interpretations of exactly what occurred. One comparatively recent analysis concludes that Schwerner and Goodman died after each was shot once through the heart. Chaney, who was Black, was severely beaten and shot three times. Schwerner and Chaney worked for the Congress of Racial Equality, part of COFO. Goodman was a summer project volunteer with CORE who had been in the state only a few days before he was killed.[87]

The Mississippi Freedom Democratic Party convention was held in Jackson two days after the bodies of the three murdered civil rights workers were found. Twenty-five hundred activists from around the state attended, including a delegation from Holmes County. The convention selected sixty-eight delegates to send to Atlantic City, with Hartman Turnbow representing Holmes County.[88]

The "regular" Democratic Party delegates from Holmes County were Ed White and Wilburn Hooker, who had been leaders in the efforts to shut down Providence Farm and the *Lexington Advertiser*. Hooker was also a member of the Mississippi State Sovereignty Commission and, for a time, state director of the Citizens' Council. He was one of the "hardliners" on the Sovereignty Commission and "one of the most vigorous sponsors of segregationist bills on the House floor during the 1960 legislative session." He was the grandson of Henry Smart Hooker, who had been one of Holmes County's delegates to the 1890 convention.[89]

The "regular" Democrats, including Hooker, had passed a resolution before the convention that read in part, "We opposed, condemn and deplore the Civil

Rights Act of 1964. . . . We believe in separation of the races in all phases of our society. It is our belief that the separation of the races is necessary for the peace and tranquility of all the people of Mississippi and the continuing good relationship which has existed over the years."[90]

The Democratic National Convention was called to order on August 24, eighteen days after the state convention and just three weeks after the bodies of Chaney, Goodman, and Schwerner were discovered. The seating of the Mississippi delegations was referred to the Credentials Committee, which televised their hearings. At the hearings, Fannie Lou Hamer, from Sunflower County, told of her life as a sharecropper; her efforts to register to vote for which she was kicked off the plantation where she lived and evicted from her home; and how she was jailed, beaten, and brutalized as punishment for her activism. Hartman Turnbow told the story of the First Fourteen and the firebombing of his home in Mileston.

Southern delegations—each virtually all white—said they would walk out if the Mississippi Freedom Party delegation was seated. President Lyndon Johnson was worried that he might need a "solid South" to win in November. Democratic leaders offered FDP delegates a compromise of two at-large seats, which were fundamentally guest passes as they did not carry a vote. The FDP delegation turned down the compromise.[91]

The experience was radicalizing for many in SNCC. They had hoped their alliances with liberal Democrats in Congress would aid their efforts in Mississippi. After a summer in which they felt unprotected by the federal government, the compromise offer from their perspective meant no voice and no power. It signaled to them that the Black community was still on its own.

CHANGE OF SEASONS

Back in Holmes County in the fall of 1964, all but five of the summer project volunteers and staff left, mostly to return to college. The efforts of the summer project—opening a community center and expanding voter registration—continued, with organizational progress on voter registration but without much success on increasing the number of Black people registered to vote, which would not happen before additional federal action. The Freedom Schools closed temporarily, but new and renewed education initiatives began. Mississippi had made little progress integrating schools—or improving education for African American children—and the state still spent less than any other on its public schools. The Holmes County activists focused increasingly on education, expanding access to preschool, and working closely with attorneys on efforts to implement school desegregation.

The structure of the civil rights movement had changed. SNCC was undergoing internal debate on its next strategic steps. From one perspective, 1964 had been a success for the organization—it had catapulted a youth-led effort to the forefront of the civil rights movement and along with it an emphasis on local leadership and organizing. The Voting Rights Act would soon be under debate in Congress, and the SNCC-centered events of 1964 are widely acknowledged as responsible for the act's passage in the middle of the following year.[92]

Still, despite organizational progress, the people at the core of SNCC were exhausted and demoralized by the events of 1964. They had witnessed more violence, including the murders of colleagues whom virtually all of them knew. The culmination of the summer at the Democratic National Convention in Atlantic City, and the weak compromise proposal, deepened doubts in SNCC about how much progress could be made from within the political system. They had obeyed the law, practiced nonviolence, communicated with federal law enforcement, the media, and federal officials. They had not achieved political success within that system. The violence had continued, and most Black people in Mississippi who went to register to vote were not being allowed to do so. They had learned they could not rely on their liberal allies around the country, whose allegiance now seemed divided at best between the civil rights movement and the Democratic Party. Key individuals—from SNCC and from CORE—left at the end of 1964.[93]

SNCC did not pull out of organizing in Mississippi, but it did broaden its agenda. It launched a new project in Alabama, and it moved in a more national direction to put pressure on Congress to pass the Voting Rights Act. SNCC was struggling to raise money as many of its traditional liberal donors had moved on. A more national focus helped fundraising. Still, SNCC launched a project in both Mississippi and Alabama in the fall of 1964 to encourage African American farmers to participate in Agriculture Stabilization and Conservation Service elections.

The ASCS had been formed during the Roosevelt administration as a replacement for the AAA. It was, however, another example of a federal program that wittingly or not discriminated against African American farmers. The ASCS played a key role in who received federal loans and in how much cotton they could grow. All representatives to the ASCS were white at that time and favored white farmers on loans and allotments. Participation in an ASCS election did not require the farmer to be registered to vote, only that they be a farmer, including farm owner, tenant farmer, or sharecropper. The ASCS, however, was not in the habit of informing Black farmers of the elections nor explaining the relatively complex process of voting in them. The process began with community-level elections. Then community representatives voted to select the county level board. SNCC launched a program to gain representation on the ASCS boards in twelve majority Black counties, including Holmes.[94]

Unsurprisingly, there were apparent election shenanigans. In Holmes County, the African American candidates received fewer votes than there were Black farmers who participated. Holmes did manage to elect one Black person at the community level—one of five counties that succeeded in doing so that year—but no Black farmers were elected on the county level in 1964.[95]

Overlapping with the ASCS elections, SNCC challenged the Mississippi congressional delegation, arguing that the members had been elected illegally since Black people had been barred from participation in the election. Strategically, the congressional challenge would help bring the Mississippi fight—and SNCC—to Washington. It began with another Freedom Vote that would elect FDP members of Congress in three of the five Mississippi congressional districts who would challenge the regular delegation. Fannie Lou Hamer was the candidate from the Second Congressional District, which included Holmes County. She received 33,009 votes to 59 votes for incumbent congressman Jamie Whitten. In Holmes County, 2,598 people participated in the congressional challenge.[96]

The broader civil rights community supported the challenge but with misgivings. They agreed that the regular delegation had been elected illegally, but the election of the three FDP members did not follow all legal guidelines either. SNCC modified the challenge to oppose seating the regular delegation until fair and inclusive elections could be held. One hundred forty-nine members of Congress, including members from both parties, voted not to seat the regular delegation as busloads of Mississippians—with a full bus of one hundred Holmes County activists—watched on the Capitol grounds.[97]

The strong showing gave the challengers the right to pursue their case. With the help of 150 lawyers from the National Lawyers Guild, white officials in Mississippi were deposed, including Governor Ross Barnett, who declared that "he did not know of a single negro who had been discriminated against." The congressional challenge effort collected six hundred depositions in three thousand pages of testimony. The challenge did not prevail, but it shook up the Mississippi establishment to see the level of support for the challenge in Congress.

President Johnson was personally angered by the congressional challenge, which came on the eve of his addressing the nation to announce his War on Poverty. Johnson's anger gave permission to moderate voices within the civil rights movement to split from SNCC. National NAACP president Roy Wilkins, who had long felt SNCC was too radical and disruptive to institutional relationships, joined the chorus. He claimed Chinese communist elements had infiltrated SNCC. His remarks divided the state NAACP and contributed to the collapse of the COFO coalition, accelerating the departure of key organizers from Mississippi. COFO would disband in the summer of 1965.[98]

During COFO's final days, Ed Brown became the Holmes County project director. Brown, originally from Baton Rouge, had been expelled from Southern University in Louisiana for civil rights activity and had transferred to Howard University in Washington, DC, where he became active in the Nonviolent Action Group (NAG), a SNCC affiliate. He had come to Mississippi for Freedom Summer and stayed first as SNCC and COFO staff and then with the FDP. He remained in Mississippi even after SNCC moved away from organizing and became a founder of Mississippi Action for Community Education (MACE), which worked on community-based enterprises.[99] MACE is still an active organization today, best known as the sponsor of the annual Mississippi Delta Blues and Heritage Festival.

The core of the movement remained the local people. The Holmes County group continued on its own. An independent volunteer, Sue Lorenzi, wrote later, "Philosophically and politically, each of us was developing a consciousness and growing understanding of the distinct roles of outside workers and local people. The Holmes County movement people had already organized themselves and knew their own needs, desires, and direction. . . . The drive and force of the local movement was the most exciting and tantalizing aspect of our independent stance in Holmes. We worked directly and only for them."[100]

The Holmes County activists continued to push forward. Building a new community center across from the New Jerusalem Church had begun over the summer in a soybean field owned by Mileston farmer Dave Howard. Volunteers completed it at the end of 1964. Sue Lorenzi and her husband Henry lived in the community center and staffed it, working full-time for the Holmes County movement.[101]

A makeshift kindergarten, initially unfunded, opened in the community center that fall. Children who had not had any access to preschool were provided hot meals and taught their letters, numbers, personal hygiene, and group songs and dances. Teachers were struck by the depth of poverty of some children who still lived on white-owned plantations. The children came to school hungry and often unkempt. Treasured toys were a tin box with rocks that made noise when you shook it. Rosie Head tells of one little boy who cried not wanting to come on the first day, but they came and picked him up anyway. Then when he went back home, he told his grandma, "That's the best school in the world! Because they will feed you three meals every day you go to school, and then they'll let you lay down and go to sleep, and still bring you back home!"[102] The Mileston Community Center Kindergarten operated for six months without outside funding, relying entirely on the local Black community.[103]

Soon Head Start came to Holmes County. As part of President Johnson's War on Poverty, the new Office of Economic Opportunity (OEO) funded Head Start programs around the country, with $1.5 million allocated to Mississippi for an initial seven-week program through the Child Development Group of Mississippi (CDGM). It was the largest initial award in the Head Start program.[104]

The head of the CDGM was Tom Levin, who first came to Mississippi as a Freedom Summer volunteer. He advocated for Head Start with SNCC. He argued that the preschools could become community centers that would be central to organizing efforts. SNCC at that point was suspicious of federal government programs, believing they were veiled efforts to curtail or control the civil rights movement. They remained officially neutral on Head Start. The local Holmes movement, however, fully embraced Head Start and its potential for the community as well as its children.

Many of the initial Mileston Community Center volunteers became teachers and teachers' aides at the Head Start centers. Head Start centers included the original Mileston effort plus centers in Tchula, Old Pilgrim's Rest, Sunnymount–Poplar Springs, Second Pilgrim's Rest, Lexington, and Durant. Together, the seven centers served more than a hundred students in Holmes County.[105] Head Start centers fed children two meals a day and readied them for school. They provided professional medical exams for children, many of whom had never seen a doctor before. The centers also provided jobs and expanded outreach as teachers traveled to some of the lowest-income communities—often still on plantation property—to recruit children for the Head Start programs. Head Start employees were paid fifty to sixty dollars a week and teachers were paid seventy-five dollars a week at a time when farm labor paid about fifteen dollars a week.[106]

Community engagement with Head Start was part of the programmatic philosophy at the OEO, which coordinated President Johnson's War on Poverty. At its core was the Community Action Program that sought to develop neighborhood and community-based solutions to problems. Rather than attacking poverty from the top down, or with a "one size fits all" model, the programs called for "maximum feasible participation of the poor in the solutions of their own problems." Levin's proposal to OEO, written with Head Start program analyst Polly Greenberg, purposefully built on the grassroots organizations nurtured by the civil rights movement to maximize local involvement.

Head Start and CDGM aroused the ire of the white power structure in Mississippi, who considered federally funded preschool a waystation to integrated schools. The *Jackson Daily News* called the poverty programs, which included Head Start, "one of the most subtle mediums for instilling the acceptance of racial integration and ultimate mongrelization ever perpetuated in this country." As far as the white establishment was concerned, the federal government was funding the civil rights movement through CDGM.[107] Or, as Shadrach Davis proclaimed, "That thang was brangin' too many poor peoples together. . . . It was the biggest thang going for poor people."[108] The Holmes County program received an award its first summer of operation as the best in the country. Rosie Head, who worked at the Head Start after her time at the Mileston Community Center kindergarten, said:

> It was wonderful! The funding money was enough so that everything you needed to operate was covered. . . . We had been using equipment and stuff that the farmers, the different carpenters, built for us. But we got everything we needed, and it was so beautiful. . . . We had to get [the children] used to coming out and being away from home and familiar people. . . . We had a shower at the center. . . . They had never seen a shower. Some of them had never seen commodes in the bathroom before. They had outside toilets. . . . We would teach them by letting them tell us things about, that they knew, and we would write it down. And then, the next day, we would read it back to them. . . . We taught them how to use a toilet, how to bathe themselves. We taught them how to just share with other children, just everything. . . . And after they had been there for, I'd say, about that first two weeks, it was like they didn't want to go home in the evening time. They were just so proud of being there. And when we had the first little graduation, we were so proud that what they had learned.[109]

Mississippi senator John Stennis believed Head Start and CDGM were too close to the civil rights movement. Stennis was a member of the US Senate Appropriations Committee and chair of the subcommittee through which funds for the war in Vietnam flowed, which meant he had President Johnson's ear. Stennis insisted on an investigation of CDGM. He sent his own staff who engaged with the Mississippi Sovereignty Commission, which placed informers in the CDGM office.

The investigation found administrative problems in the hastily constructed organization. There were questionable expenditures, like paying bail for a handful of activists, and staff had occasionally been reimbursed for minor expenses without complete receipts. But the questionable financial decisions totaled less than $5,000 of the $1.5 million grant. OEO sent auditors to help put in place better procedures, but that did not placate Stennis.[110]

Head Start funding was suspended for six months. Most centers, including those in Holmes County, continued during that period with volunteer staff. Activists also brought seventy-three Head Start students from Mississippi, along with their parents, to a congressional hearing to lobby for funds.

Forty-five of the children were from Holmes County. Head Start continued, but Levin was removed and CDGM received only two more grants. CDGM closed at the end of 1967, and a rival group without the same depth of connection to the civil rights movement became the recipient of Head Start funds.[111]

ALEXANDER V. HOLMES

The suspicion that Holmes County activists were planning to integrate the schools was valid. It had been nearly a decade since the US Supreme Court decision that schools must integrate "with all deliberate speed." But in 1964, fewer than one in five school districts in the South had desegregated. In most cases where school districts allowed Black children to attend historically white schools, the school district followed a "freedom of choice" plan. The district did not refuse the admission of a Black child who applied to attend a previously all-white school, but it did not assign a Black child to that school nor combine Black and white schools. Holmes County had not gotten even that far: In the 1964–65 school year, there were no Black children attending school with white children in Holmes County.[112]

In February of 1965, students at the Lexington and Tchula Black high schools petitioned their school principals to leave the Black schools and attend the white schools in their areas. The principals, who would have lost their jobs, ignored the students.[113] Then, in April, nearly five hundred parents and children signed petitions to enroll the children in previously all-white schools. The petitions were the product of extensive canvassing led by Ralthus Hayes, Norman Clark, Howard Taft Bailey, Earvin Gibson, and others from across the county. The petitions asked Superintendent Lester Thompson to use his influence with the board for their compliance with federal desegregation laws.[114]

The Holmes County Board of Education responded expeditiously to the April petition, taking only five days to turn down the request. The board also leaked the petition signatories to the *Holmes County Herald*, the newspaper started by the Citizens' Council, so that people knew which Black families were seeking to integrate. Superintendent Thompson, to whom the petition was directed, was the brother-in-law of county attorney Pat Barrett Sr., who was a leader of the Lexington Citizens' Council and instrumental in founding the *Herald*.

It was time for the Holmes County parents group to seek legal counsel. Their first stop was a consultation with attorneys Jack Young, Jess Brown, and Carsie Hall, who together were three-fifths of the African American attorneys in the state. Law schools in Mississippi did not admit Black students—nor did many in the South. Jess Brown became an attorney after graduating from Texas Southern University Law School. Both Hall and Young had studied law with

Sidney Redmond and then passed the Mississippi Bar exam. Redmond, the son of a wealthy lawyer and physician in Jackson, was a graduate of Harvard Law School who maintained offices in Jackson and in St. Louis.[115] His grandparents, Charles and Esther Redmond, had been born enslaved in Holmes County, where members of the extended Redmond family live today.[116]

Young, Brown, and Hall conferred with attorney Marian Wright, whom the NAACP Legal Defense Fund had sent to open their Jackson office in 1964, in time for Freedom Summer and shortly after her law school graduation. Wright, a Spelman College and Yale Law School graduate, has written about how much she learned from Young, Brown, and Hall on how to negotiate Mississippi. When Wright took the Mississippi Bar exam in 1965, she became the sixth Black lawyer and only Black woman attorney in the state. Wright was joined in the Jackson LDF office by fellow Yale Law graduate Henry M. Aronson and, that summer, by law student Melvyn Leventhal from the New York University School of Law.[117]

Leventhal lived with Sue and Henry Lorenzi at the Mileston Community Center for a good part of the summer while he did the legal legwork needed to compile a case. Leventhal, who is white, was splattered with invectives from white people he encountered in Holmes County that summer, and later said, "If I had ever studied up on exactly how dangerous it was to try to end segregation in Mississippi, I might not have had the courage to go. I could not have imagined the level of racism down there. My ignorance is what saved me."[118]

Leventhal developed lasting respect and affection for his plaintiffs. Ralthus Hayes, he notes, was "a special person," pointing to how Hayes had put up his land to secure release of civil rights workers in jail. Leventhal also tells the story of being stuck on a very dark night on a side road with no headlights. Someone saw him and called Shadrach Davis, "a man of quiet but determined bearing," who showed up in the middle of the night and pulled Leventhal's car into town.[119] Leventhal returned to Mississippi after that summer, first as an intern and then as a staff attorney after he finished law school. He then served as lead counsel at the Legal Defense Fund's Jackson office until 1974.

The first Holmes County lawsuit was heard in mid-July of 1965 in US District Court in Jackson by Judge Harold Cox. Cox's segregationist views are legendary, but prior rulings apparently left him little choice: He ruled for the plaintiffs and ordered the Holmes County School Board to present a desegregation plan in thirty days. The county reluctantly responded with the minimum plan likely to satisfy the court: "Freedom of Choice" for the first four grades. That fall, 189 Black children enrolled in white schools in Holmes County.[120] They represented nearly 20 percent of the roughly 1,000 Black students in white schools in Mississippi that year, further testament to the success of the Holmes County movement.[121]

The *Holmes County Herald* editorialized that the county had fine schools for both Negro and white children and that the teachers in both schools are "a very special segment of society." While standing up for the schools and teachers, the paper slammed the parents who had brought the suit by saying, "We think those who would label our Negro schools as inferior are those who are themselves inferior in their way of life and in their standards of behavior," calling on them to "seek education rather than integration."[122]

In Durant, flyers were posted all over town listing the names of parents who were enrolling their children in the white school. On the day one child enrolled, her mother lost her job and the local bank called in her loan. The mother was jailed for not paying her debt to the bank until the Legal Defense Fund got the charges dropped. Another parent, Robert Cooper Howard, told young interviewers from the Rural Organizing Committee years later: "It was kind of rough; it was kinda dangerous, but after I made up my mind, I just went 'head on and did it. I had a hard shell. I was harassed; some of everythan' happened. They burned crosses; they put out leaflets tellin' me what I bet' do, not do. My house was shot into. My wife was shot in the right leg. They did everythan' for me to take those children out of school, but I did not. After they went that year, all the whites left, left only eighteen li'l Blacks up there. And they stayed there the whole year." Howard showed where the bullet holes were on the side of his house and noted that his eleven children were in the same room as his wife when shots came through the window.[123]

T. C. Johnson placed his youngest son, Leander, in the previously all-white Lexington Elementary School. "They came and told me a group was comin' to see was I being paid by the government. I told 'em I just wanted my child to get a good education so he'd be able to make it through the world." Johnson told of Leander being hit and coming home with a bleeding lip and receiving calls from the school that the child just didn't have the ability and that he should take him out and let him work on the farm. Johnson stopped by the school and "they would have him out in the hall standing up on one leg or something like that." Johnson would try to give him courage: "You'll have to take a few punches. This help you to grow and learn. Now, you get your education, you'll get through the world much better." The next year, Johnson sent his daughter Sylvia as well. Both children would graduate from Lexington Elementary.[124]

A near-contemporaneous academic analysis cites a 1966 poll of Black parents whose children desegregated schools during the period. It reports widespread harassment as 28 percent of African American parents were pressured or fired by their employer and 22 percent lost bank credit. A full 47 percent experienced threatening phone calls or physical intimidation. The percentages may be deflated since the interviewers were likely white. The analysis argues persuasively that resistance was much greater in districts, like Holmes, where there was a Black majority.[125]

While its schools were reluctantly integrating under court orders, Mississippi passed a state law charging tuition of up to $360.75 a year for students whose parents lived out of state, a law that would require tuition of an estimated seven thousand children statewide, 85 percent Black, and an estimated five hundred children in Holmes County who were being raised by someone other than their parents. A *New York Times* story on the impact cited Flora Howard of Holmes County, who was raising five children. The monthly tuition of $25 per child was more than her monthly income. Wright and Aronson went back to court in the case of *Willie Earl Carthan et al. v. Mississippi State Board of Education* to win a permanent injunction against the state charging Mississippi children for public school attendance.[126]

In 1967, the Supreme Court ruled that freedom of choice—by then the integration strategy of nine out of ten southern schools—was insufficient. Instead, school districts needed to replace racially identifiable schools with a unitary system. Holmes County remained resistant. The Holmes County case was combined with that of twenty-nine other districts and filed by the NAACP Legal Defense Fund as *Alexander v. Holmes*. Beatrice Alexander was at the top of the alphabetical list of Holmes County plaintiffs, one of twelve children of Peter and Essie Alexander, and a student at Tchula Attendance Center.[127] After some additional legal and political maneuvering, the Supreme Court issued a unanimous ruling in the case that "the obligation of every school district is to terminate dual school systems at once and to operate now and hereafter only unitary schools." It was no longer legal in Holmes County or elsewhere to operate separate school systems for Black and white children.[128]

The decision was a firm and largely final legal word, but the matter did not end there. One in four white children left the thirty school districts that had been part of the case during the very first year following the decision.[129] White parents in counties like Holmes, with strong African American population majorities, were the most likely to embrace private education rather than send their children to school with Black children. That was especially true in counties that lacked a white leadership infrastructure committed to public schools.[130] In the late 1960s, new private schools—"seg academies"—opened in West, Lexington, and Cruger. By the fall of 1970, 97 percent of the children enrolled in the Holmes County public school districts were African American.

Today, two of the three original academies have closed. Cruger-Tchula Academy closed in 2001 as the Delta population dwindled. East Holmes Academy, in the town of West, closed in 2006 after making national news for refusing to play an opposing sports team because it had a Black player.[131]

In 1983, the United States Supreme Court ruled that schools could not keep their tax-exempt status if they operated "contrary to established public policy." The remaining school, Central Holmes Academy, became Central Holmes Christian School. It has an 87 percent white enrollment after awarding "a limited number of minority scholarships to qualifying applicants."[132] In the 2021–2022 school year, none of the public schools in Holmes County had more than a single-digit percent white enrollment, and several had no white students at all.[133]

FEAR AND POWER

In the mid-1960s, the Holmes County movement had turned its focus to school integration, but the fight for voting rights had not ceased. It had, however, drawn the federal attention required to advance. On August 6, 1965, the Voting Rights Act was signed into law. It suspended poll taxes, abolished literacy tests, provided for federal examiners, and required preclearance of practices in places that were denying access to the ballot based on race. The law accelerated change, but it would take another twenty years before Mississippi would elect its first Black member of Congress since Reconstruction.

In Holmes County, the circuit clerk initially just ignored the new law and proceeded in his customary pattern with the same lengthy registration form and his own often quixotic questions that served to deny voter registration. Only 690 Black people had succeeded in registering in Holmes County by October of 1965—two months after the law had passed. Those who could not read or write were denied the assistance to which they were entitled by law. One man had his registration rejected because he left out the "l" in Holmes. The circuit clerk disqualified a woman on the residency requirement, although she met it.[134]

Ralthus Hayes and others collected affidavits and petitioned the Justice Department for help with the circuit clerk "to show that, even with the 1965 Act, he plans to make it difficult for our Negro citizens to register to vote."[135] Later that month, the Justice Department announced that it was sending additional federal examiners to counties in the South, including Holmes County, given the continued use of literacy tests there. The US attorney general explained, "Negroes have been required to complete the application form unaided and were required in addition to prove their literacy by reading the oath aloud."[136] By the end of the year, federal examiners registered an additional 2,100 Black citizens in Holmes. By June of 1966, 5,000 had been registered by federal examiners. By 1967, more than 72 percent of Black citizens in Holmes County were registered to vote, far higher than the statewide average.[137] Still, fears about participation lingered and legal barriers to representation remained, including how legislative and congressional lines were drawn to limit majority Black districts.

The Freedom Democratic Party ran candidates in the 1966 federal elections as an organizing effort in preparation for state and local elections in 1967. Ralthus Hayes was the FDP candidate in the Second Congressional District against incumbent Jamie Whitten. In gerrymandering the Second Congressional District out of a Black majority, however, Holmes County had been removed to the Fourth Congressional District. Hayes was still eligible as a candidate, but the district in which he was running no longer included his home county. Hayes garnered 4,590 votes to 39,855 for Whitten. Voter turnout was low in the Democratic primary, drawing support from only about a quarter of the Black voters who had registered.

Fear of electoral participation had been underscored by the shooting of James Meredith. James Meredith, from neighboring Attala County, had been the first Black student admitted to the University of Mississippi in 1962. His admission to the University of Mississippi had turned the campus into a "war zone" with federal troops and tear gas needed to quell rioting.[138]

In 1966, days before the Democratic primary, Meredith began a 220-mile solo March Against Fear, from Memphis to Jackson, to demonstrate to Black Mississippians that they no longer needed to fear voting. But then, on the second day of the march, the day before the primary, Meredith was shot. A white man from Memphis named Aubrey James Norvell hid in the brush along the side of the road and fired three loads of buckshot. The shooting occurred in full view of reporters and law enforcement who were accompanying Meredith in anticipation of an incident. Meredith survived the shooting. What had begun, however, as an individual and perhaps quixotic venture, turned the attention of the civil rights community and the media toward Mississippi once again. Heightened fears of violence were to find further justification a few weeks later in Canton, down the road from Holmes in Madison County.[139]

After Meredith was shot, national civil rights leadership converged at his bedside to discuss continuing the march. The leaders included the Reverend Martin Luther King, Floyd McKissick from CORE, and national leaders of SNCC and the NAACP. Stokely Carmichael had become the chair of SNCC after ousting the less confrontational John Lewis. The NAACP at that point had a contentious relationship with SNCC. The rift had extended to Mississippi, where leadership of the state NAACP and of the Freedom Democratic Party were at odds.[140]

Roy Wilkins of the national NAACP and Whitney Young of the Urban League wanted the march to become a show of support for President Johnson's civil rights legislation. Carmichael aggressively challenged the more moderate leaders with the result that they stormed out, which had apparently been

Carmichael's intention.[141] Those who remained, including Carmichael, King, McKissick, and local leaders like Ralthus Hayes, agreed on a statement of purpose that included enforcement of existing federal laws, and expanding federal examiners to all counties in the Deep South to assist with voter registration.[142] One historian describes the statement: "Strident in tone, the manifesto was nonetheless a realistic assessment of the problems facing African Americans, calling attention to federal foot dragging in dealing with poverty, voting rights, and law enforcement." The national NAACP never signed the document. The state NAACP did, but some of its leadership later recanted.[143]

The march had successes. It engaged over ten thousand people to join parts of the march and registered thousands along the way and at rallies like one in Lexington. The rallying cry of "Black power" at the march was not new to activists but had its first engagement with the national press as part of Carmichael's speech in Greenwood. SNCC staffer Willie Ricks jumped on the stage next to Carmichael and began a call and response: "What do we want?" and a crowd of thousands responded, "Black power." Black power—the economic and political empowerment of Black people—became the rallying cry of the civil rights movement in the late 1960s and beyond. It was not an anti-white cry, but a call for independent rather than codependent power, as Carmichael and others wrote of it.[144]

Holmes County was not on the route of the march. The route was west of Holmes through the Delta to pass through communities that were less organized than Holmes County. But Willie Ricks led a rally in Lexington. He pointed to Sheriff Andrew Smith, the sheriff who had arrested civil rights workers, intimidated prospective registrants, and refused to accept poll taxes from the few who did register to block their capacity to vote. Ricks's example of Black power was that Smith could be replaced and that Black people in Holmes could have their own sheriff.[145]

The March Against Fear turned violent in Canton. As the *New York Times* wrote, "Mississippi highway patrolmen routed 2,500 civil rights demonstrators tonight with a thick fog of tear and irritant gas after the demonstrators had attempted to pitch camping tents on public property. . . . The gas sent men, women and children running and crying from the tents they had been trying to erect for members of the rights march through Mississippi who arrived here today. . . . 61 gun-wielding state troopers moved in with gas masks, grabbed them by the feet and hands and dragged them into the streets." King and McKissick urged the marchers to cover their faces but not to fight back as the troopers continued to hurl gas canisters. One priest from New Jersey who had joined the march said, "It was sick, evil and inhuman. . . . It spoke of the sickness of our society. It made me wonder if democracy in Mississippi, and perhaps in the United States, was dead."[146]

The violence in Canton was national news, but unlike earlier instances of violence, it was also covered in-state: "Clouds of tear gas routed a crowd of Negroes and whites trying to set up the tents of the Mississippi march," wrote the *Clarion-Ledger*. "The charging officers, wearing gas masks and helmets, knocked down one of the big revivalist style tents . . . and began pulling it into a pile." The *Clarion-Ledger* quoted CORE's McKissick saying, "Those bastards never gave any warning. There were women and children in there. It was barbarism that has never been equaled."[147]

Moderate Mississippi recognized and condemned the violence. Some seemed to believe the violence was new and, whether with irony or naiveté, called for patience. "Fear, that state of mind common to all man which Meredith wishes to overcome, now envelopes every section of the state. The only antidote, if there is one, is temperate words and actions from leaders, black and white, and a patience born of time," wrote a columnist in Greenville.[148]

The Holmes County movement shifted as planning for the 1967 elections began. Sue and Henry Lorenzi, who had worked for the movement full-time since the fall of 1964, announced they were transitioning out. SNCC sent a couple of volunteers to Holmes, and the FDP had a full-time organizer there, Edgar Love. Meanwhile, over six thousand African Americans had registered to vote in Holmes County—a sea change from the ten who had been registered by the end of 1963.

A FULL SLATE

The effort for political participation grew additionally in the year after the March Against Fear and the low-turnout 1966 primary. By the middle of 1967, there were organized activists in all five "beats" of the county.[149] The ongoing presence of federal examiners meant people no longer felt their livelihood was at risk if they participated in the political process. Monthly meetings in fifteen different communities in the county drew solid attendance. The African American farmers were still central, but the effort at this point had been joined by more "preachers and teachers." It had grown well beyond, as Jodie Saffold had described the 1963 efforts, "the dumb people" up from the grassroots.[150]

The FDP was able to recruit a full slate of African American candidates for the 1967 elections. There were twelve offices on the ballot needing twenty-two candidates, as some offices were by beat. In the end, twenty-one candidates were recruited for the FDP independent slate. There was no candidate for county attorney against Pat Barrett because there was no Black attorney in Holmes County at that time.

The process of putting together the slate began at monthly meetings in Mileston held between January and June. Candidates included those who had been movement activists since the "First Fourteen"—like T. C. Johnson and Ralthus Hayes as candidates for supervisor in their beats and John D. Wesley for justice of the peace in his beat. Mary Hightower, who had organized in Durant around school desegregation, was the countywide candidate for circuit clerk.

The slate had new faces as well. The candidate for sheriff was Bob Smith, a math teacher from Lexington. Others who had been active longer had contemplated running for sheriff but withdrew their names in favor of Smith, who was well-qualified, handled himself well, and had been brought into the effort by T. C. Johnson.[151] The deadline for filing nominating positions was in June. As the deadline approached, Robert G. Clark decided to run for state representative.

Clark had attended earlier coalition meetings and was recognized as a strong candidate. He was well known in the community with very deep roots in the county. He had been educated there through high school and then at Jackson College for Negro Teachers, now Jackson State University. He obtained his master's degree from Michigan State, as there were no advanced degrees available to African Americans at that time in Mississippi. He taught briefly on Mackinac Island in northern Michigan and then returned to Mississippi. He taught in Humphreys County for a time and then taught and coached in Holmes. In both places his contract was terminated when he challenged the school board. After his Holmes County contract ended, he began an adult education program at Saints College with Arenia Mallory.[152]

Clark's family history in Holmes began before the Civil War. His great-grandfather had been born in Greene County, Alabama, the son of the plantation owner and an enslaved woman named Rachel. After the mistress of the plantation saw the new baby, she sent Rachel, still recovering from the birth, some supper. The next morning, Rachel was dead. She had been poisoned by the mistress's apparent alms. The baby was sold to the Jones family in Holmes County, with the understanding that he would not be a field hand but would be taught a trade. The child, who would be known as Henry Jones, became a blacksmith. With money he earned as a blacksmith, Henry Jones later bought a plantation from the Jones family. The Clark-Jones family still owns that land.[153]

The FDP strategy in 1967 was to skip the Democratic primary and run FDP candidates as independents in the November general election. Asking new voters to participate once instead of twice made sense, and participation in the Democratic primary the year before had been low. Hazel Brannon Smith sideswiped the strategy by deciding to run for state senate in the August primary. She lost that effort in part, perhaps, by losing the support she might have otherwise received from the Black community.

The African American FDP candidates ran as a slate financed by the Holmes County Independent Campaign Fund and also ran individual campaigns. An extant flyer led with the headline "Help Elect a Negro Sheriff" and listed candidates backed jointly by the FDP, the Holmes County NAACP, and the Interdenominational Ministerial Conference. The flyer does not include all the candidates for constable or justice of the peace and does not include Clark, who largely relied on his own material.[154]

Election Day brought considerable confusion and multiple conflicts. Henry Lorenzi reported that about two hundred people showed up at the Lexington FDP office not knowing where or how to vote, although in Durant, local people fielded such questions from a nearby café. A couple of poll watchers were arrested, and there were reports from Tchula of surprising Black support for a white candidate and complaints that an election commissioner refused to allow observers from the FDP slate into the room where votes were counted.[155] Still, Holmes County had higher participation and more success than most counties in that first post–Voting Rights Act state election.[156]

The headline-grabbing result was that on November 7, 1967, Robert G. Clark became the first African American elected to the Mississippi State Legislature since Reconstruction, and the first from Holmes County since Greenbacker Tenant Weatherly had left office in 1881. He defeated J. P. Love, who had earlier won a Democratic primary against Wilburn Hooker. Clark won with 3,528 votes to 3,416 votes for Love, a 51 percent to 49 percent win.[157]

The candidates for supervisor, justice of the peace, and constable fared less well, possibly owing to confusion on who was running in what beat or simply because of less exposure to the candidates. Only one of them won: Griffin McLaurin in Thornton, which included Mileston.

Countywide, there were more votes cast down-ballot—for sheriff, state representative, and circuit clerk—than for governor, and each of those county-wide races was close. All three countywide FDP candidates won in Pickens, Thornton, and Ebenezer, although Clark won by a wider margin in Ebenezer, his hometown. Clark also won in Lexington and Goodman, while the others did not. Clark did not win Durant, but Love's total was lower there than that of other Democratic candidates. Clark's 150-vote margin in Lexington suggests he may have won votes from whites there, or his margin reflected support from Arenia Mallory and the COGIC leadership. Clark had not been part of earlier local confrontations on civil rights, which may have allowed broader comfort with him in Lexington.[158]

Clark became the first African American representative-elect, but he still had to fight for his seat through a series of lawsuits in which Marian Wright and the NAACP Legal Defense Fund represented him. Even after he was finally seated, the leadership of the House refused to recognize him. "I couldn't get the floor of the House. If I would stand for recognition, somebody would make a motion. I'm already standing . . . but he'd recognize somebody else. They cut me out, and I couldn't get the floor. So, one night, this was my first term, I walked out." Clark described how legendary Mississippi correspondent Bill Minor told him he was doing what the white legislators wanted him to do and he walked back in. "And when I walked back in on the floor of the House, man, they was having a hooray! They was wolf-whistling, they was clapping, and they was doing everything! And when I walked back in, they just got as quiet as a mouse."[159]

Clark remained the only African American state legislator in Mississippi until legislative redistricting following the 1970 Census allowed election of three more Black state legislators. Clark was a leader on the Education Reform Act of 1982 under Governor William Winter, which established public kindergarten for the first time in Mississippi.[160]

Education continued as a centerpiece of Black community efforts in Holmes County. In the 1970 elections, Dr. Arenia Mallory became the first African American member of the Holmes County School Board and was joined on the board by Eddie James Carthan in 1973. The school board had an African American majority beginning in 1974, with the addition of William Dean to the five-member board.[161]

Dean had been hired by Arenia Mallory to teach math and science at Saints School beginning in 1961. He met and married another teacher there, Margie McGowan, in 1962, and their wedding was the first held on the Saints School campus. Beginning in 1964, Dean taught college-level night classes at Saints while serving as math and science coordinator and then director of instruction for the Holmes County Public School System. Dean became the superintendent of education for the Holmes County Public School System, the first African American elected superintendent of education in Mississippi since Reconstruction, serving four consecutive terms. In 1986, Dean became the pastor of St. Paul Church of God in Christ—the denomination Mother Church—and was appointed president of Saints School by presiding bishop Louis Henry Ford. After Dean's wife of fifty-two years passed, he married JoeAnn Dean, a native of Lexington and licensed missionary. William Dean is now the jurisdictional bishop of the Northern Mississippi Ecclesiastical Jurisdiction of the COGIC.[162]

Since 1982, most of the countywide elected officials have been African American. Early activists on voter registration and school integration have been elected to leadership positions. Howard Taft Bailey became the first African American member of the board of supervisors in 1975. He had been chair of the FDP from 1966 to 1972 and became an election commissioner in 1968. James Johnson, a farmer and an early activist with SNCC from the Howard Bottom community, was the second supervisor elected, winning election in 1979.[163] The board of supervisors became majority Black after the

1983 election, when Odell Hampton Jr., who had been a student at Fannye Booker's camp school, was elected.[164]

Bailey had been a farmer all his life. He trained at Tuskegee Institute and went on to complete a program in co-op organizing between 1967 and 1972. The Federation of Southern Cooperatives retained him to help organize co-ops in seventeen southern states. At his 1987 retirement dinner, Bailey read a poem entitled "Anyway," a variant of which is attributed to Mother Theresa. It ended with, "Give the world the best you have, and you'll get kicked in the teeth. Give the world the best you've got anyway."[165]

RETENTION

The success in the 1970s and 1980s in electing local African American representatives did not mean the white power structure of Holmes County went away. In Holmes County, the Citizens' Council stayed active until the 1980s, as the Cruger-Tchula-Thornton Citizens' Council was still raising funds at a barbecue supper in 1980.[166] In Mississippi, the State Citizens' Council ran a statewide white voter registration drive in 1971. The council argued that "an energetic white voter registration effort is an absolute necessity if the specter of black dominance is to be halted."[167] Nationally, the Council of Conservative Citizens was founded in 1985 using Citizens' Council membership lists. That group is still an active white supremacist organization today.[168]

Stories of police harassment of Black citizens in Holmes County continued. In 1978, two white officers in Lexington arrested a young woman, Shirley Boyd, and allegedly struck her after she turned down their sexual advances. Police chief Ed Ellison denied that Boyd was beaten or that his officers had sexually harassed her. Boyd, however, was hospitalized after the incident and Ellison privately acknowledged that she had been struck. Others saw photographs showing she had been beaten severely and whipped. The case ended when Shirley Boyd was found hung in her mother's home in 1979, an apparent suicide.[169]

Tales of police harassment and the economic imbalances in Holmes County led to a series of boycotts against local merchants in Lexington. In the latter half of 1978, local citizens' and merchants' groups published dueling letters in the *Lexington Advertiser*. In June, the Concerned Citizens of Holmes County noted that a "visual survey" of stores on the Lexington courthouse square showed some had no Black employees and others had no Black management or cashiers. They demanded action to correct the situation.[170]

The response from the merchants showed little openness to change: The merchants argued that the stores were managed by their owners, who were white, and that one did have a Black cashier. They also noted that Black-owned businesses did not have white managers. The merchants castigated the citizens' group for adding to a perception of racial tensions in Lexington, arguing racial tensions would hold back economic development. The merchants' response was not well received by the citizens' group.[171]

By August, the local group was boycotting white businesses on the square and had added a demand for additional training of the Lexington police in the wake of the controversy over Shirley Boyd's arrest. The merchants denied charges against the police and called on "the better concerned citizens" to ignore the protest. The local group joined the United League of Mississippi, formed that year to fight back against reemerging Ku Klux Klan activity and police brutality. The Holmes County leader of the citizens' group, and later of the United League chapter, was Arnett Lewis. Lewis had been raised in the COGIC and graduated from Saints School in 1966. After a tour of duty in Vietnam with the Marine Corps he returned to Holmes County to organize for change, leading the boycott in the late 1970s and later founding health clinics named for Dr. Arenia Mallory.[172]

There were divisions within the African American political leadership over the boycotts and the style of the protests. On the board of supervisors, Howard Bailey tried to be a modulating influence, while James Johnson stood up for the protestors' right to be heard. State representative Robert Clark suggested the appointment of either a committee with equal representation selected by the protestors and the merchants or an arbitrator selected by the US Civil Rights Commission. Neither of those suggestions were taken. Instead, arrests of protestors continued, and the mayor of Lexington appointed a "bi-racial" committee with the Black representatives chosen from among those who opposed the protests. Throughout the boycott, it seems that whites in Holmes County presumed they held authority or, at best, that whites and Blacks would govern together on equal terms in the majority Black county.[173]

The boycott ended with court injunctions against the protestors. The United League of Holmes County evolved into the Rural Organizing and Cultural Center in the mid-1980s. Leroy Johnson succeeded Lewis as the head of ROCC. In 1989, Johnson was part of the early development of Southern Echo. Hollis Watkins, who had been a SNCC organizer at Mileston, enlisted Johnson and SNCC veteran and attorney Mike Sayer to develop Southern Echo and train young people to continue organizing efforts in African American and low-income communities.[174]

Even winners of electoral battles faced challenges from the status quo; perhaps none more than Eddie James Carthan. In 1977, Carthan, who had served on the Holmes County School Board, was elected mayor of Tchula at age twenty-seven, the town's first Black mayor since Reconstruction. Carthan had been active in the civil rights movement—after being a student at the Mileston

Freedom School in 1964—and was a cousin to Emmett Till, whose mother, Mamie Till Mobley, was born Mamie Elizabeth Carthan.[175] The year Carthan was elected, the town also elected four Black candidates to the five-member town board, three of whom were Carthan supporters. That gave Carthan a working majority on the board. The remaining two board members were John Edgar Hayes, a longtime conservative white board member, and Roosevelt Granderson, who had supported Carthan's white opponent.

At the time of Carthan's election, streets and roads on the side of town where Black people lived were unpaved and Black unemployment was 30 percent. In a town that was 85 percent Black, all city department heads were white. Carthan launched an aggressive program paving streets, employing Black people in city jobs, and directing state and federal money where it was needed most. According to Jessie Banks, then on the board of aldermen and mayor of Tchula in the 1990s, "Eddie did more in one year as far as bringing money to town and opening meetings than the previous administrations did in eight years. He started a day-care center, a housing weatherization program, got a van for senior citizens and talked seriously with several small factories about locating here."[176]

Then Carthan lost a working majority on the board. One of Carthan's supporters, who was employed by a former white county supervisor, resigned from the board and was replaced in a special election by a Black candidate who had opposed Carthan.

Shortly after that, Carthan's troubles began. First, the board replaced the police chief whom Carthan had chosen and named an officer who had helped lock Carthan out of city hall when he was first elected. Carthan, accompanied by a supportive board member, plus Carthan's police chief–designate and a police officer who supported Carthan, accosted the board's choice at the police station and asked him to surrender his gun while the matter was resolved. The discussion became heated, a shot was fired, and there were blows, although no one was seriously injured. A mostly Black jury convicted Carthan and his six followers of assault. A politically connected white judge, Webb Franklin, sentenced each to three years in jail, then suspended the sentences for Carthan's six followers but not for Carthan himself.[177]

Whether Carthan's conviction was legitimately for a felony or not remains in dispute. Simple assault would be a misdemeanor. Assault on a police officer would be a felony. Even a few of the jurors believed they convicted the seven of simple assault since the disputed chief was not sworn in. From the judge's perspective, Carthan was convicted of a felony and forced to resign as mayor as well as serve time in jail. Roosevelt Granderson, a member of the town board and Carthan opponent, became acting mayor.

Next, a bank fraud case against one of Carthan's associates included allegations of bribery and led to state and federal audits of city expenditures, which turned up sloppy bookkeeping, missing funds, and inappropriate expenditures. Carthan acknowledged he allowed associates to take advantage of him and of the city treasury but denied the bribery charge. Still, the matter led to the defeat of his supporters on the town board and the election of a white mayor who had previously run against Carthan.

Then Roosevelt Granderson was murdered. Granderson was taken to the back of the grocery store where he worked and shot twice by two gunmen who also stole from the store. Granderson had been involved with drug dealing with people in St. Louis who had an indirect relationship to Carthan. In a plea bargain to avoid capital punishment, one of the killers said Carthan had paid them to kill Granderson. Except for the plea agreement charge, there was no evidence against Carthan, who was acquitted. Later, his accuser recanted.[178] In 1983, Governor William Winter suspended Carthan's remaining sentence on the assault charge after hearing from jurors who qualified their determination of guilt. A federal judge released Carthan from prison on the fraud charges.

Civil rights and Black leadership nationally and in Mississippi mostly stood by Carthan, although the series of controversies gave Tchula citizens pause and gave local opponents opportunities. Carthan himself acknowledges he trusted people he should not have and made mistakes. Some of his most serious troubles, however, were not of his own making. Travis Clark, attorney to the now deceased John Edgar Hayes, the man who recruited Granderson to the council, is quoted in a *Washington Post* article saying Hayes was fed up with Carthan. "It got to the point Eddie did whatever he wanted to do," and vetoed what Hayes wanted,[179] a comment that suggests Hayes failed to accept that Carthan was mayor and thereby had the power of the veto. Others have quoted an anonymous source saying, "Carthan may have been elected, but he will never run this town."[180]

Carthan was again elected Beat 5 supervisor in 2015. While he was in office—having had his candidacy certified after winning election—the Mississippi state auditor charged his certification was not valid because he had been convicted of a felony and ordered him to vacate the office and repay his salary.[181]

The struggles to elect an African American member of Congress played out at a higher level but took longer. The congressional seat is especially crucial as Holmes County and the Delta rely on the federal efforts toward equity and for basic financial assistance, including agricultural subsidies. For twenty years after passage of the Voting Rights Act, Holmes County was represented by a white conservative member of Congress until successive federal court cases resulted in a congressional district with a Black majority.

The state had reconfigured its congressional districts after passage of the Voting Rights Act to divide the Delta—with its heavily African American majority—into multiple districts so no congressional district had a Black majority. After a successful challenge in federal court, the 1984 lines for the Second Congressional District had a Black majority but not a Black voting age majority. Robert Clark ran for Congress in 1982 and 1984, losing very narrowly to Republican Webb Franklin, the former judge who had sentenced Eddie Carthan to a felony. In 1986, the district had a very narrow Black majority, and Mike Espy, an African American Democrat, defeated Franklin. Mike Espy is the grandson of T. J. Huddleston, the founder of the Afro-American Sons and Daughters fraternal organization, which built the first African American hospital in Mississippi.[182]

When Espy became United States secretary of agriculture in 1993, Hinds County supervisor Bennie G. Thompson, who had been active in the civil rights movement, including in Fannie Lou Hamer's campaign for Congress, became the second Black congressman from Mississippi since Reconstruction. Thompson is the third Black member of Congress popularly elected in the state's two-hundred-year history, during most of which the state had a Black majority.[183] Thompson became chair of the Homeland Security Committee in the US House of Representatives and chair of the US House Select Committee on the January 6 Attack.

Greenwood, MS, 1963. SNCC field secretary Sam Block (figure on phone) in SNCC office as field workers plan voter registration in nearby town of Belzoni. Credit: Matt Herron/Take Stock/TopFoto.

Tougaloo, Jackson, MS, November 24, 1963. Tougaloo College students singing Freedom Songs. Hollis Watkins is on the left. Credit: 1976 Matt Herron/Take Stock/TopFoto.

Mileston, MS, June 1, 19665. Community center construction, Freedom Summer 1964. Meeting of Mileston to plan the center. Robert Head and Ozell Mitchell sit up late to discuss the center. Credit: 1976 Matt Herron/Take Stock/TopFoto.

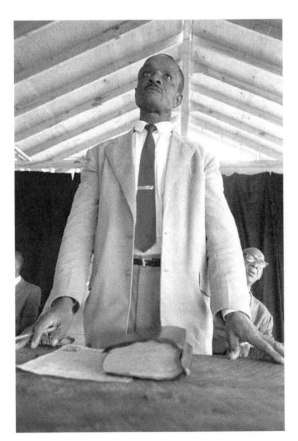

Mileston, MS, June 1, 1964. Community center construction, Freedom Summer, 1964. Mileston Dedication of Community Center. Reverend J. J. Russell giving invocation: This is not the first time the good Lord has sent a Jewish carpenter down to help the poor folks. Credit: 1976 Matt Herron/ Take Stock/TopFoto.

Mileston, MS, 1964. Farmer Hartman Turnbow picking his own cotton field. Credit: Matt Herron/Take Stock/TopFoto.

Mileston, MS, June 1, 1964. Community center construction, Freedom Summer, 1964. Dedication of Community Center. Summer volunteers and locals listening to dedication speeches. Credit: 1976 Matt Herron/Take Stock/TopFoto.

Mileston, MS, August 1, 1964. Freedom School Summer Project, Edie Black, volunteer from Smith College, teaches Freedom School at Mileston. The student in the white shirt sitting next to the Freedom Summer volunteer is Eddie James Carthan, who would become mayor of Tchula. Credit: 1976 Matt Herron/Take Stock/TopFoto.

Lexington, MS, August 15, 1965. Federal Voter Registrars enforce Voting Rights Act of 1965. Black citizens waiting in line at the Holmes County Circuit Clerk's office in Lexington to attempt to register to vote. Credit: 1976 Matt Herron/ Take Stock/TopFoto.

Chapter 5

THE SECOND REDEMPTION— 1960 TO PRESENT

One reason for the soaring output of American agriculture is the increase in farm mechanization. Just as World War I spurred the adoption of the tractor and the combine, World War II, with its demands and labor shortages, led to the widespread adoption of the combined harvester thresher and the cornpicker . . . and acceptance of the cotton picker."

—FORMER CONGRESSMAN JAMIE L. WHITTEN, IN *SO WE MAY LIVE*, 1966, P. 8

It has taken 67 years for the number of minority operated farms to decrease 94 percent and in the recent 5-year agriculture census year the decline is continuing the downward spiral totaling 11.9 percent. Besides the drastic decline in the number of minority operated farms, land loss has been so severe that 50 percent of all minority operated farms are no larger than 49 acres in size. Nearly 68 percent of all minority operated farms have agricultural products with sales valued at less than $10,000.

—FROM 101st CONGRESS HOUSE REPT. 101–984, 1990

PUTTING COTTON FIRST

Back in the nineteenth century, the white leaders who took back power called for "redemption," their counterpart to Reconstruction. At that time, "redemption" meant the elimination of voting rights for Black people and a return to white control. In the last half of the twentieth century and into the twenty-first century, the land in Holmes County changed hands again—as it has elsewhere in Mississippi and, indeed, throughout the rural South. African Americans own less land now than they did a hundred years ago—and even fewer cultivate the land they do own. African Americans regained their right to fully participate in civic life because of the civil rights movement of the 1960s. Immediately following, many lost their land and the economic independence it brought them. The latter half of the twentieth century was, in effect, a second period of redemption, but this time, land and economic vitality rather than political rights were "redeemed."

In 1945 in Holmes County, over 900 African Americans owned farms. The number declined to 780 full or part owners in 1964 and to 562 by 1969. Now there are fewer than 200 African American farmers in Holmes County. The total value of farmland is about the same as it was in 1969, but Black farmers own less of it and white farmers own more.[1]

The federal government bears considerable responsibility for the loss of African American land. Although the federal government largely sided with African American efforts to achieve equality on voting rights and desegregation, it has not sided with African Americans on land ownership. On civil rights, the US Supreme Court sided with the plaintiffs on *Brown v. Board of Education* and on *Alexander v. Holmes*. The US Department of Justice, after prodding, sent federal examiners to help enforce the Voting Rights Act once it was passed by Congress. When it came to land in the rural South, however, the federal government—and particularly the USDA—acted against the interests of African American farmers.

Once again, the profitability of cotton underlies the story. This part of the cotton story begins right after World War II. Cotton was in trouble. First, overproduction during the war meant there were cotton surpluses, just as there had been after World War I. Additionally, synthetic fabrics were grabbing market share. A scientist at DuPont developed nylon in 1939, the first entirely synthetic fabric. With the development of nylon, nylon stockings replaced silk ones. The same research at DuPont led to the development of polyester a few years later. DuPont bought the rights to the new fabric and began producing Dacron. The new fabrics were less expensive than cotton, and so cotton began losing its dominance as a lightweight fabric.[2]

The response to the challenges facing the cotton industry was to make production less costly and more efficient. The industry had formed a National Cotton Council in 1939. The Cotton Council, representatives of the USDA, and other experts held a first meeting at Stoneville, near Greenville, in Washington County, in 1947 to discuss farm mechanization as a way of making cotton more profitable.[3] "The key," as one agricultural historian wrote, "was to substitute capital for labor," and, quoting a member of the National Cotton Council, displaced workers "should not be allowed to stand in the way of progress."[4] At the 1947 Stoneville meeting, cotton planters were urged to enlarge their fields and farms to take advantage of new equipment and techniques. Larger farms would bring efficiencies and economies of scale, and larger fields made for more efficient mechanical picking. The age of mechanization and corporate farming had arrived.

Farmers had used tractors since the 1930s. There were still mule-drawn plows in Holmes County in the 1940s—but far fewer than the five thousand mules counted there in 1930. Tennessean John Rust invented a cotton picker in 1928. John Rust's brother, Mack, had been a trustee of Providence Farm and saw the invention as replacing the need for farmworkers to spend twelve-to-fifteen-hour days in the back-breaking work of picking during harvest season. The Rusts were concerned about the potential for job loss because of their cotton picker and were thoughtful about how the cotton picker might be distributed, including potential leases to sharecroppers.[5] Then International Harvester developed a cotton picker designed for even greater efficiency. International Harvester had begun development during the Great Depression but delayed introduction until labor costs had recovered, figuring higher labor costs would increase demand for their product. International Harvester launched their cotton picker in December of 1942. It was not only more efficient but far better financed than the Rust model.[6]

As mechanization developed, maximizing progress took "the combined contributions of engineers, chemists, and fertilizer specialists, plant breeders, entomologists, agronomists, and other scientists" often under contract to the USDA.[7] A new strain of cotton was developed by the USDA with bolls higher on the stalk for easier mechanical picking, new chemical weed killers and pesticides were introduced, loans were available for the purchase of new equipment, and the Delta Branch Experiment Station, about an hour's drive from Holmes County, received millions in funding for research and development and to disseminate new information to Delta planters.[8]

The process of ginning cotton—removing the seeds—also changed. Larger-capacity gins were needed as mechanical picking was quicker than hand picking. New enhanced equipment could also capture byproducts that had value, like cotton seeds for oil and lint for stuffing. As a result, large companies took over the ginning process while small local gins went dormant.[9]

By the 1970s, capital had indeed replaced labor: In 1900, it took 248 person-hours to produce a bale of cotton. Even in 1950—after tractors and early mechanical pickers became standard equipment—it took 100 person-hours to produce a bale of cotton. Delta planters still needed low-cost labor. But by the early 1970s, low-cost labor had been replaced by mechanization as producing a bale of cotton took about 5 person-hours.[10]

The facile explanation for the poverty of Holmes County is that farm mechanization and modernization were necessary to protect the profitability of the Delta's principal commodity—cotton. In that explanation, mechanization inevitably brought job loss to farm laborers and, along with it, similarly inevitable population loss that made other businesses unsustainable.

There is truth to the facile explanation, but it leaves out important parts of the story that had deep impacts on Holmes County—and on much of the Delta. The first element it omits is what modernization did to the land itself, which has not recovered. The second is that white leadership wanted African Americans to leave, motivated at least in part by a desire to regain political control. The third is that while modernization and mechanization are central to Delta history, discriminatory policies forced many African American farmers out of business, thus weakening the independence, self-sufficiency, and prosperity they represented to the larger Black community.

THAT WE MAY LIVE

Delta land sustained massive change before and after it was first occupied by human beings. The Mississippi River developed from a braided river to a singular deep channel that continued to change course—quite visibly even since the Civil War. Once the Delta became the cotton kingdom, human labor cleared much of its forests. The wetlands fed by natural aquifers were drained into irrigation ditches while man-made levees held back the flooding that had a role in replenishing the aquifers. The river itself was dredged and deepened so more water would pass down it and less into its swampy plains. Then, cotton takes a lot out of the soil and the land becomes less fertile. Cotton monoculture invited the boll weevil, which made cotton less profitable. Putting cotton first required protecting it from weeds and weevils.

More pesticides were used in the Mississippi Delta than virtually anywhere else from the 1950s onward. The Mississippi Delta has absorbed more than a third of all the cotton insecticides used in the United States. In one intensively studied tri-county area near Holmes County, the equivalent of seven to twelve pounds of insecticides per acre were applied each year, plus additional herbicides to control weeds. Until it was banned in 1972, DDT was one of the most widely used insecticides, along with toxaphene, until it too was banned in 1992.[11]

Toxaphene, while less well known than DDT, is at least as dangerous. It stays in the soil or in the bottom of lakes and streams, where it breaks down very slowly. It tends to accumulate in the fatty tissue of fish and animals. People who consume those fish and animals are exposed as well. It can "damage the nervous system, liver, and kidneys, and even cause death."[12] Both DDT and toxaphene are still found in much of the water in Holmes County, and fish advisories remain in effect as a result. Toxaphene is still present in the soil in Holmes County. The amount varies by location and by the type of soil. Soils with more clay hold chemicals longer, although the chemicals are also less likely to leach into the water supply than from more friable soil.[13]

Chemicals were sprayed directly on cotton fields, but there was toxic drift to nearby land. Spraying of insecticides also occurred when there were people working in the fields. The youth of the Rural Organizing and Cultural Center (ROCC) interviewed Mrs. Alice Rule for *Bloodlines*. Mrs. Rule was born in 1944, the oldest of ten children in the Sims family, who were day laborers. She started working in the field as a child of "round nine or ten" from first light to dusk. The children wore cotton stockings in the fields.

> When I got older, I discovered it was good protection because of all the poison and stuff they were putting on the crop then. . . . When we was going to the field . . . if they decided to spray the cotton that day, whether you was chopping or not, they sprayed the cotton. . . . I think that's where my eye problem came from . . . when they came through on the plane, with the plane spraying cotton, the choppers stayed in the fields, just like nothing was happening. You were just black people. You was just like cotton out there. You know, we were labelled in the encyclopedia as a commodity, one of the things that they growed. Soybeans, cotton, and Negroes.[14]

One of the leading advocates for the expanded use of agricultural chemicals was Congressman Jamie L. Whitten. Whitten served in Congress from 1941 until 1995. Holmes County was in his district until 1972. No one—certainly no one in Congress—had a greater impact on agricultural policy during that period than Whitten. He was chair of the Subcommittee on Agricultural Appropriations from 1949 to 1978, with one brief interruption when Republicans were in the House majority. He was chair of the full Committee on Agriculture from 1979 to 1992. When he left Congress in 1995, the Department of Agriculture building was named the Jamie L. Whitten Building in his honor.

Whitten's politics were typical of white southern policymakers during the period. He supported Roosevelt's New Deal legislation and clashed with President Ronald Reagan over efforts to cut funding for agricultural programs. He also signed the Southern Manifesto opposing integration of the public schools and opposed all the Civil Rights Acts of the 1950s and 1960s.[15]

Whitten was a staunch supporter of USDA efforts to improve cotton production; indeed, agricultural policy initiatives during his leadership could not be operationalized without his support for funding as chair of the Agriculture Appropriations subcommittee. Whitten also advanced the policy that a pesticide could not be removed from use unless it had been proven to cause damage to human health, prolonging the use of pesticides and herbicides even after suspicions of their dangers developed. He authored a book defending the use of DDT and other pesticides and herbicides. The book, entitled *That We May Live*, was published in 1966. It was a response to environmental scientist Rachel Carson's widely read 1962 book, *Silent Spring*, which questioned the use of pesticides, particularly DDT.

Whitten's book expresses pride in the quantity of pesticide used in the Delta: "The cotton growing Mississippi Delta region has one of the highest rates of pesticide application in the country. . . . [I]n the growing season, hundreds of motor vehicles and aircraft apply tons of insecticides to the cotton fields; other crops receive less regular applications. The roar of spraying and dusting aircraft is as common as the noise of tractors."[16]

Whitten denied a negative impact on wildlife, arguing that DDT was good for birds by eradicating bothersome mites. Fish, he asserted, were unaffected as they formed a genetic resistance to pesticides. His overriding conclusion was that "if pesticides cannot claim credit alone for the many remarkable advances in agriculture, nevertheless they can boast a major share."[17]

Typical among white leadership at the time, Whitten evinces little concern about the impact of agricultural policy on those who worked the land. He fantasizes that "most of the 'hands' have left the farm and now work in factories in town, making radio and television sets, providing electricity and butane gas, manufacturing refrigerators and other conveniences that add to the comfort of life." Whitten's only regret over those who were evicted from the land is that rural population loss lessened the political clout of the agriculture industry in Congress.[18]

DISPLACEMENT

Like Whitten, most of those responsible for mechanization in the 1950s and 1960s felt little responsibility for the people being displaced. There was no meaningful effort to bring in industry to replace the loss of agricultural jobs. Instead, the attitude then—and lingering in some quarters now—is that the people remaining in the Delta—without the jobs they used to have—are the problem. Those who continued to see African Americans principally as a labor force—not as full citizens—thought the solution was for them to leave. There had been support earlier for the departure of African Americans from Mississippi—a few enslaved people were sent to Liberia in an effort led by missionaries in the 1830s—but while labor was needed and the lack of voting rights inhibited Black political power—efforts at retention were more common.[19] By the 1960s, there was less demand for labor and greater concern over African American political empowerment if the Black majority in places like Holmes County remained.

Mississippi Public Broadcasting has a popular TV show called *Mississippi Roads*, which has now run more than twenty seasons, narrated by folksy fifth-generation Mississippian Walt Grayson from Greenville. Back in season 15, Grayson hosted a show on Highway 61, the north-south road through the Delta that runs parallel to Highway 51 but west of it. Grayson quotes "an old time Delta planter" who had told him "one Sunday morning years ago" that "one man on a tractor by himself could do what it used to take ten families sharecropping to do; and he went on to say the problem with the Delta is the families are still there with nothing to do." Grayson further quoted the farmer as saying that is "the contradiction of the Delta—progress is choking it."

If what the Delta needs is population loss, then Holmes County should be booming. The Holmes County population was nearly forty thousand in 1940. It fell to twenty-three thousand by 1970 and is now under seventeen thousand people.

The all-white leadership structure of the 1950s and early 1960s wanted Black people to leave. Like Grayson's Delta planter, the Holmes County establishment of the time welcomed the outmigration of African American citizens. In 1963 the *New York Times* interviewed Don Barrett, the son of county attorney Pat Barrett, and then a twenty-year-old college student. Don Barrett is now one of Lexington's most prominent citizens. He has long since repudiated his remarks in 1963. They do not reflect his modern-day thinking but do reflect the times in which the article was written. Back then, Don Barrett was more proud of being a Mississippian than being an American and did not believe the federal government had the right to say that Black people could vote. According to the article, "Barrett sees an eventual solution in the departure of all Negroes for the North 'to live on welfare,' since the planters and automated land no longer need them. He also believes the Delta will be 'forever agrarian,' though partly industrialized with small, imported industries employing whites in a prosperous blend of his beloved old way of life and new Yankee paychecks."[20]

The imported industries Whitten wrote about and Barrett envisioned have not materialized. Many Black people felt the Delta was their home and wanted to stay and farm.[21] According to the US Census, more white people than Black people have left Holmes County, which was 72 percent African American in 1960 and is 83 percent African American now.[22] Population loss and business decline are circular. People left because there were no jobs for them. Holmes County does not now have the population to sustain the businesses it once had, causing more job loss. When it had double the population that it has now, it had movie theaters and clothing stores, all of which have now closed. Once-vibrant businesses—Black and white owned—are shuttered because there are not enough people to sustain them.

Changes in transportation have not uniformly helped either—at least at this point. Trains no longer stop in Holmes County. Highway 51 still passes through the main commercial corridor of Durant—and a block from those of Goodman and Pickens. Back when it was a main road, Bob Dylan had sung of Highway 51 on his 1962 debut album, a cover of Durant native Tommy McClennan's earlier recording, "Yes, I know this highway like I know the back of my hand, running up from Wisconsin; way down to no man's land." Then the Federal-Aid Highway Act passed in 1956 and began building Interstate 55 in 1957. By 1973, it was completed and effectively replaced Highway 51. The new interstate put Holmes County less than an hour from Jackson and provides a straight shot north to Memphis, St. Louis, and Chicago. It is a travel boon—and aid to commercial trucking—but it bypasses small-town main streets that used to thrive in part on through traffic.

Some Holmes County leaders are hopeful that new development in Madison County—located between the city of Jackson and Holmes County—will spread up Interstate 55, finally bringing the new industry that many have long envisioned as a replacement for agricultural jobs. In the meantime, population loss and the new highway have brought business and job loss, particularly for Black people. The county now has only 236 employer establishments, but in a county that is 83 percent African American, only 31 employer businesses are Black owned.[23]

DISCRIMINATION

African American farmers experienced decades of policies that made it more difficult to keep their farms. In some cases, the intent was discriminatory, including efforts to punish those active in the civil rights movement. In other cases, the intent may not have been discriminatory but the result most certainly was. African American farmers suffered disproportionately as farming became more industrialized. Farms with less acreage—or farms on more hilly land—were less able to take advantage of the efficiencies of new equipment.

On average, African Americans had smaller farms, but farm size alone does not account for the loss of African American farms in Holmes County. In most places, the impact of farm size is difficult to tease out with available data, leading some to conclude that it explains the disproportionate loss of African American farms. The USDA did not keep records in the 1960s of the size of farms owned by whites and African Americans. In Holmes County, however, a 1968 study allows rough comparisons and shows that race was a crucial factor in farm loss in Holmes County.

One culprit of outright discrimination was the Agriculture Stabilization and Conservation Service. The ASCS had its roots in the agricultural programs of the 1930s but evolved into its civil rights era form in 1961 and remained in place until 1994. Under the ASCS system, committees elected at the local and then county level were empowered to make decisions on farm loans and allotments. Black farmers were generally not informed of these elections, although any farm operator—owner or tenant—was supposed to be able to participate. Holmes County activists—and SNCC—had tried to impact the elections in the 1960s and succeeded in electing local but not county-level representatives. The ASCS Committee in Holmes—and virtually everywhere—remained dominated by white owners of larger farms and plantations.

The US Civil Rights Commission complained about ASCS elections. and secretary of agriculture Orville Freeman, from Minnesota, took token action. Posters produced in 1967 encouraged African American participation in ASCS elections, but the posters were not displayed in the Black community and may not have been put up at all.[24] As the civil rights movement became more nationalized in the later 1960s, the struggles of African American farmers were no longer in the headlines, or much in the consciousness of many unfamiliar with the rural South.

Black farmers who were active in the civil rights movement—and in the ASCS elections—faced immediate negative consequences for their actions. Several were denied credit by the ASCS or found they could not get their cotton ginned. T. C. Johnson, who ran to represent his community on the ASCS board, owned nearly 1,000 acres near Lexington, with 315 acres cleared for farming. He had a 45-acre cotton allotment, which he had tried to increase. Instead, the ASCS compliance fieldworker remeasured his fields. One field that had always measured as three acres suddenly measured as four acres. Johnson was forced to plough under an acre of cotton.[25]

African American farmers long complained that USDA loans—which were processed through ASCS committees—were denied or delayed. Loans are critical in farming row crops since the harvest comes once a year and the size and quality of crops are variable. As recently as 1990, former Mileston Co-op president Shadrach Davis applied for a loan in February but didn't receive it until May, well after planting season, and had to borrow from friends to get seed and plant cotton.[26] Jimmy Lacy started farming in Holmes County back when he had only a mule-drawn plow, but by the 1990s he was leasing over six hundred acres. He tried to talk to USDA about buying a plot of land they owned, but "the guy I want to talk to is in the office until he finds out I'm Black, then he's out of the office all the time."[27] The USDA has an assistant secretary for civil rights, but complaints filed in his office at that time were taking an average of nearly three years to process.[28]

Black farmers also faced credit issues—and challenges to their ownership—due to heirs' property issues. Heirs' property refers to any property, including land, held in common by multiple heirs because the original deed holder did not leave a will. If someone bought land several generations back, and there was no will, siblings in successive generations have a claim to the land, which can force a partition sale in which the land is broken up into smaller parcels. One Holmes County resident who has tried to consolidate ownership of family land said her great-grandfather's land now has nearly a hundred heirs, only a handful of whom live in Holmes County. And when it comes to her family's land, her brothers do not want to recognize the claims of cousins who have never farmed it. Often the heir who farms the land cannot get credit or use the land as collateral for the purchase of equipment because the title remains unclear.

Stories abound in Holmes County of so-called property poachers who either take advantage of a recent death in the family to buy land from cash-strapped heirs for less than it is worth or locate a long-gone heir and force a partition sale because they have a client who wants the land in question. While there are other ways of addressing heirs' property issues, until recently, partition sales were the default in Mississippi. It takes a modest amount of genealogical research to find the second cousin of a farmer in Holmes on behalf of a client who wants that farmer's acreage. One Holmes County leader tells of a group of whites from outside the county who have been trying to buy his land for over twenty years through a purported heir in California to use as a hunting camp.

In 1997, the USDA held hearings and issued a report that found widespread discrimination and underrepresentation of minority farmers by the USDA. The report concurred with the complaints of Black farmers that the Office of the Inspector General had been used for retaliations against them. The old ASCS Committees had been restructured when Mike Espy, who had represented Holmes County and the Delta in Congress, was secretary of agriculture. Espy had tried earlier, as a member of Congress, to diversify the county-level USDA structure but could not pass his legislation through the House of Representatives. Even the new Farm Service Agency Committees, established as part of the restructuring, had just over 1 percent African American representation as late as 1996. The USDA's own report on racial discrimination in loan processing said that when it came to minority and small-scale farmers the committees "deny them courtesy and respect while giving large scale farmers service and loans." A study commissioned while Mike Espy was secretary of agriculture found that while 90 percent of white producers felt their county committee represented their interests, only half of African American farmers who completed the USDA survey felt the same way.[29]

Class action suits followed in the late 1990s. The courts found in two cases of *Pigford v. Glickman* that the USDA had systematically discriminated against Black farmers from 1983 to 1997 by denying loans, program access, representation, and information. Farmers who had loans from the period could get a cash payment of $50,000 while others with documentary evidence of discrimination could seek compensation in a separate process, one that often took years. As one scholar noted, the *Pigford* cases "allowed farmers the opportunity to bring the issue before the country and the world, but it didn't help get their land back."[30]

Despite the court rulings that the USDA discriminated against African American farmers, some still argue that the loss of African American farms is because Black farmers owned smaller farms. In most places, the capacity to trace farm loss by farm size and the race of the farmer is stymied by a lack of data. The USDA did not consistently record farms by the race of the owner. They counted farm *operators* by race. Farm operators included tenant farmers and sharecroppers. The National Agricultural Statistical Service (NASS) does, however, now count ownership by race. Data by race and size of farm is available by special request and then made publicly available.

A rough comparison over time is available in Holmes County because there was such a special request for recent data and because a student at the University of Illinois, Michael Morgalla, spent the summer of 1968 in Holmes County collecting data on farm ownership by race, including farm size. As Morgalla explained, his "paper consists largely of the compilation of data collected by me in the field; the goal is not always analysis but the creation of statistical figures not available from other sources." Morgalla copied address plates from ASCS offices, then went to the communities to determine the race of the owner. His data have a few gaps but are complete enough for rough comparison with recent NASS data.

Using NASS data and Morgalla's report, we see that only a handful of farms with 50 acres or fewer—owned by people of any race—remain operational in Holmes County today. At the opposite end of the spectrum, most farms over 500 acres, which have always been owned disproportionately by whites, remain. Currently in Holmes, there are 90 white-owned farms over 500 acres, and half of those have over 1,000 acres. There are 21 Black-owned farms over 500 acres, with only a handful over 1,000 acres. The number of African American owners of large farms is thus about what it was in 1968. Large white-owned farms have similar total acreage as in 1968 but have consolidated into fewer properties.[31]

In the middle are farms between 50 and 500 acres, and differences by race are clear. Roughly half the number of midsize white-owned farms are still operational. Only about a fifth of Black-owned farms with 50 to 180 acres are still in business, and only about a third of Black-owned farms with 180 to 500 acres are operational. The comparison demonstrates that factors other than farm size were at play in the disproportionate loss of Black-owned farms in Holmes County.

LAND OF MY FATHERS

One of the notable stories of land loss in Holmes County is that of the Hart family in Lexington, who at one time had one of the biggest farm operations in the Delta. In 2013, the Hart family was forced to sell off most of its land and cattle to USDA. Rodalton Hart, who had been the main proprietor of the farm, had been cleared of alleged wrongdoing after being caught in political crossfire in the 1990s. Still, the family was forced to sell the land after his death to avoid the USDA taking his widow's home.

The story of the Hart family's land begins in 1890 when Michael Smith, born in slavery in 1860, purchased 110 acres. Smith bought an additional 100 acres in 1928 together with Dan Kimbrough.[32] Michael Smith's granddaughter Sarah Kimbrough married a man named Cleveland Hart, the son of a sharecropper and former slave named Green Hart. Cleveland Hart, too, owned land, which he had purchased in 1917, shortly after the Federal Land Bank was established. Cleveland Hart was Rodalton Hart's grandfather. Rodalton and his brothers became the fourth generation of their family to farm in Holmes County.[33]

Rodalton Hart did not originally intend to run the family farm, but after his 1972 graduation from Jackson State, his father, Harrison Benjamin Hart, known as H.B., talked him into it. Rodalton fell in love with farming. He developed his own strain of cotton and convinced his brothers to join his growing enterprise. By 1986, he and his brothers were farming more than two thousand acres. The farm was "a highly mechanized enterprise using the best herbicides, insecticides, labor and farm machinery" with "a fleet of seven modern tractors, . . . two combines, four cotton pickers, a bulldozer . . . an 18-wheeler for hauling produce to market—and a herd of registered Beef Master cattle."[34] In 1987, he was elected to the Holmes County Board of Supervisors, where he was active on a range of issues from the supervision of young offenders to waste management and road and bridge repair.

Hart continued to expand his holdings. His farming operation became one of the largest in the Mississippi Delta, farming up to seven thousand acres with his brothers, including land in Washington County.[35] "Getting bigger," he explained, "is the only way to survive."[36]

Rodalton Hart and Mike Espy became friends. When Espy first ran for Congress in 1986, he wanted to learn more about farming. Espy was an attorney, not a farmer, and his family still operated the chain of funeral homes that had been developed by his grandfather T. J. Huddleston. Rodalton Hart became one of Mike Espy's mentors as part of his advisory committee on farm issues. Hart testified in Washington on issues facing Black farmers and on reducing agricultural paperwork and bureaucracy for all farmers.[37] Espy and Hart became personally close. They rode horses together on weekends on Hart's property near Lexington.[38] As Hart said, "Every time he comes here, we go to my parents' house for greens. My mother is trying to teach him how to cook them right. . . . He's a pretty good cook. I went up to Washington, and he made me some gumbo. Did a good job, too."[39]

Espy became secretary of agriculture in 1993. Espy replaced the old ASCS Committees with a new structure, although still county based, as part of an overhaul of the Department of Agriculture. His successor, Congressman Bennie G. Thompson, set up a fifteen-member advisory committee on agricultural issues to serve as a "pipeline" to his office in Washington. The committee included both larger and smaller farmers, both Black and white. Thompson named Rodalton Hart as the chairman. Hart said of Thompson and the committee at the time, "He's trying to involve people with an interest in agriculture. The people on this committee also belong to other groups, and they can offer a lot of feedback."[40]

Espy was forced to resign his cabinet post at the end of 1994 as questions arose about token gifts—sports tickets—he had allegedly accepted from agricultural interests. While Espy was indicted in 1997, he was cleared of all charges the following year. The charges against Espy, however, sparked investigations of some of his friends. Hart was confronted by investigators who threatened to put him out of business if he did not cooperate with their investigation of Espy.

After weather-related problems in 1993 and 1995, the Harts were eligible for disaster relief from USDA, but their application was denied as their file had been transferred to the Office of the Inspector General of USDA in connection with the Espy investigation. Without the file, the request for disaster relief could not be processed. Without assistance in 1996, Hart worked closely with the county FSA agent in 1997 and 1998 and signed loan documents on his own behalf and that of his brothers.[41]

Then Rodalton Hart's farm was raided by the FBI. Agents with horses and all-terrain vehicles arrived without warning to assess the property. They chased Hart's cattle, a few to exhaustion and death. Hart and two of his brothers were indicted on charges of bribing a USDA official and misrepresenting assets and debts on the loan applications. In October of 2000, Rodalton Hart was found guilty and sentenced to two years in prison. He was imprisoned for fourteen months before a new trial was ordered on appeal, based on problems with USDA testimony against him. The court of appeals ruled that a USDA witness had testified generally about loan applications but that USDA did not provide specific evidence that Hart misreported debts or assets on his loan applications. The judge ordered a new trial. At the new trial in 2002, Rodalton Hart was acquitted of all charges.

Despite the acquittal, years of legal difficulties took their toll on Hart's personal health and on his finances. Most of the Hart family land was sold to pay legal debts and loans. Rodalton Hart died of a heart attack at age fifty-six in

2007. As partner in the farm, his wife Carmella assumed his debts, but USDA determined she did not have the income from what remained of the farm to pay off the remaining $350,000. They were going to take her house. The Hart family sold most of the remaining land and cattle to USDA to clear the debt, leaving only a few hundred acres and about one hundred head of cattle.

Rodalton Hart's sons hope to build back over time. They say they are starting with far more than their ancestors did when they first purchased land in Holmes County in the nineteenth century.[42]

THE NEW EARTH[43]

After the first "redemption" began in 1875, the Black community in Holmes County dug in. They built their own institutions and helped each other. Twenty-first-century African American farmers cannot undo the land loss and displacement of the late twentieth century. Few can compete economically with the corporate farm operations that dominate row crop agriculture in the Delta. Instead, some are seeking another way, turning instead to producing food. Food production takes less land. It also fills a need for healthy food in the Mississippi Delta when plot-by-plot it begins to correct the damage done to the land by twentieth-century farm practices.

Expansion of food production and cooperative farming had a resurgence in the late 1960s as a reaction to the weaponization of food during the civil rights movement. The Greenwood Food Blockade drew a connection, as SNCC's Bob Moses had said, between politics and food on the table. A surge of federal anti-poverty programs of the 1960s missed their mark in some cases and in any case did not last long. The food stamp program, phased into Mississippi in 1965, originally did more to help grocers than sharecroppers. While surplus commodities had been distributed free of charge, food stamps needed to be purchased before providing a discount for food purchases. Sharecroppers lacked the cash for food stamps. A 1967 NAACP report outlined resultant discriminatory practices. With a captive market, some plantation commissaries added the cost of the food stamps—plus interest as high as 25 percent—to the sharecroppers' "furnish," the plantation owners' accounting of what the sharecropper owed him after harvest.[44] Profits of the Lewis Grocer Company, which had merged into SuperValu, burgeoned from the food stamp program.

Fannie Lou Hamer inaugurated an effort to expand cooperative farming in 1967 in nearby Sunflower County. She began the Freedom Fund Cooperative (FFC) saying, "Down where we are, food is used as a political weapon. But if you have a pig in your backyard, if you have some vegetables in your garden, you can feed yourself and your family, and nobody can push you around."[45]

Hamer's co-op planted cotton and soybeans as cash crops and gave away vegetables for free. The National Council of Negro Women contributed fifty pigs and Heifer International provided expertise on pig husbandry. By 1969, the pig bank had provided over a hundred families with pigs and more than eight hundred families four years later. Then in 1974, the business manager suffered a fatal heart attack and Hamer herself fell ill. The farm thus lost both her marquee value as a fundraiser and her skill as an organizer. The FFC had to sell its land to pay taxes in 1976. Hamer died in 1977.[46]

Other efforts from that era are still operational. The North Bolivar Co-op, also formed during the civil rights movement, grew into the North Bolivar County Good Food Revolution, which grows and distributes food in the Delta. The Federation of Southern Cooperatives was formed in 1967, originally with funding from the Ford Foundation. It now serves over one thousand members, all African American farmers, in efforts to keep their land and to develop co-ops.[47] Their mission "is to be a catalyst for the development of self-supporting communities through cooperative economic development, land retention, and advocacy."[48] They assist in the development of co-ops and coordinate resources to remediate heirs' property issues for African American farmers.

Changes in techniques of food production since that time offer new opportunities to grow food productively on less land. To learn more, I visited Otis Wright Jr., an agricultural consultant and the farm manager at Tougaloo College's Agri-Growth Initiative. He is working with several Holmes County farmers on sustainable agriculture techniques. Wright showed me the high tunnels at Tougaloo, which grow produce to help feed the campus. High tunnels, also known as hoop houses, are tall enough to walk around in, covered in fabric or plastic. The cover helps protect the plants from severe weather and pests—and pesticide drift from spraying nearby—while plants are grown directly in the ground. Drip irrigation and venting the tunnels provide ideal growing conditions and extend the growing season. The soil within the high tunnel can be amended with organic matter and natural minerals to accelerate the breaking down of pesticide residues.[49]

With an initial investment of $10,000 to $20,000 per tunnel, each one can produce $20,000 of produce a year, allowing profit by the second year with a modest initial investment. Wright says he "wants to plant seeds in the younger generation about what my version of freedom is like; seeds of love, I guess. That's where the real revolution is, getting us back to the system where we take care of each other. That's what I want my community to be."

In Holmes County, the Mileston Co-op is still operational and turning to food production. The effort is driven by economic development—job creation and generated revenue—and a new health consciousness about the impact of pesticides and herbicides on the community's health. Calvin Head, the son of civil rights activist Rosie Head, is the current executive director of the co-op. Only about a dozen families are still active in the co-op while others rent out their land or have allowed it to lie fallow to reduce property taxes. The co-op cultivates about half of the original nine thousand acres. Mileston Co-op farmers still share infrastructure—insurance, equipment, food safety compliance procedures—and put 25 percent of their profits back into the co-op. A separate Mileston nonprofit trains young people and employs a staff of seventeen. It looks particularly for those young people who need help; for some it is their first regular job.

Head says the mindset at Mileston has changed. The co-op still grows seed corn and soybeans but is setting aside increasing acreage for vegetable gardening and experimenting with growing food hydroponically. Members are working at amending the soil to lessen the presence of pesticides and hope to get to the point where their vegetables can be certified as "naturally grown," a designation fewer than a dozen Mississippi farms have achieved. The "naturally grown" certification is provided by a not-for-profit, which also gives advice on soil quality and provides peer review of farming practices. The "naturally grown" certification is easier to obtain than the USDA "organically grown" label.[50]

Farmer Sarah Horton, whose land in Holmes County has been in her family since early in the century, is also growing organically in a high tunnel and seeking certification. Horton sells her produce locally and at the farmer's market in Jackson. I have been buying her sweet potatoes, beans, and bok choy since I moved here, before I had ever heard of high tunnels.

Mac Epps, who was raised by his sharecropper grandparents in Holmes County, is returning to farming. His grandparents, who never owned their own land, discouraged him from "the harsh hard work of farming." They wanted him to leave and go to school. Epps went to Jackson State and obtained a master's degree in social work. He became a community organizer with Mississippi Motivating and Organizing Voters for Empowerment (MOVE), mentored by SNCC activist Hollis Watkins. He says his "upbringing motivated me to get back to my roots. During COVID, we got produce and gave it away. Having your own is the way to go."[51]

Earcine Evans is one of the few farmers whose produce is fully organic. Evans grew up in Holmes County. She attended Lexington High School in one of the early classes under voluntary integration but left halfway through as the pressures intensified. She graduated instead from Saints Academy in 1969. Evans left Mississippi after graduation, first living in Chicago and then in Northern California, where she owned and operated two beauty salons. After becoming ill, she returned to Holmes County, where her grandfather was still living. She says, "When I didn't live here, I felt disconnected from my grandmother, my grandfather, my great-grandparents. The moment I came back here I could feel their spirit."[52]

Evans founded Francis Flowers and Herbs Farm, named for her grandmother who was a renowned midwife and herbalist in the community. Her land has been in the family for about 150 years, although much of the original five hundred acres was lost through a partition sale. She grows flowers and herbs for her own line of natural beauty care products, Pure Ciné, on a former cotton field of six and a half acres. Evans is active teaching young people and other farmers about natural and organic growing, working with the Mileston Co-op, holding workshops, and lecturing on organic growing in area schools and colleges. Evans says, "I've been taught this: not to look at the land as a cash cow, like something you're just going to generate money off of, but if you give the land the love, the land is going to give you all the wealth you need, but you have to love it first." Evans adds, "My goal is just to be able to encourage and motivate young people—and particularly African Americans who are interested in sustainable farming—to really get on some land and do it."

African American farmers in Holmes County may not regain the acreage lost or the wealth that went with it. The challenges remain formidable, although some conditions have improved. USDA offices are diversified and both federal and not-for-profit efforts support the expansion of food production. Meanwhile, the African American farmers of Holmes County retain dedication to the community and its advancement, and to building their own independence and self-sufficiency.

Holmes County Courthouse with Confederate statue erected in 1906. Photograph by the author, 2024.

Dr. Sylvia Reedy Gist, historian and president of the Migration Heritage Foundation, at Durant Station through which thousands departed Holmes County before, during, and after the Great Migration. Dr. Gist notes the door below the sign was "the white folks door." The waiting room for Black people was through the door to the left. Photograph by the author, 2024.

Mileston historic marker ceremony, September 17, 2022. Master of ceremonies Supervisor LeRoy Johnson (right) presenting a plaque to Reverend Melvin Russell, youngest son of Reverend J. J. Russell. Photograph by the author.

Mileston historic marker ceremony, September 17, 2022. Elected officials and veterans of the civil rights movement in Holmes County and others. Seated, from left to right: Reverend Burns, Edmund Clark, Rosie Head, Griffin McLaurin, Matilda Burns. Standing, left to right: Calvin Head (with camera), state senator David Jordan, state senator Barbara Blackmon, James Wells (on the truck), and state representative Bryant Clark. Photograph by the author.

Earcine Evans in her "hoop house" at Francis Flowers and Herb Farm in Pickens. Photograph by the author, 2024.

Epilogue:

STILL HERE

When I first drove through Holmes County, I was struck most by its poverty. Today, when I drive through the county, its history forms a backdrop for what I see. In some ways, Holmes County is a very rich place. Still, many of the challenges—and much of the spirit—of Holmes County today directly reflect its past.

Driving north on I-55 from Jackson, the first Holmes County exit is for Pickens. There, the railroad station and much of downtown are boarded up, but a community group of current and former residents has renovated and supplied the library there. A new historical marker on Highway 51 honors Reconstruction-era state legislator Edmund Scarborough and his son-in-law, Jack Scott, who was born enslaved in Pickens, graduated from Tougaloo College, and became one of the county's most prosperous landowners.[1]

The town of Goodman is next up the road, named for the first president of the Mississippi Central Railroad, Walter Goodman, although he did not live there. The buildings across the street from the railroad station in Goodman are boarded up too. The main campus of Holmes County Community College is in Goodman, with smaller branches in other nearby counties. It is the modern heir to the agricultural high school founded for white students in 1911. It offers multiple majors in agricultural science, plus programs in technology, health sciences, and academics. It serves a multicounty area through satellite campuses. In at least one set of recent statistics, a narrow majority of its students are white.[2]

North on Highway 51, near Durant, the road crosses the "Choctaw line," defining the land ceded in the Treaty of Doak's Stand from the final cession in the Treaty of Dancing Rabbit Creek. A mile before Durant is the Kaffay Mileoway. It was a lively juke joint back in the 1950s, when illegal liquor so disturbed Hazel Brannon Smith. It is now one of the few non-chain sit-down restaurants in eastern Holmes County.

Another mile brings you to downtown Durant, named for Louis Durant, whose descendants with Choctaw lineage were expelled to Oklahoma, founding a town of the same name there. Durant is the most populous town in Holmes County these days, with a population of 2,231, a decrease of 400 people from 2010.[3] Durant has more industry than the other towns. A three-hundred-acre industrial park has parcels available for development. The combination of the industrial park and proximity to I-55 provides potential for attracting more employers, perhaps as part of the supply chain for the Nissan factory down the road in Madison County.

Passenger trains stopped in Durant until 1995. Many who left Holmes County during the Great Migration went north to Chicago from Durant Station. Across the street from the partly renovated station and along Highway 51 are commercial corridors that include the Howell & Heggie Drug Company and Durant Building Supply. The location of the Durant Commercial Company, the Farmer's Alliance store, is uncertain, but Durant Building Supply could be its heir. It is owned and run by family members of Shadrach Davis, who was president of the Mileston Co-op in the 1960s.

Back to I-55, Highway 17 takes you eleven miles to Lexington. Starting down Highway 17, the first right is the road to Falls Cemetery, where Robert Augustus Simmons, Holmes County's second Black sheriff, is buried along with members of the Falls family who sold land after the Civil War to people they had previously enslaved. Across from Falls Cemetery Road is the Little Red Schoolhouse, where the Order of the Eastern Star began, and which was a school for white children before the Civil War. During Reconstruction, it was a school for African American children where Simmons taught before he became sheriff. It stayed an African American school until 1960. It was returned to the Order of the Eastern Star in 1968 and was renovated by them in 1979.

Further on is a cluster of buildings and a dirt road to Franklin Church. The church shows damage from Civil War minié balls in its clapboard siding from the clash in which the Third Colored Cavalry defeated the Holmes Volunteers. The families of those buried in the churchyard hold an annual reunion. The church is surrounded by dense woods, where much of the battle of Franklin Church was fought and where some who died there are buried still. There is an African American graveyard too, behind the church, with markers dating back to at least 1870 and with graves that likely date back further still.

Continuing down Highway 17, past the old cotton gin, closed now, is the turn for Ebenezer. The town was originally named "Bucksnort Landing" and renamed by Jacob Sontheimer, one of Holmes County's first Jewish residents. Ebenezer was home to Robert Clark, the first African American state representative since Reconstruction. Robert Clark's son, Bryant Clark, won the seat in 2003 after his father retired. He had received his juris doctor the year before and practices law in Lexington. He was not the first African American lawyer in Holmes but is still one of the very few. He represents most of Holmes and parts of Attala and Yazoo Counties in the state House of Representatives and is deputy leader of the Democratic Caucus and president of the Holmes County NAACP. Clark credits his father's win in 1967 to the African American landowners in Holmes County and believes Holmes County's unique history is part of what makes it distinctive to this day.[4]

Along the road to Ebenezer is Newport Missionary Baptist Church, where blues guitarist Elmore James is buried. James has been called "a radically innovative genius."[5] Rolling Stones guitarist Bill Wyman has said there would be no Rolling Stones without Elmore James.[6] James is the most prominent of the blues musicians born in Holmes, although B.B. King lived in the county for a few years. In his autobiography, King tells of witnessing a lynching at the courthouse square in Lexington.[7]

Lexington is the next stop down Highway 17. The population of Lexington was over 2,000 twenty years ago and is currently just over 1,600. The white population is less than half what it was twenty years ago. Lexington is now more than 80 percent African American, compared to 67 percent in the year 2000. People of both races have left, but more Black people than white people have stayed.

Right before downtown and the courthouse square, Saints School, the school spearheaded by Arenia Mallory for so many years, is on the right. The buildings of Saints School are closed and shuttered, but there are plans for an upcoming renovation and a job training center. Next door to Saints School is St. Paul Church of God in Christ, the Mother Church of the denomination, where Bishop Dean, who was president of the school in the early 1990s, is pastor now and where Bishop Mason, founder of the Church of God in Christ, was pastor until 1949.

Holmes County Central High School is across the street. The school has about eight hundred students, only a handful of whom are white. Virtually all the white students in Holmes County attend Central Holmes Christian School, the only one of the three private academies founded in the 1960s that remains open. It was renamed and added a minority scholarship program after the US Supreme Court ruled private academies could not exclude children based on race.

The *Holmes County Herald,* the newspaper founded by the Citizens' Council as an alternative to the *Lexington Advertiser*, still publishes, and its offices are on the square. It provides a great deal of coverage of local schools—divided about equally between the roughly 250 students at CHCS and the approximately 2,500 in the public school district. The public school district was, however, the subject of a *New York Times* piece on rural schools in 2021.[8] The district had received an F from the state for low proficiency in both English and math. Schools had leaks, sewage backup, and no air-conditioning. A state takeover of the school district was imminent then and has happened now. The school board was disbanded, and the state appointed an interim superintendent.

The district has difficulty recruiting teachers, especially as it pays less than fast-growing and more affluent Madison County just south of Holmes. The federal government supplements education for low-income students, and the Holmes County school district has among the lowest-income student bodies in the state. However, the federal formula relies in part on per pupil state expenditures. Since Mississippi spends less than other states on schools, its low-income school districts receive less of a supplement from the federal government.[9] The result is that per pupil expenditures in Holmes County are about one-third less than the national average, while the costs of meeting the educational needs of a dispersed rural student body—with a concentration of students from low-income families—are higher.

Still, student learning and scores on state tests have improved. The district rated a C rather than F in 2022 and now rates a B. The district and its interim superintendent attribute success in part to building teacher capacity and expanding early learning with prekindergarten slots now available at all elementary schools in the county through a partnership with Head Start.[10]

On Highway 17 just past the Holmes County Central High School, immediately before the courthouse square, there is a historic marker celebrating Hazel Brannon Smith, the Pulitzer Prize–winning publisher of the *Lexington Advertiser*. The marker was unveiled August 20, 2022, and drew an array of elected officials, with a photo featured in the *Holmes County Herald*.[11]

The courthouse square looks much as it did a century ago, especially after a recent renovation. The square is where Charles Harrison Mason first preached in Holmes County and founded the Church of God in Christ in 1897. The entire downtown district of Lexington has been on the National Register of Historic places since 2001. The historic buildings around the square add to the sense of place and of history.

A statue of a Confederate soldier, designated as a historic object since 1994, is still on the northwest side of the square. The young activists who now lead the Mississippi Freedom Democratic Party in Holmes County have demonstrated for its removal. The county board of supervisors, all five of whom are African American, voted to take the statue down but have not appropriated the $80,000 it would cost to do so. They are loath to make cuts in programs that provide direct service to people to relocate the statue as required by its national registry status.

Supervisor Leroy Johnson, who headed ROCC, is a member of the FDP and works to continue the organizing tradition in Holmes County. On moving the statue, he asks, "What services are you not going to provide" while noting the board has solicited proposals to remove the statue that would meet the historic preservation requirements. Johnson's family has roots in Holmes from before the Civil War. His ancestors were among the early twentieth-century landowners when land in the hills sold for around ten dollars an acre. His family is from Howard, where the first local unit of the National Federation of Colored Farmers was founded. His maternal grandfather, Walter Jones, was active in the Southern Tenant Farmers Union. As a supervisor, Johnson is focused on bringing new economic growth to Holmes County. He says that local government does not receive the help from the state it needs, such as the often-generous state tax incentives for business provided in some other communities.[12]

A far newer statue on the opposite side of the square commemorates African American Holmes County native and Medal of Honor winner Private First Class Milton Lee Olive III, who grabbed a grenade and fell on it during the Vietnam War, sacrificing himself for his fellow soldiers. The statue is engraved, "Erected by the United Black and White Citizens of Holmes County and Dedicated July 4, 2017." Attorney Don Barrett and former Lexington mayor Clint Cobbins helped organize the monument to Milton Olive.[13]

The courthouse square is surrounded by historic buildings, some shuttered but many not. They preserve the town's early twentieth-century aura. One of the historic buildings, the Rayner Building, constructed in 1915, houses the Barrett Law Group. Pat Barrett, the county attorney in the 1950s who was active in the Citizens' Council, began his practice in 1933. Don Barrett joined his father's practice in 1969. Since that time, Don Barrett has become a preeminent trial attorney with a national client base and reputation. Barrett has had thousands of clients but is perhaps best known for his role in the tobacco litigation that led to the 1998 settlement with the tobacco industry.

Barrett represented Lexington native Nathan Horton and his family in 1987 in a suit against the American Tobacco Company, one of several suits by individuals against big tobacco in the 1980s. Horton was a carpenter who did some work on Barrett's farm and fished in his lake—and had smoked Pall Mall cigarettes for thirty-seven years. When he became ill with lung cancer, he went to Barrett to discuss suing the tobacco companies. He wanted people to know about the "sickening pain" his cigarette-induced cancer caused him. Nathan Horton would die before the case went to trial, but his wife, son, and Barrett continued what he had started.

The first trial, in the Lexington courthouse, ended in a hung jury after Horton's character was impugned for drinking and gambling. A second trial, in Oxford, found the tobacco company at fault but did not award damages to the family. The jury believed both Horton and the company were at fault. Under Mississippi law, that should have brought partial damages.[14]

The Horton case was a landmark win as it opened the potential for unending cases against the tobacco companies. It also led to Barrett's involvement in litigation the State of Mississippi later brought to recover money spent on Medicaid expenses for patients who had smoked cigarettes. In 1999, the lawsuit that originated in Mississippi turned into a $365 billion national settlement.[15]

The Barrett law firm has reached national prominence while continuing as a family enterprise. Don Barrett still practices from the Lexington office. His son, Richard Barrett, opened the firm's Oxford office, while his daughter, Katherine Barrett Riley, works out of the Lexington office and serves as the attorney for the City of Lexington and attorney for the Holmes County Board of Supervisors.

Riley graduated from Central Holmes Christian School in 1990, well after the high heat of the 1960s. Riley had little awareness of the controversies of the civil rights era as she was growing up in Holmes County and does not recall discussion of the civil rights movement or the Reconstruction era when she was in school. Asked about her racial attitudes, Riley says that she was "raised a Christian and to say yes ma'am, no ma'am white or Black." She adds, "The Lord said I made everything perfect, and that includes Black people." She recognizes that the state of race relations in the county is not perfect now, "but we are headed in the right direction." Riley does not perceive that Black leadership votes differently than she would on the issues facing Lexington, as "we all want a community we can all live in, be safe, and be proud of." Her perspective is that "for my county to move forward, we have to let go of the past."[16] She acknowledges that many in the African American community may feel differently and wish to celebrate parts of their history.

After college, law school, and a few years in Nashville, Riley married a Lexington man and returned home. "Lexington has always been home. This is where I am supposed to be," she explains. Riley recognizes the deep challenges of the shrinking tax base in Holmes County. Not only has retail moved out, but the retail that remains often does not have local ownership. Lexington, she believes, needs more businesses and specifically more businesses owned by people who live in the county and are invested in the community. Riley recognizes that the quality of public schools is a barrier and improvement is needed, saying, "I want it to be an A school district—mostly for the children, but also economically."

Racial conflict in Lexington has been in the news the last couple years surrounding the behavior of white police chief Sam Dobbins and the Lexington Police Department (LPD). Dobbins had been hired as a police officer in August of 2020 after serving in law enforcement in two other counties. He was appointed chief in Lexington by Mayor Robin McCrory, who is white, and confirmed by the board of aldermen, all but one of whom is African American.

Once Dobbins became chief, the dollar value of fines and tickets in Lexington, under $5,000 a month before Dobbins became chief, skyrocketed to over $15,000 in July, then to over $30,000 in both February and March of 2022. There was a perception among some that Dobbins was making Lexington safer, although there were also complaints that he was harassing people and denying them their rights.[17]

The matter came to a head after former police officer Robert Hooker, who is African American, taped a sixteen-minute conversation with Dobbins in which Dobbins used the "N" word, ejaculated homophobic slurs, and claimed to have shot thirteen people in the line of duty. He was fired immediately on a 3–2 vote of the board of aldermen, with one African American member joining the one white member to produce the close vote. The mayor concurred with the majority.

Dobbins had not, apparently, been thoroughly vetted. He had previously served in law enforcement in Yazoo County and in Humphreys County. There had been complaints about him in both. In Yazoo County, a sheriff's deputy described defamatory statements against Black fellow officers saying, "He's just not a person that should have been in law enforcement." In Humphreys County, Dobbins arrested one man who was severely beaten, held for three months, and denied medical care. Charges against the man were eventually dropped. The complaint was settled out of court; Dobbins's employment was terminated. Dobbins was also involved in a highly questionable shooting in Humphreys County in which he and another deputy put ninety-six bullet holes in a man's car and allegedly shot the man dead after he surrendered.[18]

Hooker, the former officer who taped Dobbins, was born in Chicago, but his parents were from Holmes County, and he returned to be with them in their retirement after serving in the marines and working for a security firm in Chicago. Holmes County was familiar turf as the family would visit for annual reunions. His mother was a member of the Russell family and valedictorian of her class at Saints School. He figures that at one time his father's family must have lived on Hooker land. Hooker describes himself as "a southern country boy by heart but a city boy by mind."

Hooker released the tape of Dobbins's comments through the Freedom Democratic Party to force the issue and to bypass the political establishment. He believed some elected officials were aware of the problem but unwilling to act until the issue was more public. He says he "was not trying to incite any kind of violence or negativity about what I was trying to do" but felt Dobbins should not be in law enforcement.[19] Robert Hooker and I met at the Southern Barrel, a restaurant just off the square, where much of the community gathers for a home-cooked meal at lunchtime and after church on Sunday, and where Hooker was greeted warmly by other patrons.

After the story about Dobbins broke in August of 2022, the US Department of Justice launched an investigation into the behavior of the Lexington Police Department. On September 26, 2024, the Civil Rights Division in conjunction with the US Attorney's Office for the Southern District of Mississippi released a report describing ongoing violations by the Lexington Police Department and the City of Lexington. The report found that "through a combination of poor leadership, retaliation, and a complete lack of internal accountability, LPD has created a system where officers can relentlessly violate the law." The report detailed the use of excessive force, illegal search and seizures, and discrimination against Black people, finding "striking differences in how LPD officers treat Black people compared to white people." The Department of Justice found the whole system of collecting fines an illegal conflict of interest and in violation of the public trust. The report closes by commending the city and the LPD for agreeing to make necessary reforms and enumerates actions they must take.[20]

Leaving Lexington and driving west on Highway 12 brings a dramatic change in the landscape. The road undulates through a series of small rises, then plunges about two hundred feet to the flat land of the Mississippi Delta. The undulation is from peaks of the loess hills, formed from wind blowing up silt from the flood plain in prehistoric times. The road to Howard cuts off in the bluffs, and Tchula is at the base of the hills.

When Tchula was officially settled in the 1830s it was a river port. Back then, Tchula Lake, a horseshoe-shaped body of water, was a bend in the Yazoo River. The river changed course and became a lake, although it is under a fish advisory now from the runoff that has polluted it.

The town of Tchula grew in the middle of the twentieth century as sharecroppers left plantation farms deeper in the Delta. Its population doubled between 1960 and 1970 and peaked at just under 3,000 at the start of the twenty-first century. The current population is 1,652. It has lost 21 percent of its population in the last decade alone. Former mayor Eddie James Carthan still lives in Tchula in a historic home just off the main street.

In 2015, the *Guardian* newspaper dubbed Tchula "the lowest income town, in the lowest income county in the lowest income state."[21] The moniker has stuck, although other smaller towns may have even lower household incomes. In Tchula, the agricultural base of employment has dissipated. The town faces serious issues with flooding. It is in the floodplain of the Yazoo River, and water comes down the streams in the bluffs to feed the Yazoo, which makes Tchula more subject to flooding than much of the Delta during heavy rains.[22]

The Mileston Co-op is just a few miles from Tchula. The State of Mississippi recently recognized the Mileston Co-op and its activists with a historical marker honoring its role in the civil rights movement.[23] Celebration of Mileston's history has not always translated into support for the co-op and its programs, however, although the new investment in food production shows promise.

If instead of driving southwest on Highway 12 toward Tchula, you continue north from Lexington on Highway 17, the road follows the top of the bluffs, once dotted by Native American villages. That is the way toward Black Hawk, in Carroll County where the Twenty-Second Infantry of the Confederate army—the Black Hawk Rifles—once trained before some of its members formed Heggie's Scouts.

The area around Highway 17 north of Lexington is heavily wooded as its hillier terrain has been subject to erosion and is difficult to farm with modern machinery. Many African American farmers in this area have sold part of their land to the Natural Resources Conservation Service of USDA, which has replanted it with trees as conservation land in perpetuity. Taharga Hart, Rodalton Hart's younger son, is the area conservation officer for the Mississippi Delta, including Holmes County, while he continues to raise cattle part-time on the piece of land his family still owns just outside of Lexington.

About eight miles north of Lexington, over creeks that run down the loess bluffs, is Bell Bottom Road. Another couple miles down Bell Bottom Road, past the cotton field on the left, is Sweet Canaan Church of God in Christ. Sweet Canaan is the second-oldest Church of God in Christ in the world. It was founded shortly after St. Paul Church of God in Christ—the country church to the in-town location of St. Paul's. It was originally called simply "the colored sanctified church" and chose the name Sweet Canaan in 1909. As a teenager, Isaac Randle, who would become a leader in the NFCF, brought sweet gum logs to serve as seats for the congregation at Sweet Canaan Church of God in Christ. Louis Henry Ford, later the pastor to the Till family and eventually the presiding bishop of the Church of God in Christ, preached there as a student at Saints School.

Dr. Percy Washington is the pastor of Sweet Canaan and a student of history. He grew up in Leflore County and lived for a time in Money, where Emmett Till was killed. Dr. Washington collaborated with the local community to help make the sites related to the Emmett Till murder a national monument, which was established in July of 2023. He has produced a song honoring Emmett Till and the Till family.[24]

A little farther north on Highway 17 is Mt. Olive–Rosebank Road. The fork to the left takes you to the site of Mt. Olive Negro Freedmen's School, organized by the Mt. Olive Missionary Baptist Church in 1871. It was later also the location of a Rosenwald School where African American children were taught until 1965. Dr. Sylvia Gist, who wrote her dissertation and a later book on education in Holmes County, graduated from Mt. Olive. She now runs the

Migration Heritage Foundation, which awards scholarships to students in Holmes County who author essays on their family history.[25]

The right fork off Mt. Olive–Rosebank Road becomes Providence Road, taking you down the bluffs to what was once Providence Farm, with its burial mound from the Mississippian period. This is the land that Will D. Campbell traced to Louis Leflore, back when the Yazoo River ran through it. It was bought and sold by the Chocchuma Land Company as the cotton kingdom rose and enslaved people were brought to Holmes County to clear and cultivate it. A hundred years later, the land was home to the idealistic experiment launched by Christian Socialists until they were forced out by the Citizens' Council for favoring integration.

Most of the land that was Providence Farm is now owned by the State of Mississippi. It has been virtually unoccupied for nearly seventy years. The land is reforesting itself—taking itself back from all who borrowed it, shrouding the contours of much that happened on this land.

ACKNOWLEDGMENTS

I could not have written this book without help from people in Holmes County. There are many relevant archival and secondary sources available, but my understanding of the material was shaped by people who have lived or worked in the county.

I want to particularly thank Dr. Sylvia Reedy Gist, whose scholarship and careful readings of drafts of this manuscript were invaluable to me. Similarly, my understanding of the Church of God in Christ derives from the tutelage of Bishop William Dean Jr., Elder William Kenneth Dean, and Pastor Dr. Percy Louis Washington. I thank them and their congregations at St. Paul Church of God in Christ and Sweet Canaan Church of God in Christ for warmly welcoming me to services, answering my questions, and sharing their time and perspectives. Dr. Washington's broad and deep interest in county history, and his engagement with this book, provided me with encouragement as well as insight.

Sheriff Willie March was one of the first leaders to meet with me. He seems to know every corner of the county and every family in it and was always helpful; Supervisor Leroy Johnson is from a family with especially deep roots in the county, and he developed my understanding of its organizing tradition; state representative Bryant Clark has read, led, and experienced a great deal of Holmes County history and was always generous with his time. Chancery clerk Charlie Luckett and her staff helped guide me through the county's voluminous land records. Former Tchula mayor Eddie James Carthan spoke of his time as mayor and his family's history in the county; Lexington alderman Joshua Davis and his cousin Melissa Coats met with me about their grandfather's role in the Mileston Co-op in the 1960s; Mileston executive director Calvin Head explained how the co-op functions now; Taharga and Rashad Hart shared their family history and their expertise on agriculture; farmer Sarah Horton recounted the history of her family farm; Earcine Evans spoke of her love of the land and the people of Holmes County; Mac Epps told me of his return to farming; Katherine Barrett Riley reflected on growing up in Lexington in the post–civil rights era and on the county's current challenges; Phil Cohen shared his experiences as a prominent merchant in Lexington; Robert Hooker shared perceptions from his time in the police department; former Holmes County residents Rosemary Ingram DuMont, Meredith Gowan Le Goff, and Susan Stern Hart recalled for me their childhoods in Durant, Pickens, and Lexington, respectively; and my friend Judge Latrice Westbrooks welcomed me to her home in Lexington and heard out many of my reflections on what I was learning. Finally, William Minter shared material from his personal collection and his perspectives on Holmes County both as a sociologist and from growing up on Providence Farm.

Others outside Holmes County were helpful as well. I thank Congressman Bennie G. Thompson and former secretary of agriculture Mike Espy for their interest, insights, and counsel. Others who shared expertise or material include Courtland Cox, chairman of the SNCC Legacy Project; author, scholar, and SNCC veteran Charles Cobb; SNCC veteran Hollis Watkins; civil rights movement veteran Frank Figgers; urban farmer Cindy Ayres-Elliott; agriculture consultant Otis Wright; attorney Melvyn R. Leventhal; geologist James Starnes; and historians Omar Ali, James Taylor Carson, Douglas Chambers, Valerie Grim, Steven Hahn, David Hargrove, Mary Carol Miller, Jarod Heath Roll, and Faye Yarbrough. Professor Carson also took a look at early draft chapters on Native Americans; Professor Eric Kades looked at the chapter on Supreme Court cases that impacted Indian lands; civil rights historian Emilye Crosby provided a careful review. Her parents, Patty and David Crosby, lent me advice, counsel, and their personal copies of *Bloodlines*. Virginia Harris provided data and insights from the US Department of Agriculture; and Stephen Bingham, Marshall Ganz, and Susan Nichols Roughton recalled their time in Holmes County as Freedom Summer volunteers. Louis Hall and his niece visited Wilkinson County with me on the trail of Oliver Cromwell, and Barbara Williams shared her knowledge of Cromwell's family history; Arekia Bennett-Scott, Ted Strickland, Charles Taylor, and Corey Wiggins are good friends and patient and helpful sounding boards.

The staff at the Mississippi Department of Archives and History helped me find and understand material on everything from Native American artifacts to twentieth-century schools. Caroline Gray-Primer of the MDAH staff, who lives in Holmes County, Jeff Giambrone, and Michael Morris, now the director of the Mississippi Two Museums, were especially helpful. Alex Brower and Betty Moore at the Mississippi Library Commission tracked down a diverse array of books and materials. My friends Michael Fitzgerald, Jere Nash, Dave Espo, Virginia and Luther Munford, Karin Johanson, and Beth Orlansky read early drafts with critical eyes and helped improve the text.

I would like to thank the University Press of Mississippi for their support and the readers who reviewed the manuscript for their cogent corrections and suggestions. Editor Emily Bandy, who helped guide me through the process, has my warm appreciation. Emily and I would have found each other eventually, but I also thank Emily and her husband Zeke's dog, Brother, and my own dog, Tchula, who began the relationship by introducing us all one day in Belhaven Park. My thanks also to Cassie Winship for the evocative cover design, Elizabeth Farry for smoothing so many rough edges in copyediting, and project editor Laura Strong for shepherding the manuscript into a book.

Finally, I want to recognize two people who instilled in me an appreciation of African American history, although both passed before I even thought about this book: My father's friend since college Judge Robert L. Carter took an interest in me when I was still in high school and introduced me to an African American intellectual world I might not otherwise have met. My longtime business associate Ivanhoe Donaldson provided consistent advice and support for almost thirty years—accompanied by nearly constant instruction on a variety of matters, including an education on the 1960s civil rights movement. I am deeply grateful to them both and I miss them.

APPENDIX

Herbert Beatty, Company D, Fifty-First Regiment
Albert Clark, Company G, Fifth Regiment
Jack Cochran, Company H, Third Cavalry
Barnes Ellis, Company I, Third Cavalry
Osborn Fairfax, Company E, Forty-Eighth Regiment
James Harvey, Company C, Sixty-Sixth Regiment
Wesley Henley, Company H, Forty-Eighth Regiment
William Johnson, Company M, Third Cavalry
Lewis Mason, Company M, Third Cavalry
Joseph Parker, Company H, Forty-Eighth Regiment
Abram Randall, Company M, Third Cavalry
Dick Robinson, Company C, Forty-Seventh Regiment
Silas Washington, Company E, Sixty-Sixth Regiment
William Wilson, Company H, Fifty-Third Regiment

Note: The redundancy in the companies in which men from Holmes served is no accident. The Third Colored Cavalry was recruited in Mississippi. The first company recruited in Vicksburg became Company A. The Third came to the Yazoo area a little later, and likely Johnson, Mason, and Randall joined at the same time. All three were born in Holmes and likely joined from there. Ellis and Cochran lived in Holmes after the war at the time they applied for accounts with the Freedman's Bank, but Ellis was born in Claiborne County and Cochran was born in Georgia and raised in Alabama. They likely joined the Third Cavalry before the three who were originally from Holmes.

Additionally, the widow of Providence Barris, a member of Company M, put his birthplace as Holmes County when she applied for a widow's pension after moving to Memphis, which she then received.

Those who died during their service have even fewer records by place of origin. The fourteen USCT veterans from Holmes who survived the war, remained in Mississippi at least for a time, and applied for accounts or pensions through the US government are a small fraction of those who served. At a time of massive displacement of people and property, recordkeeping is unsurprisingly incomplete.

BLACK LANDOWNERS IN HOLMES COUNTY: 1870 CENSUS[1]

District	Name	Age	Occupation	Real Estate $	Personal Estate $	Born in	Read?	Write?
Richland	Ambrose, David	40	Farmer	500	350	NC	N	N
Richland	Boyette, John R	29	Farmer	400	250	MS	N	N
Richland	Brown, Jno	51	Farmer	600	400	LA	Y	Y
Richland	Byrd, Jacob	44	Farmer	1,500	500	MS	N	N
Richland	Cowen, Wm	30	Farmer	300	300	AL	N	N
Richland	Crawford, Tom	60	Farmer	300	N/A	VA	N	N
Richland	Dulany, Virgil	35	Laborer	250	100	SC	N	N
Tchula	Early, Loor	48	Farmer	200	100	GA	N	N
Durant	Edmundson, Lew	23	Farmer	400	N/A	AL	N	N
Lexington	Evans, Edward	33	Blacksmith	2,000	300	NC	Y	Y
Richland	Falls, Willis	70	Farmer	2,000	250	NC	N	N
Tchula	Franklin, Adam	50	Farmer	500	300	SC	N	N

District	Name	Age	Occupation	Real Estate $	Personal Estate $	Born in	Read?	Write?
Lexington	Hodges, Jackson	55	Farmer	700	900	SC	N	N
Lexington	Hodges, Lewis	61	Farmer	2,000	1,000	SC	N	N
Lexington	Hoskins, Phil	36	Farmer	400	200	VA	Y	Y
Durant	Jefferson, Samuel	60	Farming	360	360	VA	N	N
Richland	McGuire, Milton H.	26	Farmer	3,000	1,000	MS	N	N
Richland	Miller, Jos	45		200	150	SC	N	N
Durant	Sproles, Alfred	29	Ditcher	200	50		N	N
Durant	Sproles, Carter	69	---Farmer	500	200	NC	N	N
Durant	Sproles, Dave	45	Farmer	300	250	NC	N	N
Durant	Stewart, Fred	38	Blacksmith	400	200	VA	Y	N
Richland	Taylor, Louis	30	Laborer	250	350	MS	N	N
Lexington	Truehart, Harrison	30	Blacksmith	400	200	VA	Y	Y
Lexington	Walton, George	54	Farmer	400	300	GA	Y	Y
Richland	Williams, Thomas	25	Farmer	260	1,000	MS	Y	Y

ROSENWALD SCHOOLS IN HOLMES COUNTY

Historic Name	Plan Type	Budget Year	Acres	Application #	Cost	Funding Sources			
						Negroes	White	Public	Rosen
Balters Store School	Two-teacher	1929–30	2.00	2-I	$2,800	$2,300	-	-	$500
Bee Lake School	Two-teacher	1922–23	4.00	70-B	$2,500	$700	$900	$200	$700
Bethlehem School	Two-teacher	1921–22	4.00	38-A	$2,400	$1,250	$250	$100	$800
Bowling Green School	Three-teacher	1929–30	3.00	16-I	$3,620	$2,620	$300	-	$700
Christmas School	Two-teacher	1923–24	2.00	58-C	$2,300	$1,000	$400	$200	$700
Clower School	Two-teacher	1922–23	2.00	113-B	$2,400	$1,000	$200	$500	$700
County Training School	Five-teacher	1924–25	10.00	91-D	$8,600	$1,200	$1,100	$5,000	$1,300
Durant School	Two-teacher	1921–22	4.00	23-A	$2,625	$1,625	$100	$100	$800
Egypt School	Two-teacher	1925–26	2.00	29-E	$2,200	$800	$300	$400	$700
Georgeville School	Two-teacher	1921–22	3.00	35-A	$2,650	$1,600	$75	$175	$800
Gibson School	Two-teacher	1924–25	4.00	62-D	$2,200	$900	$300	$300	$700
Gum Grove School	Two-teacher	1922–23	4.00	69-B	$2,400	$600	$900	$200	$700

Historic Name	Plan Type	Budget Year	Acres	Application #	Cost	Funding Sources			
						Negroes	White	Public	Rosen
Holly Grove School	Three-teacher	1923–24	2.00	57-C	$2,950	$1,800	$100	$150	$900
Holy City School	Two-teacher	1926–27	2.00	19-F	$2,400	$1,300	$200	$200	$700
Lebanon School	Two-teacher	1921–22	4.00	37-A	$2,500	$1,000	$100	$600	$800
Lexington School	Two-teacher	1921–22	4.00	100-A	$2,550	$1,450	$50	$250	$800
Liberty Hall School	Three-teacher	1921–22	4.00	43-A	$3,600	$2,200	$100	$300	$1,000
Meeks Chapel School	Two-teacher	1925–26	2.00	28-E	$2,200	$1,000	$300	$200	$700
Mt. Olive School	Three-teacher	1921–22	6.00	55-A	$4,200	$3,000	$200	-	$1,000
Newport School	Two-teacher	1930–31	2.00	5-J	$2,375	$1,425	$300	$250	$400
Poplar Springs School	One-teacher	1920–21	-	7	$1,800	$1,075	$125	$100	$500
Richland School	Three-teacher	1922–23	10.00	97-B	$4,100	$2,000	$200	$1,000	$900
Salem School	Two-teacher	1921–22	2.00	28-A	$2,650	$1,500	$200	$150	$800
Shiloh School	Two-teacher	1926–27	2.00	27-F	$2,600	$1,000	$700	$200	$700
Shop at Mt. Olive	Shop	1927–28	-	16-G	$2,200	$900	$50	$850	$400

Spring Hill School	Two-teacher	1921–22	5.00	6-A	$2,425	$1,200	$175	$250	$800
Tchula School	Three-teacher	1928–29	2.00	7-H	$4,350	$3,150	$500	-	$700
Trinity School	Two-teacher	1922–23	4.00	72-B	$2,500	$700	$1,000	$100	$700
Union School	Two-teacher	1921–22	3.00	22-A	$2,400	$1,500	$100	-	$800
West School	Three-teacher	1926–27	2.00	56-F	$3,500	$1,600	$500	$500	$900

From the Fisk University Rosenwald Fund Card File Database

THE MILESTON CIVIL RIGHTS FAMILIES

The Blackmon Family
The Brown Families
The Bruce Family
The Burn Families
The Byrd Families
The Carnegie Families
The Carthan Families
The Clark Families
The Cooper Families
The Davis Families
The Dulaney Families
The Ferguson Family
The Fort Families
The Hayes Families
The Head Family
The Hogan Families
The Howard Families
The Johnson Families
The Jordan Families
The Louis Families
The Love Families
The Mason Families
The McLaurin Family
The Mitchell Families
The Moore Family
The Reed Family
The Russell Family
The Sago Families
The Turnbow Family
The Wells Families
The Wesley Families
The White Families
The Williams Families
The Vance Family

From the Mileston Community Historical Marker Unveiling Program,
September 17, 2022

NOTES

INTRODUCTION

1. United States Census Bureau, "Quick Facts."
2. MDAH, "Durant Illinois Central Railroad Depot," 3–4.
3. MDAH, subject file, David Holmes.

CHAPTER 1: THE LAND IS MINE—BEFORE 1860

1. Galicki and Schmitz, *Roadside Geology of Mississippi*, 108–21. See also Mississippi Department of Environmental Quality, Geologic Map of the Tchula Quadrangle, 2018, https://geology.deq.ms.gov/Publications/OFR/0290/OF0290.pdf, showing the Cockfield formation in Holmes County.

2. Galicki and Schmitz, *Roadside Geology of Mississippi*, 138–40.

3. *Mississippi Archeology Society Newsletter* 57, no. 2 (June 2021). See also Starnes and Rego, "Prehistoric Kosciusko Quartzite Quarry."

4. Brown, *Archeological Survey*, 5–47.

5. Bowne, *Mound Sites*, 63–70, 138.

6. Brown, *Archeology of Mississippi*. On Providence mound, see also MDAH, National Register of Historic Places Inventory—Nomination form, January 16, 1987.

7. Akers, *Culture and Customs*, 68, 78.

8. Brown, *Archeology of Mississippi*, 73–75.

9. Clayton, Knight, and Moore, *De Soto Chronicles*, 445–88; Hudson, *Knights of Spain*, 340–52; Barnett, *Mississippi's American Indians*, 59.

10. For a fuller discussion of La Salle's impact, see Galloway, *La Salle and His Legacy*.

11. Galloway, *Choctaw Genesis*, 338–60; Akers, *Culture and Customs*, 94–95.

12. Wells, *Native Land*, 2.

13. Akers, *Culture and Customs*, xvi.

14. Carson, *Searching for the Bright Path*, 15–17.

15. Carson, *Searching for the Bright Path*, 17–23. See also Akers, *Culture and Customs*, 61–91.

16. Swanton, *Indian Tribes of the Lower Mississippi Valley*, 292 97.

17. Wells, *Native Land*, 125; Cushman, *History of the Choctaw, Chickasaw and Natchez Indians*, 187; Galloway, *La Salle and His Legacy*, 155.

18. Several additional sources were useful in producing this brief review of eighteenth-century history: Englebert and Teasdale, *French and Indians in the Heart of North America*; Galloway, *La Salle and His Legacy*; O'Brien, *Choctaws in a Revolutionary Age*; Pinnen and Weeks, *Colonial Mississippi*; Reeves, *Choctaw before Removal*; Smithers, *Native Southerners*; Usner, *American Indians in the Lower Mississippi Valley*; Woods, *French-Indian Relations*, 94–109; Noley, "Early 1700s."

19. Swanton, *Indian Tribes of the Lower Mississippi Valley*, 293–96.

20. Brain, *Tunica Archeology*, 303.

21. Meserve, "About Shumaka."

22. Carson, *Searching for the Bright Path*, 70–85.

23. Carson, *Searching for the Bright Path*, 44.

24. Several sources describe the history of the Leflore family, including Coleman, "Greenwood Leflore"; Deupree, "Greenwood Leflore"; Shackleford, "*Leflore Family and Choctaw Indian Removal*"; Smith, *Greenwood Leflore*; Ray, *Chieftain Greenwood Leflore*.

25. Coleman, "Greenwood Leflore"; Cushman, *History of the Choctaw, Chickasaw and Natchez Indians*, 331–32, 42–45.

26. Coleman, "Greenwood Leflore"; Shackleford, "Leflore Family and Choctaw Indian Removal," 8–9.

27. Durant, *"Footsteps" of a Durant Choctaw*, 295.

28. Deupree, "Greenwood Leflore," 141.

29. Beckert, *Empire of Cotton*, 9–11. See also Dattel, *Cotton and Race*, 27–85.

30. Beckert, *Empire of Cotton*, 85, 101.

31. Dattel, *Cotton and Race*, 34–35.

32. The following material is drawn and summarized from Kennedy, "Yazoo Land Sales"; Magrath, *Yazoo, Law and Politics*, 1–70; Robertson, *Conquest by Law*, 3–141; Saunt, "Financing Dispossession"; Saunt, *Unworthy Republic*, 173–201; Watson, *Buying America from the Indians*; Baptist, *Half Has Never Been Told*, 19–21.

33. Kennedy, "Yazoo Land Sales," 186.

34. Rothman, *Ledger and the Chain*, 7.

35. Diouf, "Clotilda."

36. Rolinson, *Grassroots Garveyism*, 27.

37. Libby, *Slavery and Frontier Mississippi*, 56.

38. Sydnor, *Slavery in Mississippi*, 67–101. Libby, *Slavery and Frontier Mississippi*, 56–58.

39. Libby, *Slavery and Frontier Mississippi*, 86–87.

40. Carson, *Searching for the Bright Path*, 70–85.

41. Kidwell, *Choctaws and Missionaries*, 22–24

42. Linceum, *Pushmataha*, 89. Durant, *"Footsteps" of a Durant Choctaw*, 195.

43. Watson, *Buying America from the Indians*, 342–58; Robertson, *Conquest by Law*, 141; Saunt, *Unworthy Republic*.

44. Author communication with James Taylor Carson.

45. Deupree, "Greenwood Leflore," 143–44. See also Shackleford, "Leflore Family and Choctaw Indian Removal," 24.

46. Kidwell, *Choctaws and Missionaries*, 116–46.

47. Recounted in chapter by Carson in O'Brien, *Pre-removal Choctaw History*. O'Brien, *Choctaws in a Revolutionary Age*, 221–32.

48. The treaty can be found at https://www.choctawnation.com/wp-content/uploads/2022/03/1830treaty-of-dancing-rabbit-creek.pdf. See also Kidwell, *Choctaws and Missionaries*, 141–42.

49. Carson, *Searching for the Bright Path*, 124.

50. Durant, *"Footsteps" of a Durant Choctaw.*

51. Office of the Chancery Clerk, Holmes County, Land Deed Records, 1827–77, 34–114.

52. Shackleford, "Leflore Family and Choctaw Indian Removal," 57–69.

53. "George W. Harkins to the American People," https://www.ushistory.org/documents// harkins.htm.

54. Mississippi Band of Choctaw Indians, "Choctaw Today."

55. Mississippi Band of Choctaw Indians, "Choctaw Today."

56. Durant, *"Footsteps" of a Durant Choctaw.*

57. Saunt, *Unworthy Republic*, 201–27. Saunt details land companies terrorizing those with preemptive rights.

58. Sumter, *Josiah Impson.*

59. Coleman, "Last Chief of the Choctaws." See also Saunt, *Unworthy Republic*, 134–35.

60. Deupree, "Greenwood Leflore," 146; Smith, *Greenwood Leflore*, 70.

61. Fletcher, "Public Land Sales."

62. Chappell, "Some Patterns of Land Speculation."

63. Saunt, "Financing Dispossession" includes a map of Chocchuma land sales. Most Holmes County land was sold through the Mount Salus office per the Bureau of Land Management.

64. Jordan, "Politician of Expansion."

65. For more on William Gwin, see Stanley, "Senator William Gwin."

66. "Frauds in Land Sales," *Niles Register*, May 2, 1835.

67. Rainwater, *Mississippi*, 10–13.

68. Office of the Chancery Clerk, Holmes County, Land Deed Records, 1827–77, 7–9.

69. *Weekly Mississippian*, October 31, 1834; See also a defense of Gwin in the *Weekly Mississippian*, August 8, 1834.

70. George R. Fall, then editor of the *Mississippian*, wrote to James K. Polk of the incident. Cited by Jerry Mitchell in the *Clarion-Ledger*, May 5, 1973.

71. Edwards, "Antebellum Holmes County, Mississippi," 134.

72. Office of the Chancery Clerk, Holmes County, Land Deed Records, 1827–77.

73. Combined across two family-owned plantations. Richard Archer was "one of the first citizens of Tchula" and part of a group that was authorized to open a bank there in 1837, although the bank never actually opened. The timing suggests a further association with the NEMLC and/or the Chocchuma Land Company. Works Progress Administration for Mississippi Source Material, copy digitized by the Mississippi Library Commission (Jackson, Record Group 60, Volume XXVI), 8.

74. Garrett Keirn likely brought slaves with him from Maryland, but on at least one occasion he bought slaves in Maryland after he moved to Mississippi. The Dorchester County Maryland Chattel Records show such a purchase in the period 1827 to 1833, http://slavery .msa.maryland.gov/html/research/slavebuy.html.

75. Haskins, *Pinckney Benton Stewart Pinchback.*

76. Edwards, "Holmes County Veterans of the Civil War Index."
This website provides an index to Holmes County residents who fought for the Confederacy in the Civil War and Confederate units raised in Holmes County. The information has been indexed from Rowland, *Military History of Mississippi* and other sources.

77. Edwards, "Antebellum Holmes County, Mississippi," 237

78. Gates, *The Black Church*, 210–11; Karade, *Handbook of Yoruba Religious Concepts*, 5–8; Raboteau, *Canaan Land*, 13–16; Mitchell, *Black Church Beginnings*, 23–45.

79. Mitchell, *Black Church Beginnings*, 16.

80. Charters, *Roots of the Blues*, 5–9; Sublette, *The World That Made New Orleans*, 56–63.

81. Charters, *Roots of the Blues*, 119–51.

82. *Lexington Union*, May 18, 1839.

83. Libby, *Slavery and Frontier Mississippi*, 41–45.

84. Johnson, *River of Dark Dreams*, 244–79.

85. Ads in the *Lexington Union*; *Weekly Mississippian* provided by Professor Douglas B. Chambers, executive director, Igbo History Foundation, LLC; Chambers, *Documenting Runaway Slaves in the Atlantic World*. Federal Writers' Project, "Slave Narrative Project," 45–46. The narratives are flawed as documentary evidence as recollections from seventy years earlier and as interviewers were white government employees of varying skill. Still, they are among the relatively few written accounts from people who had been enslaved.

86. Gist, *Mis-Educating Blacks*, 51–52.

87. MDAH, *Works Progress Administration*, 251.

88. Snyder, "Suicide, Slavery and Memory."

89. *Vicksburg Whig*, March 13, 1861. There are an additional 14 runaways from Holmes County documented by Professor Douglas Chambers, executive director of the Igbo History Foundation at the University of Southern Mississippi. That project has documented 2,487 individual runaways from Mississippi. The actual number of runaways is doubtless much higher as many slaveholders sent out a posse to look for fugitives and ads were placed only if fugitives were caught by county sheriffs. Chambers, *Documenting Runaway Slaves*.

90. Ads in the *Lexington Union*; *Weekly Mississippian* provided by Professor Douglas B. Chambers, executive director, Igbo History Foundation, LLC; Chambers, *Documenting Runaway Slaves*.

91. Sydnor, *Slavery in Mississippi*, 253.

92. See Glaude, *Exodus!*, 44–62; Gates, *The Black Church*, 88–92; traditional pre–Civil War spirituals, "Go down, Moses, "Oh Mary, don't you weep . . ."

CHAPTER 2: CIVIL WAR TO JIM CROW—1861 TO 1890

1. Precinct level results are in the *Lexington Advertiser*, November 9, 1860.

2. The description of the secession convention relies on Smith, *Mississippi Secession Convention*, supplemented by contemporaneous newspaper reports.

3. Smith, *Mississippi Secession Convention*, 202, 209; US Census, National Archives and Records Administration (1860 microfilm series M653, Roll 598), 355.

4. Smith, *Mississippi Secession Convention*, 86, 92–93, 118–20.

5. From Mississippi Declaration of Secession, https://www.mshistorynow.mdah.ms.gov/sites/default/files/2021-08/secession-causes.pdf.

6. Edwards, "Holmes County Veterans of the Civil War Index." For more history of the Thirty-eighth Infantry Regiment, see Giambrone, "Beneath Torn and Tattered Flags."

7. Edwards, "Holmes County Veterans of the Civil War Index."

8. MDAH, Governor Pettus Collection, Series 757, Box 943, Folder 12, February 10, 1863.

9. Gage, "Gage Family Collection."

10. Both the Union and the Confederacy initially allowed substitutes, although the Confederacy rescinded the policy later in the war. See Doyle, "Replacement Rebels."

11. Hahn, *A Nation under Our Feet*, 100.

12. Edwards, "Company F, 5th Mississippi Cavalry."

13. Mississippi State University, "James Z. and Elizabeth B. George"; Smith, *James Z. George*.

14. Redkey, *A Grand Army of Black Men*, 7.

15. Gladstone, *United States Colored Troops*, 120. Most had accounts in the Freedman's Bank, which asked veteran status. See US Department of the Treasury, "Freedman's Bank and Family Histories," https://home.treasury.gov/about/history/freedmans-bank-building/freedmans-bank-and-family-histories. The bank collapsed in 1873 and wiped out the savings of those freedmen who had deposits there.

16. See Main, *Story of the Marches, Battles and Incidents*.

17. Yarbrough, *Choctaw Confederates*, 75–113.

18. Deupree, "Greenwood Leflore," 150–51.

19. Main, *Story of the Marches, Battles and Incidents*, 105–06.

20. Official records do not include anyone named Leflore among the Third Colored Cavalry troops. Those who joined likely did so in civilian roles.

21. The First Mississippi Mounted Rifles, a white Union troop that formed in 1863, was also part of the raid. The troop originally had numbered about six hundred but were down to three hundred by the winter of 1864 and included only one member from Holmes County. Johnson, "1st Mississippi Mounted Rifles."

22. Surby, *Grierson's Grand Raid*, 252–53.

23. Harris, *Presidential Reconstruction*, 18–36.

24. MDAH, *Works Progress Administration*, 171.

25. See Foner, *Reconstruction*, xvii-xxv for a discussion of the historiography; also see Lemann, *Redemption*; Hahn, *A Nation under Our Feet*.

26. See Foner, *Reconstruction*; Hahn, *A Nation under Our Feet*, 150–51.

27. Hahn, *A Nation Under Our Feet*, 150–51.

28. *Lexington Advertiser*, October 23, 1968.

29. Garner, *Reconstruction in Mississippi*, 176–82.

30. Harris, *Presidential Reconstruction*, 106–14.

31. Holmes may have been one of the counties that omitted candidates from the ballot as the Daily Mississippian in reporting totals on October 5, 1865, says only that Humphreys had a majority of "about 600" over his lead opponent in Holmes County.

32. Gienapp, *Civil War and Reconstruction*, 327–29.

33. Edwards, "Holmes County Veterans of the Civil War Index."

34. Witty, "Reconstruction in Carroll and Montgomery Counties." Witty's grandfather Dr. J. W. Holman "was a boyhood chum of J. Z. George," and the Witty family was related by marriage to the Hooker family in Holmes County.

35. *Carpetbaggers* refers to northerners who came south after the war; scalawags are southerners who sided with the Union before or right after the end of the war.

36. See Hargrove, *Mississippi's Federal Courts*, 73–115 for background on Judge Hill. The quote is on page 104. See also Smith, *James Z. George*, 88 for a reference to George and Walthall's pro bono representation.

37. The author thanks Sara Brewer at the National Archives in Atlanta for her diligent search.

38. *Clarion-Ledger*, November 1, 1866. Violent incidents involving the Heggie family continued into the twentieth century. In 1902, an African American tenant farmer attempted to poison Aurelius Heggie, although the tenant "continued to deny that he had until after Mr. Heggie had loosened one of his plow lines and swung him to a limb for a few minutes." In 1907, Homer Heggie, Aurelius's son, shot a man named Will Bell, "a desperate mulatto" and "a criminal of a very dangerous type." The *Vicksburg Herald* wrote that "the killing was entirely justifiable" because Bell had previously resisted arrest in Winona and threatened to kill Heggie. *Winona Democrat*, August 19, 1902; *Vicksburg Herald*, September 14, 1907.

39. Harris, *The Day of the Carpetbagger*, 19.

40. MDAH, Freedmen's Bureau Records, 1865–1878, Assistant Commissioner, NARA Series 826, Roll 1. See also https://bioguide.congress.gov/search/bio/B000189.

41. MDAH, Freedmen's Bureau Records, 1865–1878, Assistant Commissioner, NARA Series 826, Roll 46.

42. MDAH, Freedmen's Bureau Records, 1865–1878, Assistant Commissioner, NARA Series 826, Roll 49.

43. MDAH, Freedmen's Bureau Field Office Records, 1865–1872, Roll 16, Letters received, Jul–Nov 1867, image 55 of 127, NARA microfilm publication, M1907.

44. M Howard to Coll Thomas, January 25, 1866, H-14 1866, Registered Letters Received. Series 2052, MS Assistant Commissioner, Bureau of Refugees, Freedmen and Abandoned Lands, Record Group 105, NARA.

45. Grim, "Between Forty Acres and a Class Action Lawsuit"; interview with the author, February 2, 2023. Transcribed by the Freedmen and Southern Society Project, University of Maryland.

46. Hahn, *A Nation under Our Feet*, 145–46.

47. Oubre, *Forty Acres and a Mule*, 10.

48. Hoffnagle, "The Southern Homestead Act."

49. Thomas became a significant industrialist who, according to his *New York Times* obituary and a subsequent article, left an estate of over $10 million. *New York Times*, January 12 and January 29, 1903.

50. Oubre, *Forty Acres and a Mule*, 75–76.

51. Oubre, *Forty Acres and a Mule*, 22–45.

52. Schweninger, *Black Property Owners in the South*, 146.

53. Schweninger, *Black Property Owners in the South*, 82–83.

54. Ashford, *Mississippi Zion*, 44.

55. The names of Black landowners in Holmes County in 1870 are listed in the appendix.

56. Morgalla, *Black Ownership of Farmland*; Gist, "Educating a Southern Rural Community."

57. An A. D. Ambrose bought land on July 13, 1865, which could be the sale to the Black farmer listed as David Ambrose in the 1870 Census.

58. Office of the Chancery Clerk, Holmes County, General Index to Land Deeds, Reverse, 1833–77; See also Deed Book Q, 398; Deed Book S; 536; Deed Book R, 443.

59. Will D. Campbell quotes from Mrs. Gwin's memoir in his book *Providence*, 141–42.

60. *Clarion-Ledger*, March 21, 1868.

61. See Harris, *The Day of the Carpetbagger*, 115–59.

62. Harris, *The Day of the Carpetbagger*, 157–58.

63. *Clarion-Ledger*, May 13, 1868.

64. Powell, "Correcting for Fraud."

65. The full text of the Constitution ratified in 1869 can be found at https://www
.mshistorynow.mdah.ms.gov/issue/mississippi-constitution-of-1868.

66. See Span, *From Cottonfield to Schoolhouse*, 23–116.

67. Mayes, *History of Education in Mississippi*, 282.

68. MDAH, *Works Progress Administration*, 274.

69. Holmes County, Mississippi, "Little Red Schoolhouse."

70. See Gist, "Educating a Southern Rural Community," 60–71, and Span, *From Cottonfield to Schoolhouse*, 1–116.

71. Alvord, *Semi-Annual Report(s)*, Report 1, 1.

72. Alvord, *Semi-Annual Report(s)*, Report 10, 2–8, 28–30.

73. "Marcus Morton Holmes," University of Washington University Libraries, https://digitalcollections.lib.washington.edu/digital/collection/gar/id/32/.

74. Holmes County, Mississippi, "Little Red Schoolhouse." See also Gist, *Mis-Educating Blacks*, 37–39.

75. Gist, "Educating a Southern Rural Community," 64. Also, Simmons's grave in Falls family cemetery notes he was born on St. Bart's in 1844.

76. The directory of African American students at Dartmouth College is at Dartmouth Historical Black Alumni Exhibit (badahistory.net). My thanks to Professor Matthew F. Delmont for pointing me to it.

77. Report of the State Board of Education, 1871, page 36.

78. Angell, *Bishop Henry McNeal Turner*, 268–69.

79. Wharton, *The Negro in Mississippi*, 259–60.

80. Fitzgerald, *The Union League Movement*, 9–112.

81. Vogt, "James D. Lynch."

82. Fitzgerald, *The Union League Movement*, 111.

83. *Grenada Sentinel*, June 27, 1868.

84. *Clarion-Ledger*, April 15, 1869.

85. "A Howl from Lynch" reprinted on March 23, 1869, by the *Tri-Weekly Clarion* from the *Colored Citizen Monthly*, a newspaper Lynch founded.

86. *Tri-Weekly Clarion*, May 27, 1869.

87. MDAH, 2022 historical marker.

88. Backgrounds on individual legislators include Eric Foner's 1996 book, *Freedom's Lawmakers*, supplemental material provided by historian Steven Hahn from his files, a search of all Mississippi newspapers from the period, and the record of state legislative proceedings. Newspaper articles are also included on the website Against All Odds, the First Legislators in Mississippi, maintained by DeeDee Baldwin, https://much-ado.net/legislators/.

89. Foner, *Freedom's Lawmakers*, 214. See also Baldwin, "Against All Odds."

90. MDAH, *Works Progress Administration*, 193.

91. MDAH, *Works Progress Administration*, 193.

92. Foner, *Freedom's Lawmakers*, 111. See also Baldwin, "Against All Odds."

93. Foner, *Freedom's Lawmakers*, 204. See also Baldwin, "Against All Odds."

94. Foner, *Freedom's Lawmakers*, 207.

95. *Canton Mail*, April 3, 1875.

96. MDAH, *Works Progress Administration*, 170, 489.

97. Lemann, *Redemption*, 110–19.

98. *Lexington Advertiser*, April 3, 1874. The quote is from the *Lexington Advertiser*, and the italics are theirs.

99. *Clarion-Ledger*, April 7, 1874.

100. Foner, *Freedom's Lawmakers*, 28.

101. Lemann, *Redemption*, 85–91; Hahn, *A Nation under Our Feet*, 297–98.

102. *Clarion-Ledger*, August 11, 1875.

103. *Vicksburg Herald*, October 14, 1874

104. *Weekly Mississippi Pilot*, August 14, 1875.

105. *Weekly Mississippi Pilot*, August 21, 1875.

106. Ames, *Chronicles from the Nineteenth Century*. Quotes are from letters on from Adelbert Ames on August 5, 1875 (125–26); September 3, 1875 (159–60); and September 11, 1875 (175).

107. Between August 25 and August 27, 1875, the ad appeared in the *Clarion-Ledger*, the *Vicksburg Herald*, and likely other papers as well

108. The *Lexington Advertiser* actually says they went to North Dakota, but that is not where the Black Hills are located.

109. Harris, *The Day of the Carpetbagger*, 617–18.

110. *Yazoo Herald*, November 10, 1876.

111. *Yazoo Herald*, November 10, 1876.

112. On August 15, 1885, the *Weekly Democrat-Times* in Greenville printed that several of Mississippi's federal representatives—including Senator Walthall—were urging Marshall's appointment as United States Minister to Liberia, where there were resettlements of people who had been enslaved in the United States. "Marshall is well educated, intelligent, good looking and well behaved, and if appointed will do his country and his race credit at Monrovia."

113. Gist, *Mis-Educating Blacks*, 41–42.

114. Kirwan, *Revolt of the Rednecks*, 21.

115. MDAH subject file, Absolom West.

116. Griffith, *Dauntless in Mississippi*, 75.

117. The county records at MDAH for 1884 show only the vote for winning electors. However, populist candidate Frank Burkitt a decade later received only 273 votes for governor.

118. From the *Comet*, January 17, 1880.

119. *Comet*, November 20, 1880

120. *Chronicle Star*, January 7, 1881.

121. *Clarion-Ledger*, November 18, 1880. Baxter Wilson was presumably the spouse of Mrs. Baxter Wilson, whose father enslaved Harrison Truehart.

122. Ali, *In the Lion's Mouth*, 48–77. See also Gaither, "Blacks and the Southern Farmers' Alliance Movement"; Gaither, *Blacks and the Populist Movement*.

123. Willis, *Forgotten Time*, 128–29. It operated until 1897, and none of the farmers who did business with the store lost land during the period.

124. *Winona New Farmer*, July 25, 1888.

125. Sieber, "The Black Populist Movement."

126. Albert Clark of Holmes County was also in the Fifth, although not in the same company as Cromwell.

127. MDAH, Record of Pardons Granted 1886–1888, Series 817, Box 1056, Page 33, May 14, 1886. Cromwell was pardoned by Governor Lowry at the recommendation of then former governor Stone. Cromwell apparently had considerable political skill.

128. Willis, *Forgotten Time*, 129–36. See also Pratt, *Sowing the Wind*, 56–58.

129. *Clarion-Ledger*, September 5,1889.

130. *Grenada Sentinel,* September 7, 1889.

131. Ali, *In the Lion's Mouth* and personal correspondence. Barbara Williams, descendant of the Colored Farmers' Alliance leader, does not believe he was from Wilkinson County. Her family believes he was from the Delta. Cromwell said in his Gambrell trial testimony that he was living by the Tallahatchie River. An 1889 piece in the *Clarion-Ledger* said he had lived previously in Hinds County. Louis Hall, whose great-grandmother was Hannah Levinson, recalls she had a picture of Oliver Cromwell in his Union army uniform but does not recall her discussing the Colored Farmers' Alliance. It is possible there were two men and also possible one man had two families.

132. *Weekly Democrat,* September 11, 1889.

133. For additional context on Gambrell, see Nicholas, "'The Spirit of an Age.'"

134. Duels were illegal in Mississippi but did occur. Former general Wirt Adams (the same one who fought at Franklin Church) was a character witness for Hamilton at his 1888 trial. He was later shot in a duel with John H. Martin, an ally of Gambrell. Both men died at the scene.

135. *Daily Commercial Herald,* March 30, 1888; *Semi-Weekly Leader* (Brookhaven), April 5, 1888. A discussion of the trial is also included in Nicholas, "'The Spirit of an Age,'" 137–69.

136. Nembhard, *Collective Courage.* Nembhard has written a history of economic cooperation with multiple examples from Holmes County and the Mississippi Delta.

137. *Yazoo Herald,* March 28, 1890.

138. Pratt, *Sowing the Wind,* 10–143 was especially useful on the history of the 1890 convention. See also Kirwan, *Revolt of the Rednecks,* 8–9, 59–74; Clark, "The Mississippi Constitutional Convention."

139. Pratt, *Sowing the Wind,* 51–52.

140. *Yazoo Herald,* February 21, 1890.

141. Henry Hooker's grandson, Wilburn Hooker, became a state legislator in the twentieth century and a member of the Mississippi State Sovereignty Commission.

142. McMillen, *Dark Journey,* 41.

143. Quoted in Clark, "The Mississississippi Constitutional Convention."

144. See Stone, "A Note on Voter Registration," for registration numbers in 1892 and an analysis of who passed the understanding clause.

CHAPTER 3: A NEW CENTURY—1900 TO 1950

1. Blackmon, *Slavery by Another Name,* 402.

2. *Lexington Advertiser,* March 12, 1909. See also Tuskegee University, "Monroe Work Today Dataset Compilation."

3. *Lexington Advertiser,* June 17, 1910.

4. *Vicksburg Herald,* November 21, 1905.

5. *Lexington Advertiser,* September 11, 1908.

6. *Lexington Advertiser,* February 14, 1908.

7. Tuskegee University, "Monroe Work Today Dataset Compilation."

8. Chicago Historical Society, "African Americans."

9. The title of this chapter is taken from a hymn printed in Bishop Clemmons's 1996 biography of Bishop Mason. The closing lines are "Sinner be wise. Open your eyes. Whenever He comes, I know he'll take me home. Then I shall rise, surely shall rise."

10. The COGIC began as a local church called Church of God in Christ in Lexington in 1897. Its first general assembly was in Memphis in 1907 where it was incorporated in a tristate area. See White, *The Rise to Respectability*, 39–40.

11. Church of God in Christ, "About Us," https://www.cogic.org/about-us/.

12. Roll, *Spirit of Rebellion*, 88.

13. St. Paul Church of God in Christ, http://www.stpaulthemotherchurch.org/.

14. Raboteau, *Slave Religion*, 44–92; Gates, *The Black Church*, 103.

15. Raboteau, *Canaan Land*. Note that AME churches also embraced the Holy Spirit as an empowering force, but among the other theological differences, Bishop Turner saw sanctification—or Christian perfection—as a gradual rather than a revelatory process. Angell, *Bishop Henry McNeal Turner*, 269.

16. King, *Blues All around Me*, 16. The COGIC was the home church of many well-known blues, gospel, and R&B artists and developed a unique gospel sound.

17. Most of the biographical material on Mason is from Clemmons, *Bishop C. H. Mason* and from St. Paul Church of God in Christ, "Our History," www.stpaulthemotherchurch.org/history. Both sources were authorized by the Church of God in Christ at the time they were developed.

18. Jones, *White Too Long*, 38–45.

19. Calvin White in his 2012 book on the Church of God in Christ notes that Smith endorsed the principles of sanctification and that her work was distributed throughout the South. White writes, "Mason might have read it, though no direct evidence of this has been produced." White, *The Rise to Respectability*, 17.

20. Smith, *An Autobiography*, 92.

21. Clemmons, *Bishop C. H. Mason*, 71.

22. Clemmons, *Bishop C. H. Mason*, 6. The term *slave religion* is common historical usage. Dr. Percy Washington, pastor of Sweet Canaan Church of God in Christ, has pointed out that "slave religion" is a misnomer, as the vitality of the religion of enslaved people is something they brought from Africa, not something developed during slavery.

23. Sernett, *African American Religious History*, 317–18.

24. Robeck, *The Azuza Street Mission and Revival*, 35–36.

25. Clemmons, *Bishop C. H. Mason*, 46–48;

26. Sernett, *African American Religious History*, 323.

27. *Lexington Advertiser*, January 17, 1908.

28. Clemmons, *Bishop C. H. Mason*, 70–71.

29. May, "A Survey of Glossolalia and Related Phenomena"; Mischel, "African Powers in Trinidad."

30. Catherine Beyer, "The Orishas: Aganyu, Babalu-Aye, Chango, and Eleggua," Learn Religions, February 3, 2019, https://www.learnreligions.com/orishas-gods-of-santeria-95915

31. Gates, *The Black Church*, 213.

32. St. Paul Church of God in Christ, "Our History."

33. *Jackson Daily News*, April 1, 1918.

34. Hamilton, *Sanctified Revolution*, 99–107.

35. White, *The Rise to Respectability*, 55–76.

36. For more on the Till murder and COGIC, see Tyson, *The Blood of Emmett Till*, 63–75; Gorn, *Let the People See*, 60–61; Whitfield, *A Death in the Delta*.

37. The funeral was covered in the *Chicago Tribune*, *Ebony* and *Jet* magazines, and multiple newspapers worldwide.

38. Hamilton, *Sanctified Revolution*.

39. Conversations with Dr. Percy Washington and Elder William Kenneth Dean.

40. Stuart Grayson Noble, *Forty Years of the Public Schools in Mississippi, With Special Reference to the Education of the Negro* (New York City: Teachers College, Columbia University, 1918), 108.

41. Noble, *Forty Years of the Public Schools*, 141–42.

42. *Holmes County Times*, May 11, 1906.

43. *Lexington Advertiser*, August 7, 1908.

44. Simmons and Martin, *Down behind the Sun*, 50.

45. White, *The Rise to Respectability*, 83–86.

46. Butler, *Women in the Church of God in Christ*, 129–34.

47. Simmons and Martin, *Down behind the Sun*, 1–2, 6–7.

48. Author interview with Bishop William Dean, September 7, 2022.

49. Butler, *Women in the Church of God in Christ*, 103.

50. Simmons and Martin, *Down Behind the Sun: The story of Arenia Conelia Mallory*, 18.

51. Author interviews with Pastor Dr. Percy Washington, May 18, 2022, and September 15, 2022.

52. Butler, *Women in the Church of God in Christ*, 107.

53. The film is *Twenty Pearls: The Story of the Alpha Kappa Alpha Sorority*. "History," Alpha Kappa Alpha Sorority Incorporated, https://aka1908.com/about/history/. The author thanks Holmes County AKA member Melissa Coats for the reference.

54. Michals, "Mary McLeod Bethune."

55. Butler, *Women in the Church of God in Christ*, 110.

56. Butler, *Women in the Church of God in Christ*, 129.

57. Author interviews with Eddie James Carthan and Bishop William Dean, who both served with Mallory on the board.

58. *Greenwood Commonwealth*, April 3, 1925.

59. See Baughn, "Rosenwald Schools In Mississippi"; Fisk University, "Franklin Library Special Collections." See also Hoffschwelle, *The Rosenwald Schools of the American South*.

60. Du Bois, *The Souls of Black Folk*, 23.

61. Author interview with Dr. Sylvia Reedy Gist, April 4, 2022.

62. The Rosenwald Schools in Holmes County and the value contributed to each from a variety of sources are listed in the appendix. From Fisk University, "Franklin Library Special Collections."

63. Hoffschwelle, *The Rosenwald Schools of the American South*, 236–37; conversation with Jennifer Baughn, MDAH.

64. See Hoffschwelle, *The Rosenwald Schools of the American South*, 230–38; Gist, "Educating a Southern Rural Community," 72–100.

65. Hoffschwelle, *The Rosenwald Schools of the American South*, 178–80.

66. Gist, "Educating a Southern Rural Community," 113.

67. Author interview with Dr. Sylvia Reedy Gist, April 4, 2022.

68. Adelman, *Famous Women*.

69. Gist, *Mis-Educating Blacks*, 66–72.

70. Gist, "Educating a Southern Rural Community," 240.

71. Exodus 10:12. "And the LORD said unto Moses, stretch out thine hand over the land of Egypt for the locusts, that they may come up upon the land of Egypt, and eat every herb of the land."

72. *New York Times*, September 10, 1911.

73. *Lexington Advertiser*, April 11, 1955. Perhaps Walter Leake Keirn's most prominent offspring was Nellie Sutton Keirn, who became president of the Mississippi University for Women.

74. The 1910 Census was the first that collected agricultural data by race. Of the 1,365 farm owners, 770 were African American and 591 were native-born whites. Holmes County also had 4,664 Black tenant farmers and 448 white tenant farmers.

75. Gist, *Mis-Educating Blacks*, 59–65.

76. Giesen, "'The Truth about the Boll Weevil.'"

77. *Lexington Advertiser*, August 26, 1910.

78. *Lexington Advertiser*, June 20, 1913.

79. *Lexington Advertiser*, July 4, 1913.

80. In 2017, the USDA reported that Mississippi was the third-largest cotton growing state, after Texas and Georgia, with 1,220,000 bales harvested; California was fifth with 996,000 bales harvested.

81. Geib, *Soil Survey*.

82. Geib, *Soil Survey*.

83. Beckert, *Empire of Cotton*, 377; Federal Reserve Bulletins.

84. McMurchy, "'The Red Cross Is Not All Right!'"; Barry, *Rising Tide*, 269–71, 82–89, 319–20.

85. Saikku, *This Delta, This Land*, 40–44.

86. United States Senate Hearings before the Committee on Commerce, January 23–31, 1928.

87. Part of a quotation from W. E. B. Du Bois. The full quote is "Now is the accepted time, not tomorrow, not some more convenient season. It is today that our best work can be done and not some future day or future year. It is today that we fit ourselves for the greater usefulness of tomorrow. Today is the seed time, now are the hours of work, and tomorrow comes the harvest and the playtime." It is derived from Isaiah 49:8–11. From Du Bois, *Prayers for Dark People*, 36.

88. Mikkelson, "Coming from Battle."

89. *Lexington Advertiser*, September 1, 1927.

90. Rolinson, *Grassroots Garveyism*; Roll, Jarod, "The Lazarus of American Farmers," in Reid and Bennett, *Beyond Forty Acres and a Mule*, 132–55.

91. Hill, *The Marcus Garvey and United Negro Improvement Association Papers*, 991.

92. *Negro World*, October 18, 1930.

93. *Modern Farmer*, February 16, 1931.

94. Gist, *Mis-Educating Blacks*, 84.

95. *Modern Farmer*, April 15, 1930. The article notes that the purchasing association was founded in 1911. There may therefore have been cooperative purchases prior to the 1916 Land Act. The author thanks Sylvia Reedy Gist for calling attention to the importance of the 1916 Act.

96. "Farmers End Three-Day Meeting in Mound Bayou," *Chicago Defender*, September 5, 1931.

97. Hope, "Rochdale Cooperation among Negroes."

98. McElvaine, *The Great Depression*, 134–35.

99. Conkin, *A Revolution Down on the Farm*, 57.

100. He won South Carolina with 98 percent.

101. *New York Times*, July 24, 1979 (Tugwell obituary). See also Holley, *Uncle Sam's Farmers*, 106.

102. McElvaine, *The Great Depression*, 187.

103. Rural Organizing and Cultural Center, "Bloodlines," 26–40. After the summer of 1988 and again in the spring of 1990, the interviews were published in a periodical called *Bloodlines*. The second issue, focused on the civil rights movement, was also published by Westview Press in 1991 as a book, *Minds Stayed on Freedom*.

104. Thomas and Amberson, *The Plight of the Share-Cropper*, 1.

105. Baldwin, *Poverty and Politics*, 197.

106. *Greenwood Commonwealth*, June 15, 1936.

107. The STFU also had support at Providence Farm in Holmes County, as discussed in the section "Providence Lost" later in this chapter.

108. Conversations with Supervisor Leroy Johnson. Supervisor Johnson is Walter Jones's grandson.

109. Roll, *Spirit of Rebellion*, 29.

110. *Clarion-Ledger*, August 2, 1939.

111. Mileston is about a mile from Howard; both are just a few miles south of Tchula.

112. *Winston County Journal*, June 26, 1969.

113. Holley, *Uncle Sam's Farmers*, 68–70.

114. *Hope Star*, June 29, 1935.

115. Holley, *Uncle Sam's Farmers*, 185–86.

116. *Clarion-Ledger*, February 11, 1940.

117. *Hope (Arkansas) Star*, January 27, 1937.

118. Baldwin, *Poverty and Politics*, 197–99.

119. Material on Tugwell from his obituaries: *New York Times*, July 24, 1979; *Los Angeles Times*, July 24, 1979.

120. Holley, *Uncle Sam's Farmers*, 112.

121. *Yazoo Semi-Weekly Sentinel*, August 9, 1940; *Clarion-Ledger*, August 11, 1940.

122. *Clarion-Ledger*, September 26, 1940.

123. *Yazoo Herald*, July 18, 1941.

124. Gist, "Educating a Southern Rural Community," 117.

125. Wood, "The Roots of Black Power."

126. *Hattiesburg American*, June 5, 1941. Syndicated in multiple Mississippi newspapers.

127. Press release cited in Wood, "The Roots of Black Power."

128. *Jackson Advocate*, February 18, 1950. Note that the *Advocate* article misspelled Davis's name as Shedrick, and it has been corrected here.

129. Howell, *Hazel Brannon Smith*. The biographical material in this chapter is from Jeffrey Howell's book.

130. Howell, *Hazel Brannon Smith*, 16–19.

131. Morris, *North Toward Home*, 54.

132. Tracy, *Mississippi Moonshine Politics*, 11, 26, 35–37. The Mileoway, a mile outside Durant, continues as a local restaurant.

133. Howell, *Hazel Brannon Smith*, 26.

134. Howell, *Hazel Brannon Smith*, 34.

135. Swan, "The Harlem and Detroit Riots."

136. Archer, *Growing Up Black in Rural Mississippi*, 43.

137. *Lexington Advertiser*, July 15, 1943.

138. *Lexington Advertiser*, November 7, 1946.

139. *Jackson Advocate*, November 2, 1946.

140. Ferguson, *Remaking the Rural South*.

141. Holley, *The Second Great Emancipation*, 48–53.

142. Franklin, "Early Years," 1.

143. Ferguson, *Remaking the Rural South*, 86–87.

144. Daniels, *A Southerner Discovers the South*, 149, 54.

145. Campbell, *Providence*, 96–99.

146. Ferguson, *Remaking the Rural South*, 115.

147. Interview with Fannye Booker, Tamiment Library and Robert F. Wagner Labor Archives, New York University.

148. Taylor, "I Done Made My Mind Up," 42. Taylor interviewed Hampton on January 28, 1996. Hampton was elected to the Tchula Board of Aldermen in 1977 and became a member of the board of supervisors in 1979.

149. Rushing, *Empty Sleeves*, 93–94; Taylor, "I Done Made My Mind Up," 44–48.

150. Ferguson, *Remaking the Rural South*, 132.

151. Author interview with William Minter, January 30, 2023.

152. Ferguson, *Remaking the Rural South*, 120–22.

153. Franklin, "Early Years," 64–65.

154. Campbell, *Providence*, 208.

155. Gates, "What Was Black America's Double War?"

156. *Pittsburgh Courier*, January 31, 1942.

157. "Meridian Elks in Double 'V' Drive," *Jackson Advocate*, August 15, 1942; "Over $2000 in Bonds and Stamps Sold Last Sunday at Patriotic Tea Here," *Jackson Advocate*, September 18, 1943.

158. *Durant News*, January 20, 1944.

159. Cripps and Culbert, "The Negro Soldier."

160. Davis, "When Youth Protest."

161. The LDF became completely independent of the NAACP in 1957.

162. Davis, "When Youth Protest."

CHAPTER 4: DESEGREGATION AND VOTING RIGHTS—1950 TO 1980

1. Povall, *The Time of Eddie Noel*, 4–22.

2. Tracy, *Mississippi Moonshine Politics*, 80–81; Howell, *Hazel Brannon Smith*, 67.

3. Povall, *The Time of Eddie Noel*, 52.

4. Rural Organizing and Cultural Center, "Bloodlines (Minds Stayed on Freedom)," 64.

5. Howell, *Hazel Brannon Smith*, 70–71.

6. *Mississippi Enterprise*, January 30, 1954.

7. Noel also wrote to Robert Clark, who was state representative at the time. Clark went to see Noel at Whitfield. See Povall, *The Time of Eddie Noel*, 167–68.

8. Rural Organizing and Cultural Center, "Bloodlines (Minds Stayed on Freedom)," 64.

9. 102 Congressional Record 4515–16 (1956).

10. Howell, *Hazel Brannon Smith*, 79. Howell attributes the quote to Hodding Carter in Carter's piece, *The South Fights Back*.

11. Hustwit, William P., "Thomas P. Brady," *Mississippi Encyclopedia*.

12. Howell, *Hazel Brannon Smith*, 82.

13. See Rolph, *Resisting Equality*, 62–64.

14. Neil R. McMillen, *The Citizens' Council: Organized Resistance to the Second Reconstruction* (Urbana/ Chicago: University of Illinois Press, 1971, 1994), 27.

15. Including Byron de la Beckwith, who was to assassinate Medgar Evers.

16. Berman, *A House of David*, 241–45; author interview with Phil Cohen, December 27, 2022.

17. *Lexington Advertiser*, November 4, 1954.

18. Sovereignty commission files list each of these as contacts.

19. *Durant News*, March 30, 1952; Barker, "Don Carlos Barrett," 139.

20. McMillen, *The Citizens' Council*, 235.

21. From Alicia Patterson Fellowship papers, 1983, https://aliciapatterson.org/stories/separate-unequal.

22. Howell, *Hazel Brannon Smith*, 80.

23. *Lexington Advertiser*, July 22, 1954.

24. Howell, *Hazel Brannon Smith*, 82–91. See also McMillen, *The Citizens' Council*, 255–56.

25. Ferguson, *Remaking the Rural South*, 148.

26. See Ferguson, *Remaking the Rural South*, 151–52.

27. See Ferguson, *Remaking the Rural South*, 144–56, and Howell, *Hazel Brannon Smith*, 89–92.

28. Ferguson, *Remaking the Rural South*, 154.

29. Ferguson, *Remaking the Rural South*, 164.

30. Howell, *Hazel Brannon Smith*, 98.

31. Mississippi State Sovereignty Commission, "Holmes County," November 27, 1961, SCRID# 2-54-1-58-2-1-1, https://da.mdah.ms.gov/sovcom/result.php?image=images/png/cd02/013568.png&otherstuff=2|54|1|58|2|1|1|13313|1962, Mississippi State Sovereignty Commission Records, 1994–2006, MDAH. See also Howell, *Hazel Brannon Smith*, 117–20.

32. *Lexington Advertiser*, October 17, 1963.

33. *New York Times*, November 22, 1965.

34. "Hazel Brannon Smith: 'A Product of Her Times'—and a Force for Change," The Pulitzer Prizes, https://www.pulitzer.org/article/hazel-brannon-smith-product-her-times-and-force-change.

35. "T. R. M. Howard," *Mississippi Encyclopedia*. See also Beito and Beito, *T. R. M. Howard*, 83, and Williams, *Medgar Evers*, 52–53.

36. Beito and Beito, *T. R. M. Howard*, 78–79.

37. Percy Greene advocated for voting rights in the early 1950s, but he was uncomfortable with integration and became hostile to the NAACP, which led to boycotts of the *Jackson Advocate*. The *Advocate* provided positive coverage of Garvey's UNIA, and Greene

apparently shared Garvey's separatist views and opposed the push for integration led by the NAACP. After Greene's death in 1977, his heirs discovered he had become an informant for the Sovereignty Commission. Thompson, *Percy Greene and the Jackson Advocate*.

38. Beito and Beito, *T. R. M. Howard*, 122.

39. SNCC Legacy Project and Duke University, "SNCC Digital Gateway." The SNCC Digital Gateway is the product of a collaboration between the SNCC Legacy Project, founded by members of SNCC to tell their story, and Duke University. It includes links to archived primary source materials and references secondary sources, as well as a timeline of SNCC activities. It is an invaluable resource in studying the history of the civil rights movement in the 1960s.

40. "SNCC Digital Gateway," Amzie Moore.

41. Williams, *Medgar Evers*, 53.

42. Sojourner, *Thunder of Freedom*, 58.

43. Mendelsohn, *The Martyrs*, 1–20.

44. Beito and Beito, *T. R. M. Howard*, 121.

45. Booker, *Black Man's America*.

46. *Jackson Advocate*, May 14, 1955.

47. The undertaker was T. V. Johnson, and the doctors were W. A. Walwyn, chief surgeon at the Afro-American Sons and Daughters Hospital in Yazoo City, and C. C. Battle from Indianola.

48. Mendelsohn, *The Martyrs*, 1–20.

49. Beito and Beito, *T. R. M. Howard*, 189.

50. Mississippi State Sovereignty Commission, "Memo to Director State Sovereignty Commission," January 23, 1959, SCRID# 2-54-1-5-1-1-1, 1959, Mississippi State Sovereignty Commission Records, 1994–2006, MDAH, https://da.mdah.ms.gov/sovcom/result .php?image=images/png/cd02/013388.png&otherstuff=2|54|1|5|1|1|1|13136.

51. Mississippi State Sovereignty Commission, "Memo to Director State Sovereignty Commission," April 2, 1959, 1959, SCRID# 2-54-1-9-1-1-1, 1959, Mississippi State Sovereignty Commission Records, 1994–2006, MDAH, https://da.mdah.ms.gov/sovcom/result .php?image=images/png/cd02/013395.png&otherstuff=2|54|1|9|1|1|1|13143.

52. Mississippi State Sovereignty Commission, "Report on Holmes County," June 6, 1962, SCRID# 2-54-1-62-1-1-1, 1962, Mississippi State Sovereignty Commission Records, 1994–2006, MDAH, https://da.mdah.ms.gov/sovcom/result.php?image=images/png/cd02/013577.png&ot herstuff=2|54|1|62|1|1|1|13322.

53. Rural Organizing and Cultural Center, "Bloodlines," 40.

54. "Rosie Head Oral History Interview Conducted by John Dittmer in Tchula, Mississippi, 2013 March 13," Video, Library of Congress, https://www.loc.gov/item/2015669173/.

55. There are many sources on the history of SNCC. See "SNCC Digital Gateway"; Dittmer, *Local People*, 92; Carson, *In Struggle*, 19–30; Halberstam, *The Children*, 1–234; Ransby, *Ella Baker and the Black Freedom Movement*, 239–72.

56. SNCC Digital Gateway, Voter Education Project Launches.

57. SNCC Digital Gateway, Bob Moses.

58. Rural Organizing and Cultural Center, "Bloodlines," 55–56.

59. Smith, *Food Power Politics*, 44. Smith devotes a full chapter to the Lewis Grocer Company. His citation for the quote found on page 44 of his work is Morris Lewis Jr. memo to Retail Customers, November 15, 1962, Series 3, Subseries 7, box 11, folder 11–73, James O.

Eastland Collection, Archives and Special Collections, J. D. Williams Library, University of Mississippi, Oxford.

60. Smith, *Food Power Politics*, 27–73. See also de Jong, *You Can't Eat Freedom*, 88–141.

61. SNCC Digital Gateway, Timeline: Fall 1962, Leflore County Cuts Off Surplus Commodities.

62. Smith, *Food Power Politics*, 141–42.

63. Watkins, *Brother Hollis*, 198–200.

64. *Holmes County Herald*, April 10, 1963. See also Sojourner, *Thunder of Freedom*, 24–32.

65. Rural Organizing and Cultural Center, "Bloodlines (Minds Stayed on Freedom)," 5.

66. Rural Organizing and Cultural Center, "Bloodlines (Minds Stayed on Freedom)," 5–13.

67. "Rosie Head Oral History Interview."

68. Sojourner, *Thunder of Freedom*, 31–33.

69. Watkins, *Brother Hollis*, 116.

70. Dittmer, *Local People*, 192–93.

71. Cobb, *This Nonviolent Stuff'll Get You Killed*, 138.

72. *Holmes County Herald*, June 13, 1963.

73. *Lexington Advertiser*, June 13, 1963.

74. Forman, *The Making of Black Revolutionaries*, 354–61.

75. Dittmer, *Local People*, 200–07.

76. Ivanhoe Donaldson in Dittmer, *Local People*, 209.

77. Dittmer, *Local People*, 244.

78. Dittmer, *Local People*, 242–43.

79. Rural Organizing and Cultural Center, "Bloodlines (Minds Stayed on Freedom)," 10.

80. Email to the author, August 14, 2022.

81. Bingham has posted a 2019 interview and his reflections on Freedom Summer on crmvet.org, a site maintained by veterans of the civil rights movement. His reflections include a long letter he wrote in 1965, which he also sent in an email to the author, https://www.crmvet.org/vet/bingham.htm.

82. Quoted in *New York Times*, November 7, 1986, Mario Savio Obituary.

83. Marshall Ganz biography, https://www.hks.harvard.edu/faculty/marshall-ganz; communication with the author.

84. ROCC interview with Reverend Russell.

85. SNCC Digital Gateway, Building the Mississippi Freedom Democratic Party.

86. COFO Papers accessed through SNCC Digital Gateway.

87. Dittmer, *The Good Doctors*, 56–59.

88. SNCC Digital Gateway, Hartman Turnbow.

89. Katagiri, *The Mississippi State Sovereignty Commission*, 67.

90. Dittmer, *Local People*, 273–302; *New York Times*, July 28, 1964.

91. Forman, *The Making of Black Revolutionaries*, 386–406.

92. Carson, *In Struggle*, 133–52.

93. The author has had many conversations over the years with SNCC activists about this period, most recently with Courtland Cox, chair of the SNCC Legacy Project. See also Carson, *In Struggle*, 123–29, 53–74; Forman, *The Making of Black Revolutionaries*, 396–406.

94. Sojourner, *Thunder of Freedom*, 74–75; Dittmer, *Local People*, 333–35; SNCC Digital Gateway, ASCS.

95. Dittmer, *Local People*, 333–35.

96. Andrews, *Freedom Is a Constant Struggle*, 85.

97. The details of the challenge and the response to it are described in Carson, *In Struggle*; Dittmer, *Local People*; and on the SNCC Digital Gateway under MFDP Congressional Challenge. The point about maintaining regular action is taken from Andrews, *Freedom Is a Constant Struggle*, 83–85.

98. Dittmer, *Local People*, 340–41.

99. SNCC Digital Gateway, Ed Brown.

100. Sojourner, *Thunder of Freedom*, 60–61. Sue Lorenzi later changed her name to Sojourner. The text uses Lorenzi because that is the name by which she was known in Holmes County.

101. At this writing, Dave Howard's son is the current president of the Mileston Co-op, and Robert Head's grandson is the current director.

102. "Rosie Head Oral History Interview."

103. Sojourner, *Thunder of Freedom*, 69–70, 117.

104. See Dittmer, *Local People*, 363–88; Sanders, "More Than Cookies and Crayons; SNCC Digital Gateway, Child Development Group of Mississippi Runs Head Start Programs; and Lemann, *The Promised Land*, 323–27.

105. Sojourner, *Thunder of Freedom*, 118.

106. Hale, "The Struggle Begins Early."

107. Dittmer, *Local People*, 370–71.

108. Rural Organizing and Cultural Center, "Bloodlines (Minds Stayed on Freedom)."

109. "Rosie Head Oral History Interview."

110. See Sanders, "More Than Cookies and Crayons"; Hale, "The Struggle Begins Early."

111. Sanders, "More Than Cookies and Crayons"; Sojourner, *Thunder of Freedom*, 148–49.

112. Munford, "Black Gravity."

113. Hustwit, *Integration Now*.

114. Hustwit, *Integration Now*, 41.

115. Hustwit, *Integration Now*, 69–70.

116. Sewell and Dwight, *Mississippi Black History Makers*, 355.

117. Hustwit, *Integration Now*, 75–78.

118. Hustwit, *Integration Now*, 80.

119. Author interview with Mel Leventhal, August 13, 2022.

120. Gist, "Educating a Southern Rural Community," 201. Gist's count is based on her review of school board records; Leventhal believes the board may have undercounted.

121. Melvyn Leventhal from Department of Health, Education, and Welfare reporting at the time. See also Sojourner, *Thunder of Freedom*, 112.

122. *Holmes County Herald*, August 5, 1965.

123. Rural Organizing and Cultural Center, "Bloodlines (Minds Stayed on Freedom)," 35–42.

124. Rural Organizing and Cultural Center, "Bloodlines (Minds Stayed on Freedom)," 55–64.

125. Munford, "Black Gravity," 9. Munford references an unpublished speech by Kenneth Dean, director of the Mississippi Council on Human Relations, entitled "An Evaluation of School Desegregation in Mississippi" as the source of the data.

126. *New York Times*, September 11, 1965.

127. Some sources name Beatrice Alexander as a parent and others give her mother's name as Mattie. Sylvia Reedy Gist recently interviewed the Alexanders, and I thank her for the correction.

128. United States Supreme Court, October 29, 1969, https://supreme.justia.com/cases/federal/us/396/19/.

129. Holmes County took an extra year to implement school desegregation since the Durant school district, which had a higher white percentage than the rest of the county, broke from the county school district and implemented a zoned plan for school attendance, which the NAACP Legal Defense Fund had accepted. Holmes was one of four school districts that were allowed two-stage desegregation plans.

130. Munford, "Black Gravity," 54.

131. MacLeod, "Bridging Street and School."

132. Central Holmes Christian School, https://www.chcstrojans.com.

133. National Center for Education Statistics, https://nces.ed.gov/globallocator/.

134. Sojourner, *Thunder of Freedom*, 130–31.

135. Sojourner, *Thunder of Freedom*, 131.

136. *New York Times*, October 30, 1965.

137. Andrews, *Freedom Is a Constant Struggle*, 85, 121.

138. Salamon and Van Evera, "Fear, Apathy, and Discrimination." The article argues persuasively that fear rather than apathy was responsible for depressed voter turnout in the 1960s. One consequence of strong organization, like that in Holmes County, used as an example in the study, is to help manage fear.

139. See SNCC Digital Gateway, June 1966, Meredith March.

140. Dittmer, *Local People*, 339; Halberstam, *The Children*, 527–32.

141. Dittmer, *Local People*, 393.

142. Sojourner, *Thunder of Freedom*, 175.

143. Dittmer, *Local People*, 393–94.

144. SNCC Digital Gateway, Meredith March.

145. Sojourner, *Thunder of Freedom*, 177.

146. *New York Times*, June 23, 1966, 1.

147. *Clarion-Ledger*, June 24, 1966.

148. Kenneth Fairly, "This Is Time for Tempered Words on the Part of All Racial Leaders," *Delta Democrat-Times*, June 26, 1966, 4.

149. Beats, in Mississippi, are supervisory districts, so named from the pre–Civil War period when the board of supervisors was the board of police.

150. Sojourner, *Thunder of Freedom*, 200–05.

151. Sojourner, *Thunder of Freedom*, 226–27.

152. Clark, "Oral History Interview."

153. Campbell, *Robert G. Clark's Journey to the House*, 60–61; author interview with Representative Bryant Clark, July 18, 2019.

154. See appendix.

155. Author interview with Eddie James Carthan, September 7, 2022.

156. Andrews, *Freedom Is a Constant Struggle*, 121–23.

157. Dittmer, *Local People*, 416

158. Love was also reportedly personally unpopular, as a Lexington football coach, in the rival town of Durant.

159. Campbell, *Robert G. Clark's Journey to the House*, 132.

160. Clark's son Representative Bryant Clark has sponsored legislation for universal preschool in Mississippi, but it has made little progress in the legislature to date.

161. William Dean was then the pastor of St. Paul Church of God in Christ; he remains pastor and is now bishop for northern Mississippi's 182 COGIC churches.

162. Biography provided in an email from Elder William Kenneth Dean and from the St. Paul website, http://www.stpaulthemotherchurch.org/pastor.htm.

163. Leroy Johnson, who currently serves on the board of supervisors, is James Johnson's son.

164. Hampton had been a student at Fannye Booker's Camp Schools at Providence Farm.

165. *Holmes County Herald*, December 31, 1987.

166. *Holmes County Herald*, June 17, 1971, and March 20, 1980.

167. *Clarion-Ledger*, May 6, 1971.

168. Graham, "The White Supremacist Group Which Inspired a Racist Manifesto."

169. From Gist ("Educating a Southern Rural Community"), who reviewed primary source material from ROCC. Author interview with Leroy Johnson, who saw photographs of Boyd after the beating, January 10, 2023.

170. *Lexington Advertiser*, June 29, 1978.

171. *Lexington Advertiser*, August 10, 1978, and August 17, 1978.

172. "Arnett Otha Lewis Jr.," Find a Grave, https://www.findagrave.com/memorial/189620672/arnett-otha-lewis#source.

173. *Lexington Advertiser* articles July 13, August 17, August 31, December 17, 1978; Gist, "Educating a Southern Rural Community"; Howell, *Hazel Brannon Smith*; author interview with Phil Cohen, December 27, 2022.

174. Watkins, *Brother Hollis*, 348–53.

175. Multiple biographies of Mamie Till Mobley and author interview with Eddie James Carthan, September 7, 2022.

176. Howell, "The Mayor, the Murder . . . and the Methodists," 300.

177. See *New York Times*, October 20, 1982, and November 5, 1982.

178. Gist, "Educating a Southern Rural Community," 257–60.

179. *Washington Post*, August 3, 2015.

180. Howell, "The Mayor, the Murder . . . and the Methodists," 300; interview with Eddie James Carthan, September 7, 2022.

181. *Washington Post*, August 5, 2015; *Los Angeles Times*, April 26, 2019.

182. Conversations with Secretary Mike Espy.

183. Nash and Taggart, *Mississippi Politics*, 242–45.

CHAPTER 5: THE SECOND REDEMPTION—1960 TO PRESENT

1. The most recent USDA data assesses the market value of land in Holmes at just over $66 million from 241,000 acres of farmland. In 1969, the market value was just over $67 million in 2017 dollars from 359,000 acres farmed. Thus, the value per acre farmed is higher now: about $275 per acre with an average of 487 acres per farm; in 1960 it was $189 per acre at an average of 294 acres per farm. USDA Census of Agriculture, County Profile, Holmes County Mississippi.

2. DuPont, "Our History."

3. Holley, *The Second Great Emancipation*, 128–29.

4. Fite, *Cotton Fields No More*, 177–78.

5. Holley, *The Second Great Emancipation*, 50–53

6. Holley, *The Second Great Emancipation*, 94–96.

7. Fite, "Mechanization of Cotton Production"; quoted in Daniel, *Breaking the Land*, 245.

8. See also Conkin, *A Revolution Down on the Farm*; Ransom and Sutch, *One Kind of Freedom*.

9. Daniel, *Breaking the Land*, 250–51.

10. Conkin, *A Revolution Down on the Farm*.

11. Williams, Cotton, "Chemicals and the Political Ecologies of Racial Capitalism," 14–19.

12. Agency for Toxic Substances and Disease Registry, *Toxaphene—ToxFAQs*.

13. Mississippi Department of Environmental Quality, *Total Maximum Daily Loads*.

14. Rural Organizing and Cultural Center, "Bloodlines," 10–11.

15. *New York Times*, September 10, 1995.

16. Whitten, *That We May Live*, 55–56.

17. Whitten, *That We May Live*, 10.

18. Whitten, *That We May Live*, 135, 208.

19. Sydnor, *Slavery in Mississippi*, 94. See also Dennis, "Mississippi State Colonization Society."

20. *New York Times*, November 10, 1963.

21. de Jong, *You Can't Eat Freedom*, 44–53.

22. United States Census Bureau, *U.S. Census of Population: 1960*, 33; United States Census Bureau, "Quick Facts, Holmes County."

23. US Census: only thirty-one employer establishments in Holmes County are Black owned.

24. Daniel, *Disposession*, 140. Pete Daniel's book is a thorough treatise on discrimination against Black farmers in the 1960s through the 1990s.

25. Daniel, *Disposession*, 23.

26. *Washington Post*, August 26, 1990.

27. *News and Observer*, September 23, 1990.

28. Congressional Research Service, Racial and Ethnic Equity in US Agriculture, April 1922.

29. USDA Disparity Study, D. J. Miller and Associates, 1996. The full text is available online at https://static.ewg.org/reports/2021/BlackFarmerDiscriminationTimeline/1996_DJ-Miller-Report.pdf.

30. Interview with Valerie Grim, February 2, 2023.

31. Morgalla, *Black Ownership of Farmland*. USDA did not supply information on size of farm by race in the late 1960s. Morgalla produced a 1968 report on farmland ownership in Holmes County. There are some gaps in his data, but they allow rough comparisons. Current ownership data was obtained by special request through NASS.

32. Smith's first deed was witnessed by J. M. Dyer, son of one of Holmes County's delegates to the secession convention; the second was witnessed by a member of the Hooker family.

33. Genealogical research shared with the author by the Hart family.

34. From a June 1986 profile of the Harts in *Ebony Magazine*.

35. Information provided by Rashad Hart, February 11, 2023.

36. *News and Observer*, September 23, 1990.

37. *Clarion-Ledger*, August 4, 1991.

38. Author interview with former secretary Mike Espy, December 30, 2022.

39. *Hattiesburg American*, January 30, 1994.

40. *Clarion-Ledger*, January 25, 1995.

41. Information from court records and stories in the *Clarion-Ledger*, October 26 and 29, 2000, and October 26 and 30, 2002.

42. Interviews with Taharga Hart, December 16, 2022, and Rashad Hart, December 27, 2022.

43. "For as the new heavens and the new earth that I am making stand before me, said the Lord, so shall stand your seed and your name." Isaiah 67; "Then I saw a new heaven and a new earth, for the first heaven and the first earth had passed away, and there was no longer any sea." Revelation 27.

44. Smith, *Food Power Politics*, 67.

45. White, *Freedom Farmers*, 65.

46. White, *Freedom Farmers*, 72–87.

47. See Smith, *Food Power Politics*, 109–21; Nembhard, *Collective Courage*, 193–210; de Jong, *You Can't Eat Freedom*, 141–74.

48. Federation of Southern Cooperatives/Land Assistance Fund, "Federation of Southern Cooperatives/Land Assistance Fund."

49. Interview with Otis Wright, April 1, 2024, and April 9, 2024. See also "Growing All Seasons: High Tunnels," Natural Resources Conservation Service, https://www.nrcs.usda.gov/getting-assistance/other-topics/organic/nrcs-assistance-for-organic-farmers/growing-all-seasons-high-tunnels.

50. Interviews with Calvin Head, April 25, 2022, and April 5, 2024.

51. Interview with Mac Epps, April 1, 2024.

52. Interview with Earcine Evans, April 8, 2024. See also "Manifest Your Destiny Healing Herbal Retreat," Pure Ciné, https://www.ilovepurecine.com/.

EPILOGUE: STILL HERE

1. Holmes County has more than a dozen historical markers, plus several markers that are part of the Mississippi Blues Trail.

2. "Holmes CC Student Population," Univstats, https://www.univstats.com/colleges/holmes-community-college/student-population/.

3. The Mississippi State University Extension has provided updated population statistics for small towns using data released for redistricting: http://extension.msstate.edu/economic-profiles.

4. Interviews with Bryant Clark, July 18, 2019, April 25, 2022, and September 20, 2022.

5. Woods, *Development Arrested*, 169.

6. "Elmore James: The Sky Is Crying: The History of Elmore James," PopMatters, June 17, 2004, https://www.popmatters.com/jameselmore-skyiscrying-2495952033.html; multiple interviews with various members of the Rolling Stones reference Elmore James.

7. King, *Blues All around Me*, 51.

8. The district consolidated Durant public schools into the county school system in 2018. Casey Parks, "The Tragedy of America's Rural Schools," *New York Times Magazine*, September 7, 2021.

9. Paul Boger, "Feds Are Underfunding Mississippi Schools?," Mississippi Public Broadcasting, May 2, 2016, https://www.mpbonline.org/blogs/news/feds-are-underfunding-mississippi-schools/.

10. *Holmes County Herald*, October 6, 2022; September 26, 2024.

11. *Holmes County Herald*, September 1, 2022.

12. Anna Wolfe, "These Black Residents Are Led by an All-Black Local Government. But There's Still a 'Race Problem,'" *Mississippi Today*, February 1, 2021; interview with Leroy Johnson.

13. Interview with Katherine Barrett Riley, November 4, 2022.

14. *New York Times*, August 16, 1987, January 29, 1988, and September 26, 1990; Barrett Law Group website, https://barrettlawgroup.com/.

15. *Washington Post*, December 18, 1996.

16. Interview with Katherine Barrett Riley, November 4, 2022.

17. Interviews with Holmes County leadership.

18. Neirin Gray Desai, Samuel Boudreau, and Elena DeBre, "Fired Lexington Police Chief Exposed in Racist Recording Had a Checkered Past in Law Enforcement," Mississippi Center for Investigative Reporting, August 16, 2022.

19. Interview with Robert Hooker, September 18, 2022.

20. United States Department of Justice Civil Rights Division and United States Attorney's Office for the Southern District of Mississippi, *Investigation of the Lexington Police Department*, 1, 36, 46.

21. Chris McGreal, "Poorest Town in Poorest State: Segregation Is Gone but So Are the Jobs," *Guardian*, November 15, 2015.

22. Interview with James Starnes, October 31, 2022.

23. The names of the Mileston civil rights families that were listed in the program at the dedication are in the appendix. Some share heritage with families who bought land in Holmes County in the 1860s.

24. Interviews with Dr. Washington. History quoted on the church's Facebook page from Fifty Years Achievement from 1906–1956: A Period in History of the Church of God in Christ, by Charles H. Please, 1991 reprint; https://www.facebook.com/profile.php?id=100072106328439. His song can be heard on YouTube: https://www.youtube.com/watch?v=agyNEFM72Rs.

25. See the Historic Sweet Canaan Facebook page, https://www.facebook.com/mhf2016/, and website, https://mhf-hc.org/2022/11/21/welcome/.

APPENDIX 1870 CENSUS

1. The Census form included questions on the value of real estate owned and the value of other personal property. The form also included columns to be marked by the census-taker if the respondent could not read or write. An "N" in the table for those columns means that column was marked by the census taker.

BIBLIOGRAPHY

Adelman, Joseph. *Famous Women: An Outline of Feminine Achievement through the Ages with Life Stories of Five Hundred Noted Women.* New York: Ellis M. Lonow Company, 1926.

Agency for Toxic Substances and Disease Registry. *Toxaphene—ToxFAQs.* Atlanta, GA: Centers for Disease Control and Prevention, March 29, 2016. https://www.atsdr.cdc.gov/toxfaqs/tfacts94.pdf.

Akers, Donna L. *Culture and Customs of the Choctaw Indians.* Santa Barbara, CA: Greenwood, ABC-CLIO, 2013.

Ali, Omar. *In the Balance of Power: Independent Black Politics and Third-Party Movements in the United States.* Athens: Ohio University Press, 2020.

Ali, Omar. *In the Lion's Mouth: Black Populism in the New South, 1886–1900.* Jackson: University Press of Mississippi, 2010.

Alvord, John W. *Semi-Annual Report(s) on Schools for Freedmen.* Washington, DC: Government Printing Office, 1866–1870. First to Tenth Semi-Annual Report.

Ames, Blanche Butler, comp. *Chronicles from the Nineteenth Century: Family Letters of Blanche Butler and Adelbert Ames in Two Volumes.* Clinton, MA: Colonial Press, 1957.

Anderson, James D. *The Education of Blacks in the South, 1860–1935.* Chapel Hill: University of North Carolina Press, 1988.

Andrews, Kenneth T. *Freedom Is a Constant Struggle: The Mississippi Civil Rights Movement and Its Legacy.* Chicago: University of Chicago Press, 2004.

Angell, Stephen Ward. *Bishop Henry McNeal Turner and African American Religion in the South.* Knoxville: University of Tennessee Press, 1992.

Archer, Chalmers, Jr. *Growing Up Black in Rural Mississippi: Memories of a Family, Heritage of a Place.* New York: Walker and Company, 1992.

Ashford, Evan Howard. *Mississippi Zion: The Struggle for Liberation in Attala County, 1865–1915.* Jackson: University Press of Mississippi, 2022.

Baldwin, DeeDee. "Against All Odds: The First Black Legislators in Mississippi." https://much-ado.net/legislators/.

Baldwin, Sidney. *Poverty and Politics: The Rise and Decline of the Farm Security Administration.* Chapel Hill: University of North Carolina Press, 1969.

Bancroft, Frederic. *Slave Trading in the Old South.* Columbia: University of South Carolina Press, 1996.

Baptist, Edward E. *The Half Has Never Been Told: Slavery and the Making of American Capitalism.* New York: Basic Books, 2014.

Barker, Eugene C. "Don Carlos Barrett." *Southwestern Historical Quarterly* 20, no. 2 (October 1916): 139–45.

Barnett, James F. *Mississippi's American Indians.* Jackson: University Press of Mississippi, 2012.

Barry, John M. *Rising Tide: The Great Mississippi Flood of 1927 and How It Changed America.* New York: Simon and Schuster, 1997.

Baughn, Jennifer. "Rosenwald Schools in Mississippi." Mississippi History Now. September 2021. https://mshistorynow.mdah.ms.gov/issue/rosenwald-schools-in-mississippi.

Beard, Augustus Field. *A Crusade of Brotherhood: A History of the American Missionary Association.* Boston: Pilgrim Press, 1909.

Beckert, Sven. *Empire of Cotton: A Global History.* New York: Vintage Books, 2014.

Behrend, Justin. *Reconstructing Democracy: Grassroots Politics after the Civil War.* Athens: University of Georgia Press, 2017.

Beito, David T., and Linda Royster Beito. *T. R. M. Howard: Doctor, Entrpreneur, Civil Rights Pioneer.* Oakland, CA: Independent Institute, 2018.

Berman, Robert Lewis. *A House of David in the Land of Jesus.* Charleston, SC: Booksurge On-demand Publishing, 2007.

Bettersworth, John K., ed. *Mississippi In the Confederacy.* Vol 1, *As They Saw It.* Baton Rouge: Louisiana State University Press, 1961.

Blackmon, Douglas A. *Slavery by Another Name: The Re-enslavement of Black Americans from the Civil War to World War II.* New York: Anchor Books, 2009.

Booker, Simeon. *Black Man's America.* Englewood Cliffs, NJ: Prentice-Hall, 1964.

Bowne, Eric E. *Mound Sites of the Ancient South: A Guide to the Mississippian Chiefdoms.* Athens: University of Georgia Press, 2013.

Brain, Jeffrey P. *Tunica Archeology.* Cambridge, MA: Peabody Museum of Archeology and Ethnology at Harvard University, 1988.

Brooks, Maegan Parker, and Davis W. Houck, eds. *The Speeches of Fannie Lou Hamer: To Tell It Like It Is.* Jackson: University Press of Mississippi, 2011.

Brown, Calvin S. *Archeology of Mississippi.* Jackson: University Press of Mississippi, 1992. First published 1926.

Brown, Ian W. "An Archaeological Survey of the Tchula-Greenwood Bluffs Region, Mississippi." Unpublished manuscript, 1978.

Butler, Anthea D. *Women in the Church of God in Christ.* Chapel Hill: University of North Carolina Press, 2007.

Campbell, Will D. *Providence.* Waco, TX: Baylor University Press, 2002.

Campbell, Will D. *Robert G. Clark's Journey to the House.* Jackson: University Press of Mississippi, 2003.

Carson, Clayborne. *In Struggle: SNCC and the Black Awakening of the 1960s.* Cambridge, MA: Harvard University Press, 1995.

Carson, James Taylor. *Searching for the Bright Path: The Mississippi Choctaws from Prehistory to Removal.* Lincoln: University of Nebraska Press, 1999.

Center for Southern Culture. *Mississippi Encyclopedia.* Jackson: University Press of Mississippi, 2018 (online version).

Chambers, Douglas B. *Documenting Runaway Slaves in the Atlantic World.* Vol. 5, *Runaway Slaves in Mississippi 1800–1860.* Hattiesburg: University of Southern Mississippi, 2019.

Chappell, Gordon T. "Some Patterns of Land Speculation in the Old Southwest." *Journal of Southern History* 15, no. 4, (November 1949): 463–77.

Charters, Samuel. *The Roots of the Blues: An African Search.* Salem, NH: Da Capo Press, 1981.

Chicago Historical Society. "African Americans." Encyclopedia of Chicago. 2005. http://www.encyclopedia.chicagohistory.org/pages/27.html.

Clark, Eric Charles. "The Mississsippi Constitutional Convention of 1890: A Political Analysis." Master's thesis, University of Mississippi, May 1975.

Clark, Robert G. "Oral History Interview with African American Politician Robert G. Clark." Interview by John Dittmer. March 13, 2013.

Clayton, Lawrence, Vernon James Knight, and Edward C. Moore, eds. *The De Soto Chronicles: The Expedition of Hernando de Soto to North America 1539–1543; Volume 2.* Tuscaloosa: University of Alabama Press, 1993.

Clemmons, Ithiel C. *Bishop C. H. Mason and the Roots of the Church of God in Christ.* Bakersfield, CA: Pneuma Life Publishing, 1996.

Cobb, Charles E. *This Nonviolent Stuff'll Get You Killed.* New York: Basic Books, 2014.

Coleman, Harris Leflore. "Greenwood Leflore." Vaiden. September 29, 1994. https://www.vaiden.net/greenwood_leflore_history.pdf.

Cone, James H. *Black Theology and Black Power.* Maryknoll, NY: Orbis Books, 2018.

Cone, James H. *Risks of Faith: The Emergence of a Black Theology of Liberation, 1968–1998.* Boston: Beacon Press, 1999.

Conkin, Paul K. *A Revolution Down on the Farm: The Transformation of American Agriculture since 1929.* Lexington: University Press of Kentucky, 2009.

Cripps, Thomas, and David Culbert. "The Negro Soldier (1944): Film Propaganda in Black and White." *American Quarterly* 31, no. 5 (winter 1979): 616–40.

Cushman, H. B. *History of the Choctaw, Chickasaw, and Natchez Indians.* Norman: University of Oklahoma Press, 1962. First edition 1899.

Daniel, Pete. *Breaking the Land: The Transformation of Cotton, Tobacco, and Rice Cultures since 1880.* Urbana: University of Illinois Press, 1985.

Daniel, Pete. *Disposession: Discrimination against African American Farmers in the Age of Civil Rights.* Chapel Hill: University of North Carolina Press, 2013.

Daniels, Jonathan. *A Southerner Discovers the South.* New York: Macmillan, 1938.

Dattel, Gene. *Cotton and Race in the Making of America: The Human Costs of Economic Power.* Chicago: Ivan R. Dee, 2009.

Davis, Dernoral. "When Youth Protest: The Mississippi Civil Rights Movement, 1955–1970." Mississippi HistoryNow. August 2001. https://www.mshistorynow.mdah.ms.gov/issue/the-mississippi-civil-rights-movement-1955-1970-when-youth-protest.

Degler, Carl N. *The Other South: Southern Dissenters in the Nineteenth Century.* New York: Harper and Row Publishers, 1974.

de Jong, Greta. *You Can't Eat Freedom: Southerners and Social Justice after the Civil Rights Movement.* Chapel Hill: University of North Carolina Press, 2016.

Dennis, Dawn. "Mississippi State Colonization Society." Mississippi Encyclopedia. April 24, 2018. https://mississippiencyclopedia.org/entries/mississippi-state-colonization-society.

Deupree, Mrs. N. D. "Greenwood Leflore." *Publication of the Mississippi Historical Society* 7, (1902): 141–51.

Deutsch, Stephanie. *You Need a Schoolhouse: Booker T. Washington, Julius Rosenwald, and the Building of Schools for the Segregated South.* Evanston, IL: Northwestern University Press, 2011.

Dinges, Bruce J., and Shirley A. Leckie, eds. *A Just and Righteous Cause: Benjamin Grierson's Civil War Memoir.* Carbondale: Southern Illinois University Press, 2008.

Diouf, Sylviana A. "Clotilda, America's Last Slave Ship Stole Them from Home. It Couldn't Steal Their Identities." *National Geographic*, February 2020.

Dittmer, John. *The Good Doctors.* Jackson: University Press of Mississippi, 2009.

Dittmer, John. *Local People: The Struggle for Civil Rights in Mississippi.* Urbana: University of Illinois Press, 1995.

Dobak, William A. *Freedom by the Sword: The U.S. Colored Troops, 1862–1867.* Washington, DC: Center of Military History, United States Army, 2011.

Doherty, Patric J. "Integration Now: A Study of Alexander v. Holmes County Board of Education." *Notre Dame Law Review* 45, no. 3, (1970): 489–514.

Doyle, Patrick J. "Replacement Rebels: Confederate Substitution and the Issue of Citizenship." *Journal of the Civil War Era* 8, no. 1, (March 2018): 3–31.

Du Bois, W. E. B. *Black Reconstruction in America, 1860–1880.* New York: Free Press, 1962. First published 1935.

Du Bois, W. E. B. *Economic Co-operation among Negro Americans.* Atlanta, GA: Atlanta University Press, 1907.

Du Bois, W. E. B. *Prayers for Dark People.* Edited by Herbert Aptheker. Amherst: University of Massachusetts Press, 1980.

Du Bois, W. E. B. *The Souls of Black Folk.* Coppell, TX: Millenium Publications, 2014.

DuPont. "Our History." 2023. https://www.dupont.com/about/our-history.html.

Durant, Randle. *"Footsteps" of a Durant Choctaw.* Privately published, 1999.

Edwards, Dan. "Company F, 5th Mississippi Cavalry." Holmes County, Mississippi, Genealogical and Historical Web Site. 2006. http://sites.rootsweb.com/~msholmes/military/co-f-5th-miss.html.

Edwards, Dan. "Holmes County Veterans of the Civil War Index." Holmes County, Mississippi, Genealogical and Historical Web Site. September 16, 2006. https://sites.rootsweb.com/~msholmes/military/cw-idx.htm.

Edwards, J. Daniel. "Antebellum Holmes County, Mississippi: A History." Master's thesis, Mississippi State University, 1992.

Egerton, Douglas R. *The Wars of Reconstruction: The Brief Violent History of America's Most Progressive Era.* New York: Bloomsbury Press, 2014.

Englebert, Robert, and Guillaume Teasdale, eds. *French and Indians in the Heart of North America, 1630–1815.* East Lansing: Michigan State University Press, 2013.

Federal Writers' Project. "Slave Narrative Project, Vol. 9, Mississippi, Allen-Young." Library of Congress. 1936. https://www.loc.gov/item/mesn090/.

Federal Writers' Project. *Slave Narratives: A Folk History of Slavery in the United States from Interviews with Former Slaves.* Government Report, Washington, DC: Library of Congress, 1941.

Federation of Southern Cooperatives/Land Assistance Fund. "Federation of Southern Cooperatives/Land Assistance Fund." March 2024. https://app.joinit.com/o/federation-of-southern-cooperatives-laf.

Ferguson, Robert Hunt. *Remaking the Rural South: Interracialism, Christian Socialism, and Cooperative Farming in Jim Crow Mississippi*. Athens: University of Georgia Press, 2018.

Findlay, James F. "The Mainline Churches and Head Start in Mississippi: Religious Activism in the Sixties." *American Society of Church History* 64, no. 2 (June 1995): 237–50.

Fisk University. "Franklin Library Special Collections and Archives: Julius Rosenwald Fund Archives." September 5, 2023. https://fisk.libguides.com/c.php?g=1057119&p=7710823.

Fite, Gilbert C. *Cotton Fields No More: Southern Agriculture, 1865–1980*. Lexington: Univeristy Press of Kentucky, 1984.

Fite, Gilbert C. "Mechanization of Cotton Production since World War II." *Agricultural History* 54 (January 1980): 190–207.

Fitzgerald, Michael W. *Splendid Failure: Postwar Reconstruction in the American South*. Chicago: Ivan R. Dee, 2007.

Fitzgerald, Michael W. *The Union League Movement in the Deep South: Politics and Agricultural Change during Reconstruction*. Baton Rouge: Louisiana State University Press, 2000.

Fletcher, Ryan L. "Public Land Sales, 1800–1840s." Mississippi Encyclopedia. October 14, 2017. https://mississippiencyclopedia.org/entries/land-sales-public-1800-1840s/.

Foner, Eric. *Freedom's Lawmakers: A Directory of Black Officeholders during Reconstruction*. Baton Rouge: Louisiana State University Press, 1996.

Foner, Eric. *Reconstruction, America's Unfinished Revolution 1863–1877*. New York: Harper Perennial Classics, 2014.

Forman, James. *The Making of Black Revolutionaries*. Seattle: University of Washington Press, 1997.

Franklin, John Hope. *Reconstruction after the Civil War*. Chicago: University of Chicago Press, 2013.

Franklin, Samuel H., Jr. "Early Years of the Delta Cooperative Farm and the Providence Cooperative Farm." Unpublished manuscript provided by William Minter, n.d.

Gage, Jeremiah. "The Gage Family Collection." Archives and Special Collections, J. D. Williams Library. University of Mississippi, 1863.

Gaither, Gerald H. *Blacks and the Populist Movement*. Tuscaloosa: University of Alabama Press, 2005.

Gaither, Gerald H. "Blacks and the Southern Farmers' Alliance Movement." *East Texas Historical Journal* 14, no. 1 (1976): 25–38.

Galicki, Stan, and Darrel Schmitz. *Roadside Geology of Mississippi*. Missoula, MT: Mountain Press, 2016.

Gallay, Alan. *The Indian Slave Trade: The Rise of the English Empire in the American South, 1670–1717*. New Haven, CT: Yale University Press, 2002.

Galloway, Patricia K. *Choctaw Genesis, 1500–1700*. Lincoln: University of Nebraska Press, 1995.

Galloway, Patricia K., ed. *La Salle and His Legacy*. Jackson: University Press of Mississippi, 1982.

Garner, James Wilford. *Reconstruction in Mississippi*. New York: Macmillan, 1902.

Gates, Henry Louis, Jr. *The Black Church: This Is Our Story, This Is Our Song*. New York: Penguin, 2021.

Gates, Henry Louis, Jr. "What Was Black America's Double War?" https://www.pbs.org/wnet/african-americans-many-rivers-to-cross/history/.

Geib, W. J. *Soil Survey of Holmes County, Mississippi.* Government Report, US Department of Agriculture, Bureau of Soils, Washington, DC: Government Printing Office, 1909.

Giambrone, Jeffrey. "Beneath Torn and Tattered Flags: 2017 Edition." Mississippians in the Confederate Army, December 27, 2017. https://mississippiconfederates.wordpress.com/2017/12/27/beneath-torn-and-tattered-flags-2017-edition/.

Gienapp, William E., ed. *The Civil War and Reconstruction: A Documentary Collection.* New York: W. W. Norton, 2001.

Giesen, James C. "'The Truth about the Boll Weevil': The Nature of Planter Power in the Mississippi Delta." *Environmental History* 14, no. 4 (October 2009): 683–704.

Gist, Sylvia Reedy. "Educating a Southern Rural Community: The Case of Blacks in Holmes County Mississippi, 1870 to Present." PhD dissertation, University of Chicago, 1994.

Gist, Sylvia Reedy. *Mis-Educating Blacks in a Southern Rural Community: The Case of Holmes County, Mississippi.* South Holland, IL: Accurate Publishing Company, 2023.

Gladstone, William A. *The United States Colored Troops, 1863–1867.* Gettysburg, PA: Thomas Publications, 1996.

Glaude, Eddie S., Jr. *Exodus! Religion, Race, and Nation in Early Nineteenth-Century Black America.* Chicago: University of Chicago Press, 2000.

Gorn, Elliott J. *Let the People See.* Oxford: Oxford University Press, 2018.

Graham, David. "The White Supremacist Group Which Inspired a Racist Manifesto." *Atlantic,* June 22, 2015. https://www.theatlantic.com/politics/archive/2015/06/council-of-conservative-citizens-dylann-roof/396467/.

Griffith, Helen. *Dauntless in Mississippi: The Life of Sarah A. Dickey, 1838–1904.* Northampton: Metcalf, 1965.

Grim, Valerie. "Between Forty Acres and a Class Action Lawsuit." In *Beyond Forty Acres and a Mule,* edited by Debra A. Reid, and Evan P. Bennett. Gainesville: University Press of Florida, 2014, 271–96.

Grubbs, Donald H. *The Southern Tenant Farmers' Union and the New Deal.* Fayetteville: University of Arkansas Press, 2000.

Hagge, Patrick David. "The Decline and Fall of a Cotton Empire: Economic and Land Use Change in the Lower Mississippi River "Delta" South, 1930–1970." PhD Dissertation, Pennsylvania State University, 2013.

Hahn, Steven. *A Nation under Our Feet: Black Political Struggles in the Rural South from Slavery to the Great Migration.* Cambridge, MA: Belknap Press, 2003.

Halberstam, David. *The Children.* New York: Random House, 1998.

Hale, Jon N. "The Struggle Begins Early: Head Start and the Mississippi Freedom Movement." *History of Education Quarterly* 52, no. 4, (November 2012): 506–34.

Hamilton, Ovell. *Sanctified Revolution, The Church of God in Christ: A History of African American Holiness.* São Paulo, Brazil: UPBooks, 2021.

Hargrove, David M. *Mississippi's Federal Courts: A History.* Jackson: University Press of Mississippi, 2019.

Harris, William C. *The Day of the Carpetbagger: Republican Reconstruction in Mississippi.* Baton Rouge: Louisiana State University Press, 1979.

Harris, William C. *Presidential Reconstruction in Mississippi.* Baton Rouge: Louisiana State University Press, 1967.

Haskins, James. *Pinckney Benton Stewart Pinchback.* London: Macmillan, 1973.

Hill, Robert A., ed. *The Marcus Garvey and United Negro Improvement Association Papers, Volume VII, November 1927–August 1940.* Berkeley: University of California Press, 1991.

Hoffnagle, Warren. "The Southern Homestead Act: Its Origins and Operation." *Historian* 32, no. 4 (1970): 612–29.

Hoffschwelle, Mary S. *The Rosenwald Schools of the American South*. Gainesville: University Press of Florida, 2006.

Holley, Donald. *The Second Great Emancipation: The Mechanical Cotton Picker, Black Migration, and How They Shaped the Modern South*. Fayetteville: University of Arkansas Press, 2000.

Holley, Donald. *Uncle Sam's Farmers*. Urbana: University of Illinois Press, 1975.

Holmes County, Mississippi. "Little Red Schoolhouse." https://holmescountyms.org/little-red -schoolhouse.

Hope, John, II. "Rochdale Cooperation among Negroes." *Phylon* 1, no. 1 (1940): 39–52.

Howell, Jeffery. *Hazel Brannon Smith: The Female Crusading Scalawag*. Jackson: University Press of Mississippi, 2017.

Howell, Leon. "The Mayor, the Murder . . . and the Methodists." *Christianity and Crisis*, October 18, 1982, 299–306.

Hudson, Charles. *Knights of Spain, Warriors of the Sun: Hernando de Soto and the South's Ancient Chiefdoms*. Athens: University of Georgia Press, 1997.

Hudson, Charles, and Carmen Chavez Tesser. *The Forgotten Centuries: Indians and Europeans in the American South, 1521–1704*. Athens: University of Georgia Press, 1994.

Hurston, Zora Neale. *The Sanctified Church*. Berkeley, CA: Turtle Island, 1983.

Hustwit, William P. *Integration Now: Alexander v. Holmes and the End of Jim Crow Education*. Chapel Hill: University of North Carolina Press, 2019.

Johnson, Beau. "1st Mississippi Mounted Rifles: Mississippi's Union Battalion in the Civil War." Honor's thesis, University of Southern Mississippi, 2012.

Johnson, Walter. *River of Dark Dreams: Slavery and Empire in the Cotton Kingdom*. Cambridge, MA: Harvard University Press, 2013.

Jones, Robert P. *White Too Long: The Legacy of White Supremacy in American Christianity*. New York: Simon and Schuster, 2020.

Jordan, H. Donaldson. "A Politician of Expansion: Robert J. Walker." *Mississippi Valley Historical Review* 18, no. 3 (December 1932): 362–81.

Karade, Baba Ifa. *The Handbook of Yoruba Religious Concepts*. Newburyport, MA: Weiser Books, 2020.

Katagiri, Yasuhiro. *The Mississippi State Sovereignty Commission: Civil Rights and States' Rights*. Jackson: University Press of Mississippi, 2001.

Kehoe, Alice Beck. *North America before the European Invasions*. New York: Routledge, 2017.

Kennedy, Brenden Edward. "The Yazoo Land Sales: Slavery, Speculation, and Capitalism in the Early American Republic." PhD thesis, University of Florida, 2015.

Kidwell, Clara Sue. *Choctaws and Missionaries in Mississippi, 1818–1918*. Norman: University of Oklahoma Press, 1995.

King, B.B. *Blues All around Me: The Autobiography of B. B. King*. New York: First It Books, 2011.

Kirwan, Albert D. *Revolt of the Rednecks: Mississippi Politics, 1876–1925*. Lexington: University of Kentucky Press, 1951.

Krauthamer, Barbara. *Black Slaves, Indian Masters: Slavery, Emancipation, and Citizenship in the Native American South*. Chapel Hill: University of North Carolina Press, 2013.

Lemann, Nicholas. *The Promised Land*. New York: Alfred A. Knopf, 1991.

Lemann, Nicholas. *Redemption: The Last Battle of the Civil War*. New York: Farrar, Straus and Giroux, 2006.

Liardon, Roberts, comp. *Frank Bartleman's Azuza Street*. Shippensburg, PA: Destiny Image
     Publishers, 2006.
Libby, David J. *Slavery and Frontier Mississippi: 1720–1835*. Jackson: University Press of
     Mississippi, 2004.
Linceum, Gordon. *Pushmataha: A Choctaw Leader and His People*. Tuscaloosa: University of
     Alabama Press, 2004.
Litwack, Leon F. *Been In the Storm So Long: The Aftermath of Slavery*. New York: Vintage
     Books, 1980.
Long, Howard H. "The Negro Soldier in the Army of the United States." *Journal of Negro
     Education* 12, no. 3 (Summer 1943): 307–15.
Lynch, John Roy. *The Facts of Reconstruction*. N.p.: Pantianos Classics, 1913.
Lynch, John Roy. *John Roy Lynch: Reminiscences of an Active Life*. Jackson: University Press
     of Mississippi, 2008.
MacLeod, Jay. "Bridging Street and School." *Journal of Negro Education* 60, no. 3 (1991): 264.
Magrath, C. Peter. *Yazoo, Law and Politics in the New Republic: The Case of Fletcher v. Peck*.
     Providence: Brown University Press, 1966.
Main, Edwin M. *The Story of the Marches, Battles and Incidents of the Third United States
     Colored Cavalry: A Fighting Regiment in the War of Rebellion, 1861–5*. London: Forgotten
     Books, 2012. Originally published Louisville, KY: Globe Printing Company, 1908.
Mason, R. Paul. "Neglected Histories: The Cruger Families and the Roots of American
     Independence." *Journal of the American Revolution*, 2017.
May, L. Carlyle. "A Survey of Glossolalia and Related Phenomena in Non-Christian Religions."
     American Anthropologist, February 1956, 75–96.
Mayes, Edward. *History of Education in Mississippi*. Washington, DC: US Government Printing
     Office, 1899.
McElvaine, Robert S. *The Great Depression*. New York: Three Rivers Press, 2009.
McGee, Leo, and Robert Boone, eds. *The Black Rural Landowner—Endangered Species: Social,
     Political and Economic Implications*. Westport, CT: Greenwood Press, 1979.
McMillen Neil R. *The Citizens' Council: Organized Resistance to the Second Reconstruction*.
     Urbana: University of Illinois Press, 1994.
McMillen, Neil R. *Dark Journey*. Urbana: University of Illinois Press, 1990.
McMurchy, Myles. "'The Red Cross Is Not All Right!' Herbert Hoover's Concentration Camp
     Cover-Up in the 1927 Mississippi Flood." *Yale Historical Review* (2016): 87–113.
McNichol, Dan. *The Roads That Built America: The Incredible Story of the U.S. Interstate System*.
     New York: Sterling Publishing Company, 2006.
McPherson, James M. *The Negro's Civil War: How American Blacks Felt and Acted during the
     War for the Union*. New York: Vintage Books, 1993. Originally published 1965.
Mendelsohn, Jack. *The Martyrs: Sixteen Who Gave Their Lives for Racial Justice*. New York:
     Harper and Row, 1966.
Meserve, John Bartlett. "About Shumaka, Chakchiuma, iksa Kushyapa Okla." *Chronicles of
     Oklahoma* 13, no. 3 (September 1935): 298–99.
Michals, Debra. "Mary McLeod Bethune." National Women's History Museum. 2015. www
     .womenshistory.org/education-resources/biographies/mary-mcleod-bethune.
Mikkelson, Vincent. "Coming from Battle to Face a War: The Lynching of Black Soldiers in
     the World War I Era." PhD thesis, Florida State University, 2007.

Miller, Clark Leonard. "'Let Us Die to Make Men Free': Political Terrorism in Post-Reconstruction Mississippi, 1877–1896." PhD thesis, University of Minnesota, 1983.

Milner, George R. *The Moundbuilders: Ancient Peoples of Eastern North America*. London: Thames and Hudson, 2004.

Mischel, Frances. "African Powers in Trinidad: The Shango Cult." *Anthropological Quarterly* 30, no. 2 (April 1957): 45–59.

Mississippi Band of Choctaw Indians. "Choctaw Today." 2024. https://www.choctaw.org/about-us/tribal-history/#mark_today.

Mississippi Department of Archives and History. "Durant Illinois Central Railroad Depot." *National Register of Historic Places Registration Form*. Jackson, MS: United States Department of Interior, December 4, 2015.

Mississippi Department of Archives and History. *Works Progress Administration for Mississippi Source Material*. Jackson: Mississippi Library Commission, Record Group 60, Volume XXVI.

Mississippi Department of Environmental Quality. *Total Maximum Daily Loads for the Legacy Pesticides DDT and Toxaphene in the Yazoo River Basin*. Jackson: MDEQ, November 2005. https://www.mdeq.ms.gov/wp-content/uploads/TMDLs/Yazoo/Yazoo_Basin_FINAL_Pesticide_TMDL_12247.pdf.

Mississippi State University. "James Z. and Elizabeth B. George." Mississippi Political Collections. https://www.library.msstate.edu/cprc/james-z-and-elizabeth-b-george.

Mitchell, Harry Leland. *Mean Things Happening in This Land*. Norman: University of Oklahoma Press, 1979.

Mitchell, Henry H. *Black Church Beginnings: The Long Hidden Realities of the First Years*. Grand Rapids, MI: Wm. B. Eerdmand Publishing, 2004.

Morgalla, Michael M. "Black Ownership of Farmland in Holmes County, Mississippi: A Preliminary Study." Unpublished manuscript, Land Tenure Center Library, Univeristy of Wisconsin, Madison, 1968.

Morris, Robert C. *Reading, 'Riting, and Reconstruction: The Education of Freedmen in the South, 1861–1870*. Chicago: University of Chicago Press, 1981.

Morris, Willie. *North toward Home*. New York: Vintage Books, 1967.

Munford, Luther. "Black Gravity: Desegregation in 30 Misssissippi School Districts." Unpublished senior thesis, Woodrow Wilson School of Public and International Affairs, Princeton University, 1971.

Nash, Jere, and Andy Taggart. *Mississippi Politics: The Struggle for Power, 1976–2006*. Jackson: University Press of Mississippi, 2006.

Nembhard, Jessica Gordon. *Collective Courage: A History of African American Cooperative Economic Thought and Practice*. University Park: Pennsylvania State University Press, 2014.

Newton, Michael. *The Ku Klux Klan in Mississippi: A History*. Jefferson, NC: McFarland, 2010.

Nicholas, Timothy A. "'The Spirit of an Age': The Prohibition Press of Mississippi, 1876–1890." PhD dissertation, University of Southern Mississippi, 1996.

Noble, Stuart Grayson. *Forty Years of the Public Schools in Mississippi, with Special Reference to the Education of the Negro*. New York: Teachers College, Columbia University, 1918.

Noley, Grayson. "The Early 1700s: Education, Economics and Politics." In *The Choctaw before Removal*, edited by Carolyn Keller Reeves. Jackson: University Press of Mississippi, 1985, 73–119.

O'Brien, Greg. *Choctaws in a Revolutionary Age, 1750–1830*. Lincoln: University of Nebraska Press, 2002.

O'Brien, Greg, ed. *Pre-removal Choctaw History*. Norman: University of Oklahoma Press, 2008.

Oubre, Claude F. *Forty Acres and a Mule: The Freedmen's Bureau and Black Land Ownership*. Baton Rouge: Louisiana State University Press, 1978.

Pinnen, Christian, and Charles Weeks. *Colonial Mississippi: A Borrowed Land*. Jackson: University Press of Mississippi, 2021.

Pitts, Walter. "Like a Tree Planted by the Water: The Musical Cycle in the African-American Baptist Ritual." *Journal of American Folklore* 104, no. 413 (Summer 1991): 318–40.

Povall, Allie. *The Time of Eddie Noel*. Concord, NC: Comfort Publishing, 2010.

Powdermaker, Hortense. *After Freedom: A Cultural Study in the Deep South*. New York: Viking Press, 1939.

Powell, Lawrence N. *New Masters: Northern Planters during the Civil War and Reconstruction*. New Haven, CT: Yale University Press, 1980.

Powell, Lawrence N. "Correcting for Fraud: A Quantitative Reassessment of the Mississippi Ratification Election of 1868." *Journal of Southern History* 55, no. 4 (November 1989): 633–58.

Pratt, Dorothy Overstreet. *Sowing the Wind: The Mississippi Constitutional Convention of 1890*. Jackson: University Press of Mississippi, 2018.

Providence Plantation. "The Cooperative Farm Carries On." 1947. https://egrove.olemiss.edu/civ_pubs/1/.

Raboteau, Albert J. *Canaan Land: A Religious History of African Americans*. New York: Oxford University Press, 2001.

Raboteau, Albert J. *Slave Religion: The "Invisible Institution" in the Antebellum South*. New York: Oxford University Press, 2004. First published in 1978.

Raines, Howell. *My Soul Is Rested: Movement Days in the Deep South Remembered*. New York: G. P. Putnam's Sons, 1977.

Rainwater, Percy Lee. *Mississippi: Storm Center of Secession*. Baton Rouge, LA: Otto Claitor, 1938.

Ramsdell, Charles W. *Behind the Lines in the Southern Confederacy*. Baton Rouge: Louisiana State University Press, 1972.

Ransby, Barbara. *Ella Baker and the Black Freedom Movement: A Radical Democratic Vision*. Chapel Hill: University of North Carolina Press, 2003.

Ransom, Roger L, and Richard Sutch. *One Kind of Freedom: The Economic Consequences of Emancipation*, 2nd ed. New York: Cambridge University Press, 2001.

Ray, Rebecca Florence. *Chieftain Greenwood Leflore and the Choctaw Indians of the Mississippi Valley: Last Chief of the Choctaws East of the Mississippi River*. Memphis, TN: C. A. Davis, 1936.

Redkey, Edwin S., ed. *A Grand Army of Black Men*. New York: Cambridge University Press, 1992.

Reeves, Carolyn Keller, ed. *The Choctaw before Removal*. Jackson: University Press of Mississippi, 1985.

Reid, Debra A., and Evan P. Bennett, ed. *Beyond Forty Acres and a Mule*. Gainesville: University Press of Florida, 2012.

Resendez, Andres. *The Other Slavery: The Uncovered Story of Indian Enslavement in America*. New York: Mariner Books, 2017.

Richardson, Joe M., and Maxine D. Jones. *Education for Liberation: The American Missionary Association and African Americans, 1890 to the Civil Rights Movement*. Tuscaloosa: University of Alabama Press, 2009.

Robeck, Cecil M. *The Azuza Street Mission and Revival: The Birth of the Global Pentecostal Movement*. Nashville: Emanate Books, 2006.

Roberts, Charles Kenneth. *The Farm Security Administration and Rural Rehabilitation in the South*. Knoxville: University of Tennessee Press, 2015.

Robertson, Lindsay G. *Conquest by Law: How the Discovery of America Dispossed Indigenous Peoples of Their Lands*. Oxford: Oxford University Press, 2007.

Robinson, Donald W. "Head Starts in Mississippi." *Phi Delta Kappan* 47, no. 2 (October 1965): 91–95.

Rolinson, Mary G. *Grassroots Garveyism: The Universal Negro Improvement Association in the Rural South, 1920–1927*. Chapel Hill: University of North Carolina Press, 2007.

Roll, Jarod. *Spirit of Rebellion: Labor and Religion in the New Cotton South*. Urbana: University of Illinois Press, 2010.

Rolph, Stephanie R. *Resisting Equality: The Citizens Council, 1954–1989*. Baton Rouge: Louisiana State University Press, 2018.

Rothman, Joshua D. *Flush Times and Fever Dreams: A Story of Capitalism and Slavery in the Age of Jackson*. Athens: University of Georgia Press, 2012.

Rothman, Joshua D. *The Ledger and the Chain: How Domestic Slave Traders Shaped America*. New York: Basic Books, 2021.

Rowland, Dunbar. *Military History of Mississippi, 1803–1898*. Spartanburg, SC: Reprint Company, 1999. Originally published 1908.

Ruminski, Jarret. *The Limits of Loyalty: Ordinary People in Civil War Mississippi*. Jackson: University Press of Mississippi, 2017.

Rural Organizing and Cultural Center. "Bloodlines (Minds Stayed on Freedom: Movement Veterans Speak to Holmes County Youth)." *Bloodlines*, 1990.

Rural Organizing and Cultural Center. "Bloodlines." *Bloodlines*, 1988.

Rushing, Phillip. *Empty Sleeves*. Grand Rapids, MI: Zonderman Books, 1984.

Saikku, Mikko. *This Delta, This Land: An Environmental History of the Yazoo-Mississippi Floodplain*. Athens: University of Georgia Press, 2005.

Salamon, Lester M., and Stephen Van Evera. "Fear, Apathy, and Discrimination: A Test of Three Explanations of Political Participation." *American Political Science Review* 67, no. 4 (December 1973): 1288–306.

Saloutos, Theodore. *Farmer Movements in the South, 1865–1933*. Lincoln: University of Nebraska Press, 1969.

Sanders, Crystal R. "More Than Cookies and Crayons: Head Start and African American Empowerment in Mississippi." *Journal of African American History* 100, no. 4 (2015): 586–609.

Sansing, David. "George Poindexter, Second Governor of Mississippi: 1820–1822." *Mississippi History Now*. December 2003. http://mississippihistory.org.

Saunt, Claudio. "Financing Dispossession: Stocks, Bonds, and the Deportation of Native Peoples in the Antebellum United States." *Journal of American History* 106, no. 2 (September 2019): 315–37.

Saunt, Claudio. *Unworthy Republic. The Dispossession of Native Americans and the Road to Indian Territory*. New York: W. W. Norton, 2020.

Schaller, Mary W., and Martin N., Schaller, eds. *Soldiering for Glory: The Civil War Letters of Colonel Frank Schaller, Twenty-Second Mississippi Infantry.* Columbia: University of South Carolina Press, 2007.

Schweninger, Loren. *Black Property Owners in the South, 1790–1915.* Champaign, IL: Illini Books, 1997.

Seeley, Samantha. *Race, Removal, and the Right to Remain.* Chapel Hill: University of North Carolina Press, 2023.

Sernett, Milton C., ed. *African American Religious History: A Documentary Witness,* 2nd ed. Durham, NC: Duke University Press, 1999.

Sewell, George A., and Margaret L. Dwight. *Mississippi Black History Makers.* Jackson: University Press of Mississippi, 1984.

Seymour, William J. *The Words That Changed the World: Azuza Street Sermons.* Duncan, OK: Christian Life Books, 2017.

Shackleford, Nora Jeanne. "The Leflore Family and Choctaw Indian Removal." Master's thesis, Oklahoma State University, 1967.

Sieber, Karen. "The Black Populist Movement Has Been Snuffed Out of the History Books." *Jacobin,* May 17, 2023.

Silver, James, ed. *Mississippi In the Confederacy* Vol 2, *As Seen in Retrospect.* Baton Rouge: Louisiana State University Press, 1961.

Simmons, Dovie Marie, and Olivia L. Martin. *Down behind the Sun: The Story of Arenia Conelia Mallory.* Memphis, TN: Riverside Press, 1983.

Smith, Allene De Shazo. *Greenwood Leflore and the Choctaw Indians.* Memphis, TN: C. A. Davis, 1951.

Smith, Amanda. *An Autobiography. The Story of the Lord's Dealings with Mrs. Amanda Smith the Colored Evangelist; Containing an Account of Her Life, Work of Faith, and Her Travels in America, England, Ireland, Scotland, India and Africa, as an Independent Missionary.* Chicago: Meyer and Brother, 1893.

Smith, Bobby J., II. *Food Power Politics: The Food Story of the Mississippi Civil Rights Movement.* Chapel Hill: University of North Carolina Press, 2023.

Smith, Timothy B. *James Z. George: Mississippi's Great Commoner.* Jackson: University of Mississippi Press, 2012.

Smith, Timothy B. *The Mississippi Secession Convention: Delegates and Deliberations in Politics and War, 1861–1865.* Jackson: University Press of Mississippi, 2014.

Smithers, Gregory D. *Native Southerners: Indigenous History from Origins to Removal.* Norman: University of Oklahoma Press, 2019.

SNCC Legacy Project and Duke University. "SNCC Digital Gateway." 2022. snccdigital.org.

Snyder, Terri L. "Suicide, Slavery and Memory in North America." *Journal of American History* 97, no. 1 (June 2020): 39–62.

Sojourner, Sue [Lorenzi], with Cheryl Reitan. *Thunder of Freedom: Black Leadership and the Transformation of 1960s Mississippi.* Lexington: University Press of Kentucky, 2013.

Span, Christopher M. *From Cottonfield to Schoolhouse: African American Education in Mississippi, 1862–1875.* Chapel Hill: University of North Carolina Press, 2009.

Sparks, Randy J. *Religion in Mississippi.* Jackson: University Press of Mississippi, 2001.

Stanley, Gerald. "Senator William Gwin: Moderate or Racist?" *California Historical Quarterly* 50, no. 3 (September 1971): 243–55.

Starnes, James E., and Christopher Michael Rego. "Prehistoric Kosciusko Quartzite Quarry Identified in Holmes County." *Mississippi Archeological Association Newsletter*, June 2021, 13.

Stein, Waltraut. "The White Citizens' Councils." *Negro History Bulletin* 2 (1956): 21–23.

Sterling, Dorothy, ed. *The Trouble They Seen: The Story of Reconstruction in the Words of African Americans*. New York: Da Capo Press, 1994.

Stone, James H. "A Note on Voter Registration under the Mississippi Understanding Clause, 1892." *Journal of Southern History* 38, no. 2 (May 1972): 293–96.

Sublette, Ned. *The World That Made New Orleans: From Spanish Silver to Congo Square*. Chicago: Lawrence Hill Books, 2009.

Sumter, Veller. *Josiah Impson*. Oklahoma City: Oklahoma Historical Society, 1983.

Surby, Richard W. *Grierson's Grand Raid*. Monee, IL: Big Byte Books, 2021. First published 1865.

Swan, L. Alex. "The Harlem and Detroit Riots of 1943: A Comparative Analysis." *Berkeley Journal of Sociology* 16 (1971–72): 75–93.

Swanton, John R. *Indian Tribes of the Lower Mississippi Valley and Adjacent Coast of the Gulf of Mexico*. Mineola, NY: Dover Publications, 1911. Abridged edition 1998.

Sydnor, Charles S. *Slavery in Mississippi*. Columbia: University of South Carolina Press, 1933.

Taylor, Kieran W. "I Done Made My Mind Up: The Legacy of the Providence Cooperative Farm." Master's thesis, University of Mississippi, 1998. Provided by William Minter.

Thomas, Norman, and William R. Amberson. *The Plight of the Share-Cropper*. New York: League for Industrial Democracy, 1934.

Thompson, Julius E. *Percy Greene and the Jackson Advocate: The Life and Times of a Radical Conservative Newspaperman, 1897–1977*. Jefferson, NC: McFarland, 1994.

Tracy, Janice Branch. *Mississippi Moonshine Politics: How Bootleggers and the Law Kept a Dry State Soaked*. Charleston, SC: History Press, 2015.

Tracy, Janice Branch. *The Juke Joint King of the Mississippi Hills: The Raucous Reign of Tillman Branch*. Charleston, SC: History Press, 2014.

Tuskegee University. "Monroe Work Today Dataset Compilation." Tuskegee University Archives Repository. October 23, 2017. http://archive.tuskegee.edu/archive/handle/123456789/984.

Tyson, Timothy B. *The Blood of Emmett Till*. New York: Simon and Shuster, 2017.

United States Census Bureau. "Quick Facts, Holmes County, Mississippi." 2020, 2022. https://www.census.gov/quickfacts/fact/table/holmescountymississippi,US/PST045222.

United States Census Bureau. *U.S. Census of Population: 1960. Supplementary Reports*, Series PC(S1)-52, "Negro Population, by County: 1960 and 1950." Washington, DC: US Government Printing Office, 1966.

United States Department of Justice Civil Rights Division and United States Attorney's Office for the Southern District of Mississippi. *Investigation of the Lexington Police Department and the City of Lexington, Mississippi*. September 2024. https://www.justice.gov/crt/media/1370761/dl?inline.

United States Government. *U.S. Census*. National Archives and Records Administration, 1870 microfilm series M593, Roll 3527.

United States Government. *U.S. Census*. National Archives and Records Administration, 1860 microfilm series M653, Roll 598.

Usner, Daniel H., Jr. *American Indians in the Lower Mississippi Valley: Social and Economic Histories*. Lincoln: University of Nebraska Press, 1998.

Vogt, Daniel C. "James D. Lynch." *Mississippi Encyclopedia*, Center for Study of Southern Culture, 2018. https://mississippiencyclopedia.org/entries/james-d-lynch/.

Walter, Mildred Pitts. *Mississippi Challenge*. New York: Bradbury Press, 1992.

Warnock, Raphael G. *The Divided Mind of the Black Church*. New York: New York University Press, 2014.

Waters, Andrew, ed. *Prayin to Be Set Free*. Winston-Salem, NC: John F. Blair, 2002.

Watkins, Hollis, with C. Liegh McInnis. *Brother Hollis: The Sankofa of a Movement Man*. Clinton, MI: Sankofa Southern Publishing, 2015.

Watkins, William H. *The White Architects of Black Education: Ideology and Power in America, 1865–1954*. New York: Teachers College Press, 2001.

Watson, Blake A. *Buying America from the Indians: Johnson v. McIntosh and the History of Native American Land Rights*. Norman: University of Oklahoma Press, 2012.

Watts, Jill. *The Black Cabinet: The Untold Story of African Americans and Politics during the Age of Roosevelt*. New York: Grove Press, 2020.

Wells, Mary Ann. *Native Land: Mississippi, 1540–1798*. Jackson: University Press of Mississippi, 1994.

Wharton, Vernon Lane. *The Negro in Mississippi, 1865–1890*. Chapel Hill: University of North Carolina Press, 1947.

White, Calvin, Jr. *The Rise to Respectability*. Fayetteville: University of Arkansas Press, 2012.

White, Monica M. *Freedom Farmers: Agricultural Resistance and the Black Freedom Movement*. Chapel Hill: University of North Carolina Press, 2018.

Whitfield, Stephen J. *A Death in the Delta: The Story of Emmett Till*. New York: Free Press, 1988.

Whitten, Jamie L. *That We May Live*. Princeton, NJ: Van Nostrand, 1966.

Williams, Brian. "Cotton, Chemicals and the Political Ecologies of Racial Capitalism." PhD dissertation, University of Georgia, 2018.

Williams, Michael Vinson. *Medgar Evers: Mississippi Martyr*. Fayetteville: University of Arkansas Press, 2011.

Willis, John C. *Forgotten Time: The Yazoo-Mississippi Delta after the Civil War*. Charlottesville: University Press of Virginia, 2000.

Winston, James E. "The Lost Commission: A Study in Mississippi History." *Mississippi Valley Historical Review* 5, no. 2 (September 1918): 158–89.

Witty, Fred M. "Reconstruction in Carroll and Montgomery Counties." *Mississippi Historical Society* (1908): 115–34.

Wood, Spencer D. "The Roots of Black Power: Land, Civil Society, and the State in the Mississippi Delta, 1935–1968." PhD dissertation, University of Wisconsin, 2006.

Woods, Clyde. *Development Arrested: The Blues and Plantation Power in the Mississippi Delta*. Brooklyn: Verso, 2017. Originally published 1998.

Woods, Patricia Dillon. *French-Indian Relations on the Southern Frontier, 1699–1762*. Ann Arbor: UMI Research Press, 1980.

Yarbrough, Fay A. *Choctaw Confederates: The American Civil War in Indian Country*. Chapel Hill: University of North Carolina Press, 2021.

ARCHIVAL SOURCES

Collection of the Smithsonian National Museum of African American History and Culture in
    partnership with the American Folklife Center, Library of Congress
Cornell University Digital Library Collections
CRL Digital Delivery System, Negro World
Dorchester County Maryland Chattel Records
Fisk University, Franklin Library Special Collections, Julius Rosenwald Fund Archives
Library of Congress
    Chronicling America
    Federal Writers' Project, Slave Narrative Project
    Photos, Prints and Drawings, Marion Post Wolcott
Mississippi Department of Archives and History (MDAH)
    Absolom West, subject file
    David Holmes, subject file
    Holmes County, subject file
    Freedmen's Bureau Records
    Governor Pettus Collection
    Greenwood Leflore, subject file
    Online electronic resource: Sovereignty Commission Files
    Reports of the State Board of Education
National Archives in Atlanta (assisted search)
National Archives in Fort Worth (assisted search)
National Park Service, Soldiers and Sailors Database
Office of the Chancery Clerk, Holmes County, Land Records
Schomburg Archives at the New York Public Library, UNIA Collection
SNCC Digital Gateway
Tamiment Library and Robert F. Wagner Labor Archives, New York University (online)
Tuskegee University Archives, Lynching Records
University of Mississippi, eGrove, Gage Family Collection
University of Southern Mississippi, Civil Rights in the Mississippi Delta, Digital Collection
Wisconsin Historical Society, Freedom Summer Digital Collection

NEWSPAPERS, MAGAZINES, AND NEWSLETTERS

Brandon Republican, Brandon, MS
Canton Mail, Canton, MS
Chicago Defender, Chicago, IL
Chronicle Star, Moss Point, MS
Clarion-Ledger, Jackson, MS
Colored Citizen Monthly, Jackson, MS
Comet, Jackson, MS
Daily Commercial Herald, Vicksburg, MS
Daily Herald, Biloxi, MS
Delta Democrat-Times, Greenville, MS

Durant News, Durant, MS
Ebony, published in Chicago until 2016
Greenwood Commonwealth, Greenwood, MS
Grenada Sentinel, Grenada, MS
Hattiesburg American, Hattiesburg, MS
Holmes County Herald, Lexington, MS
Holmes County Times, Lexington, MS
Hope Star, Hope, AR
Jackson Advocate, Jackson, MS
Jackson Daily News, Jackson, MS
Jet, published in Chicago until 2016
Lexington Advertiser, Lexington, MS
Lexington Union, Lexington, MS
Los Angeles Times, Los Angeles, CA
Mississippi Enterprise, Jackson, MS
Modern Farmer, national magazine of the NFCF, Nashville, TN
Negro World, publication of the UNIA, Harlem, NY
New Haven Register, New Haven, CT
New Mississippian, Jackson, MS
News and Observer, Raleigh, NC
New York Times, New York, NY
Niles Register, Washington, DC
Pickens Enterprise, Pickens, MS
Pittsburgh Courier, Pittsburgh, PA
Semi-Weekly Leader, Brookhaven, MS
St. Louis Post-Dispatch, St. Louis, MO
Times-Picayune, New Orleans, LA
Tri-Weekly Clarion, Meridian, MS
Vicksburg Herald, Vicksburg, MS
Vicksburg Whig, Vicksburg, MS
Washington Post, Washington, DC
Weekly Democrat, Natchez, MS
Weekly Democrat-Times, Greenville, MS
Weekly Mississippian, Jackson, MS
Weekly Mississippi Pilot, Jackson, MS
Winona Democrat, Winona, MS
Winona New Farmer, Winona, MS
Winston County Journal, Louisville, MS
Yazoo Herald, Yazoo City, MS
Yazoo Semi-Weekly Sentinel, Yazoo City, MS

INDEX

Page numbers in **bold** indicate figures and tables.

ABOUT THE AUTHOR

Photo by Candace Mckenzie

Diane T. Feldman was born in Washington, DC, and grew up in New York City before returning to Washington. She was president of a research company there for thirty years. She retired to Mississippi in 2018 and lives in Jackson.